LAND REFORM AND PEASANT LIVELIHOODS

LAND REFORM AND PEASANT LIVELIHOODS
The Social Dynamics of Rural Poverty and Agrarian Reforms in Developing countries

Edited by

Krishna B. Ghimire

ITDG
PUBLISHING

Published by ITDG Publishing
103–105 Southampton Row, London WC1B 4HL, UK

© United Nations Research Institute for Social
Development 2001

First published in 2001

ISBN 1 85339 527 7

A catalogue record for this book is available from the
British Library.

ITDG Publishing is the publishing arm of the
Intermediate Technology Development Group. Our
mission is to build the skills and capacity of people in
developing countries through the dissemination of
information in all forms, enabling them to improve the
quality of their lives and that of future generations.

Typeset by J&L Composition Ltd, Filey, North Yorkshire
Printed in Great Britain by
The Cromwell Press Limited, Trowbridge

Dedication

To Gerrit Huizer
with our collective thoughts

Contents

Maps

Tables

Contributors

Solon L. Barraclough is Senior Consultant at the UN Research Institute for Social Development, Geneva. He is author of numerous books on the agrarian question, including *An End to Hunger? The Social Origins of Food Strategies*, Zed Books, London, 1991.

Eduardo Baumeister is Research Associate at the Centro de Estudios del Desarrollo Rural in San Jose and Consultant at the Centro de Estudios para la Participacion Democratica y el Desarrollo in Managua. He is author of *Estructura y Reforma Agraria en Nicaragua* (1979–1989), Free University of Amsterdam, Amsterdam, 1998.

Peter Dorner is Professor Emeritus of Agricultural Economics at the Land Tenure Center, University of Wisconsin-Madison. He is author of *Latin American Land Reforms in Theory and Practice*, University of Wisconsin Press, Madison, 1992.

Krishna B. Ghimire is Project Leader and researcher at the UN Research Institute for Social Development, Geneva. He is author and editor of several books on land tenure questions and sustainable rural livelihoods, including *Agricultural Expansion and Tropical Deforestation* (with S. Barraclough), Earthscan, London, 2000.

M. Riad El-Ghonemy is a Senior Research Associate at the International Development Centre, Queen Elizabeth House, University of Oxford. He is author of *Land, Food and Rural Development in North Africa*, IT Publications, London, 1993.

Gerrit Huizer was Professor at the Third World Centre, Catholic University of Nijmegen, Nijmegen. He is author of *Peasant Rebellion in Latin America*, Marwah Publications, New Delhi, 1978 and *Peasant Movements and their Counter-forces in South East Asia*, Marwah Publications, New Delhi, 1980.

Jose Noel D. Olano is Executive Director of Philippine Development Assistance Programme. He was previously a senior official at the Department of Agrarian Reform, Quezon City, Philippines.

Abbreviations and Acronyms

ADC	Alianza Democrática Campesina (El Salvador)
AIFLD	American Institute for Labor Development
AIKS	All-India Kisan Sabha
AJAC/Z	Youth Association of the Ziquinchor Region in Senegal
ALRD	Association for Land Reform and Development (Bangladesh)
AMT	Aguman Ding Maldong Talapagobra (League of Poor Labourers, the Philippines)
ANAP	National Association of Small Cultivators
ANGOC	Asian NGO Coalition for Agrarian Reform and Rural Development
AOCFSD	African Organizations Coalition for Food Security and Sustainable Development
APM	Agriculture Peasants and Modernization Network
AR Now!	People's Campaign for Agrarian Reform Now (Philippines)
ASK	Ain O Shalish Kendra (Bangladesh)
ASOCODE	Asociación de Organizaciones Campesinas Centroamericana para la Cooperación y el Desarrollo
ATC	Rural Workers' Federation (Nicaragua)
BAIDA	Bukidnon Agro-Industrial Development Association (Philippines)
BARC	Barangay Agrarian Reform Council (Philippines)
BCCs	Basic Christian Communities (Philippines)
BHRC	Bangladesh Human Rights Commission
BHREC	Bangladesh Human Rights Enforcement Committee
BLAST	Bangladesh Legal Aid and Services Trust
BMFI	Balay Mindanaw Foundation Inc. (Philippines)

BSAC	British South Africa Company
BTI	Barisan Tani Indonesia (Indonesian Peasant Front)
BUDC	Barrio United Defence Corps (Philippines)
CARP	Comprehensive Agrarian Reform Program (Philippines)
Carruf	Carpio-Rufino Agricultural Corporation
CART	Malay Mindanao Foundation and Center for Alternative Rural Technology (Philippines)
CCHRB	Coordinating Council of Human Rights of Bangladesh
CERAS	Agrarian Reform Centres (Chile)
CIA	Central Intelligence Agency (United States)
CIERA	Centre for Agrarian Reform Research and Studies
CIMMYT	International Corn and Wheat Improvement Center
CJP	Commission for Justice and Peace
CLOA	Certificate of Land Ownership Award (Philippines)
CNTCB	National Confederation of Peasant Workers of Bolivia
COACES	Confederación de Asociaciones Cooperativas de El Salvador
COCOCH	Consejo Coordinador de Organizaciones Campesinas de Honduras
CODIMCA	Consejo para el Desarrollo Integral de la Mujer Rural (Honduras)
CONFRAS	Confederación de Federaciones de la Reforma Agraria de El Salvador
CONGCOOP	Coordinación de ONG y Cooperativas (Guatemala)
CONTAG	Confederação Nacional dos Trabalhadores na Agricultura (Federation of Agricultural Workers, Brazil)
CORA	Agrarian Reform Corporation (Chile)
CPAR	Congress for a People's Agrarian Reform (Philippines)
CPT	Comisao Pastoral de Terra (Brazil)
DA	Department of Agriculture (Philippines)
DAR	Department of Agrarian Reform (Philippines)
DARAB	Department of Agrarian Reform Adjudication Board (Philippines)
DENR	Department of Environment and Natural Resources (Philippines)

DRC	Desarrollo Rural Concentrado (Honduras)
ECLAC	Economic Commission for Latin America and the Caribbean
ECODEPA	Empresa Cooperativa de Productores Agropecuarios (Nicaragua)
ECOSOC	United Nations Economic and Social Council
EDSA	Epiphanio de los Santos Avenue (Philippines)
ESCWA	Economic and Social Commission for Western Asia
EZLN	Zapatista Army of National Liberation (Mexico)
FAO	Food and Agriculture Organization of the United Nations
FENACOOP	Federación Nacional de Cooperativas Agropecuarias y Agroindustriales (Nicaragua)
FFF	Federation of Free Farmers (Philippines)
FIAN	FoodFirst Information and Action Network
FLASCO	La Facultad Latinoamericana de Ciencias Sociales
FMLN	Frente Farabundo Martí de Liberación Nacional (El Salvador)
FRAP	Leftist Popular Action Front (Chile)
FRELIMO	Front for the Liberation of Mozambique
FSLN	Frente Sandinista de Liberación Nacional (Sandinista party)
GATT	General Agreement on Tariffs and Trade
GDP	gross domestic product
GO	governmental organization
GSS	Gonoshahajjo Sangstha (Bangladesh)
GTZ	Deutsche Gesellschaft für Technische Zusammenarbeit
HUKBALAHAP	Hukbo ng Bayan Laban sa Hapon (The People's Army Against the Japanese) (Philippines)
IBP	Integrated Bar of the Philippines
ICAD	Interamerican Committee for Agricultural Development
ICIRA	Chilean Agrarian Reform Research and Training Institute
ICJ	International Commission of Jurists
ICP	international comparable purchasing power
ICCO	Interchurch Organization for Development Cooperation

IDB	Inter-American Development Bank
IFAD	International Fund for Agricultural Development
IFPRI	International Food Policy Research Institute
IHDER	Instituto Hondureño de Desarrollo Rural (Honduras)
IICA	Inter-American Institute for Agricultural Co-operation
ILO	International Labour Organization
IMF	International Monetary Fund
INA	Instituto Nacional Agrario (Honduras)
INDAP	Instituto de Desarrollo Agropecuario (Institute for Agricultural and Livestock Development)
INPROA	Instituto de Promocion Agraria (Institute for Agrarian Promotion)
ISTA	Instituto Salvadoreño de Transformación Agraria (El Salvador)
IUF	International Union of Food, Agricultural, Hotel, Restaurant, Catering, Tobacco and Allied Workers' Associations
JCRR	Joint Commission on Rural Reconstruction (Taiwan Province of China)
KAISAHAN	Kaisahan Tungo sa Kaunlaran ng Kanayunan at Repormang Pansakahan
KASAMA	Katipunan ng mga Samahang Magsasaka (peasants' federation) (Philippines)
KMP	Kilusang Magnubukid ng Philipinas (National Peasant Movement in the Philippines)
KPMP	Katipunan Pambansa ng mga Magbubukid sa Philipinas (National Union of Peasants in the Philippines)
LAD	Land Acquisition and Distribution (Philippines)
LASEDECO	Land Settlement and Development Corporation (Philippines)
LBP	Land Bank of the Philippines
LMR	land market reform
LRC	Legal Resources Centre (South Africa)
LRF	Legal Resource Foundation (Zimbabwe)
MARO	Municipal Agrarian Reform Officer (Philippines)

MIDINRA	Ministerio de Desarrollo Agropecuario y Reforma Agraria (Nicaragua)
MNR	National Revolutionary Movement (Bolivia)
MST	Movimento dos Trabalhadores Rurais Sem Terra (Brazil)
NAFTA	North American Free Trade Agreement
NCA	Notice of Compulsory Acquisition (Philippines)
NGO	non-governmental organization
Nichinó	Nihon Nomin Kumiai (Japanese Peasant Union)
NITAPLAN	Centro de Investigaciones de la Universidad Centroamericana (Nicaragua)
NLC	National Land Committee
NLSA	National Land Settlement Administration (Philippines)
NPA	New People's Army (Philippines)
NQSRMDC	Norberto Quisumbing Sr. Management and Development Corporation (Philippines)
OAS	Organization of American States
OXFAM	Oxford Committee for Famine Relief
PAKISAMA	Pambansang Kilusan ng mga Samahang Magsasaka (Philippines)
PALAMBU	Panaghiusa sa Lalawigang Maguuma sa Bukidnon (Philippines)
PARC	Presidential Agrarian Reform Council (Philippines)
PARO	Provincial Agrarian Reform Officer (Philippines)
PCAC	Programa de Campesino a Campesino (Nicaragua)
PERA	Programa de Evaluación de la Reforma Agraria (El Salvador)
PD	Presidential Decree (Philippines)
PFSA	Programa de Formación y Seguridad Alimenticia
PhilDHRRA	Philippine Partnership for the Development of Human Resources in Rural Areas
PKI	Indonesian Communist Party
PO	people's organization
PPI	Philippine Peasant Institute
PPP	purchasing power parity

PRI	Institutional Revolutionary Party (Mexico)
PROCORAC	Programa para la Consolidación de la Reforma Agraria en Comayagua (Honduras)
PRRM	Philippine Rural Reconstruction Movement
PTT	Programa de Transferencia de Tierras, (El Salvador)
RA	Republic Act
RLR	redistributive land reform
ROD	Register of Deeds
SALAG	Structural Alternative Legal Assistance for Grassroots (Philippines)
SALIGAN	Sentro para sa Alternatibong Lingap Panlegal (Philippines)
SCAP	Supreme Commander for the Allied Powers
SENTRA	Sentro para sa Tunay Na Repormang Agraryo (Philippines)
SNA	Large Landowners' Association (Chile)
SOCRA	Sociedad de Cooperativas Cafetaleras de la Reforma Agraria (El Salvador)
TNCs	transnational corporations
TriPARRD	Tripartite Partnership for Agrarian Reform and Rural Development (Philippines)
TRO	Temporary Restraining Order (Philippines)
UGOCM	Unión General de Obreros y Campesinos de México
UNAG	Unión Nacional de Agricultores y Ganaderos (Small Farmers' Organization, Nicaragua)
UNAPA	Unión Nacional de Productores Autogestionarios (Nicaragua)
UNDP	United Nations Development Programme
UNESCO	United Nations Educational, Scientific and Cultural Organization
UNICEF	United Nations Children's Fund
UNRISD	United Nations Research Institute for Social Development
UP	Popular Unity (Chilean coalition)
UPES	Unidades de Producción Estatal (Nicaragua)
US	United States
USSR	Union of Soviet Socialist Republics

WCARRD	World Conference on Agrarian Reform and Rural Development
WCED	World Commission on Environment and Development
WFP	World Food Programme
ZANLA	Zimbabwe Nationalist Liberation Army
ZANU	Zimbabwe African National Union
ZANUPF	Zimbabwe African National Union/Popular Front
ZAPU	Zimbabwe African People's Union

CHAPTER ONE

Land Reform at the End of the Twentieth Century: An Overview of Issues, Actors and Processes

Krishna B. Ghimire[1]

BACKGROUND

The need for land reform

There is a wide consensus about the need for reforming land tenure systems and relations in order to reduce rural poverty and hunger in developing countries. This is agreed by national and international bodies, non-governmental organizations (NGOs), the academic community, as well as scores of other actors. However, they vary in their approaches to land reform: some may propose radical land reform measures involving a sweeping appropriation of large holdings and their redistribution to the landless; others want to see restitution of land rights previously taken by powerful groups. Land colonization may be considered as an alternative to widespread land expropriation and redistribution. And, recently, schemes are being developed to intervene in the land market with the aim of making more land available for purchase by the landless. The intentions of these approaches, as well as their perceived benefits, differ greatly among various bodies and actors, particularly in the degree of commitment that is attached – it is this aspect which largely explains why a genuine implementation of land reform measures is missing in most contexts.

The justifications for promoting land reform are many, and some are compelling. In many developing countries, the vast majority of the population consists of near-landless, the landless and rural workers. It is suggested that in the mid-1980s there were as many as 817 million smallholder and landless rural labourers in Asia, Africa and Latin America (FAO, 1987). According to another source, during the same period there were 180 million rural landless in India, 24 million in Pakistan, 12 million in the Philippines, 8 million in Brazil, and over 324 million in only 64 developing countries (Jazairy et al., 1992).

Small farmers, tenants, sharecroppers and landless workers are among the social groups most vulnerable to hunger and poverty, and they usually have inadequate access to land and other productive resources. An International Labour Organization (ILO) study suggests that agricultural wage labourers, for example, are the poorest sections of the rural population, and in many countries their real wages have fallen despite rising agricultural productivity and trade (Anon., 1996c). At the same time, much of the cultivated, fertile land is held by a small number of powerful landowners. Thus the social impetus for land reform is the possibility of improved social justice and equity. This may also help to reduce rural conflict and violence. Land reform should, in particular, lead to greater food security, income and family welfare for many groups of the socio-economically marginalized rural population, including women and indigenous communities. Formalization and protection of land rights also helps to reinforce local agricultural and cultural diversity.

Perhaps one of the primary reasons for advocating land reform and tenurial security is that access to land by the rural population should be seen as an essential human right. With access to land, the rural poor have the possibility of access to shelter, food, employment and improved livelihood (Plant, 1993; Künnemann, 1997, 1998). Granting of a reliable tenurial security also implies respect for minimum human dignity. This would be the case, for example, with many indigenous peoples or other population groups previously dispossessed of their land, such as the black communities in Zimbabwe and South Africa.

Even in countries where land reform policies have been implemented, human rights violations are rampant. Peasants tend to be the least powerful and vulnerable groups in society, and in their struggles to obtain and secure access to land and related resources they face numerous human rights violations in the form of police, landowner harassment, random imprisonment, unfair trials held in courts lacking an independent judiciary, not to mention repeated acts of coercion to expel them from their holdings. Many of these serious violations go unnoticed by human rights groups such as Amnesty International, as they are sporadic and under-documented. Indeed, peasants' land rights have remained fairly marginalized in international human rights discourse and legislation. For example, the UN High Commission for Human Rights and the UN Economic and Social Council Commission on Human Rights (which have emphasized special land rights for indigenous peoples, women and children) do not consider small peasants, tenants and landless agricultural labourers as a category of the rural population requiring attention (Ghimire, Chapter 6).

Land reform is also essential from the point of view of environmental protection. The possession of secure, legal land titles encourages peasants to invest more time and resources in making land more fertile and productive. This may lead them to adopt sustainable practices of agriculture, such as on-farm regeneration of useful biomass, soil and water preservation, recycling of natural nutrients, maintaining crop and livestock diversities, etc. (Reijntjes et al., 1996). The other side of the coin is that the drive for agricultural modernization, based on a high use of chemical fertilizers, pesticides, fossil fuels and capital-intensive machines for cash crop production for export by powerful landowners and agrobusiness groups, tends to adversely affect farm workers' health and displace peasants from their land. Agri modernization usually reduces the demand for wage employment in agriculture, and leaves little choice or recourse for a considerable number of poorer rural households than to resort to invading the forest or other environmentally fragile areas in order to survive.

Despite these convincing reasons, few countries have undertaken sweeping land reform measures – in most cases because the political and economic difficulties associated with land reform have been formidable. Undeniably, there has been some progress. Examples may include the agrarian reforms introduced in Mexico early in the twentieth century as a result of a popular movement; in Japan, Korea and Taiwan after the Second World War by authoritarian governments; and in China and Cuba by revolutionary governments. Many other developing countries in Asia and Africa sought to promote tenurial reforms in the 1950s and 1960s after gaining their independence. The specific role of the USA (either through bilateral means, or through its heavy weight in multilateral funding organizations such as the World Bank and the Food and Agriculture Organization, FAO) in advocating land reform as a way of deterring communism or for promoting green revolution technological packages should also be recalled. The evidence suggests, though, that the full application of legislation has been rare in most of these countries; political mobilization by the peasantry has often been weak and their leaders are co-opted; reform measures covered little agricultural land and few peasants. In South Asia, for example, the existing small-cultivator systems changed little, with the exception of the Indian states of West Bengal and Kerala. On the whole, less than 10 per cent of the rural population benefited (Barraclough, 1991, p.120). Similar outcomes have been witnessed in countries where large-estate commercial farming systems were prevalent, namely in Latin America, but also in southern Africa and the Philippines. In sub-Saharan Africa, on the other hand, where communal tenure systems have remained predominant, attempting to impose private entitlements has created confusion and weakened existing tenurial security and communal solidarity (Mafeje, 1993; Platteau, 1995).

Land reform implies intervention in local power relations. Attempts to offer greater access to, and control over, land and productive resources, and improved support services to small farmers, rural workers, women and other marginalized agrarian social groups, mean reduction of the economic and political power of the landed classes, rich merchants, elites and agro-business interests. Simultaneously, however, the process permits increased participation of the rural poor in decision-making. These changes in social relations are never easy. This explains why many land reform measures, even those initially appearing most elaborate and far-reaching, fail to produce the intended results.

Recent land reform approaches and outcomes

During the past two decades, land reform measures lost political momentum in many developing countries. This was in part due to economic difficulties – debt burden, budget deficit, and reduced public spending resulting from structural adjustment programmes. In Zimbabwe, one country to call for radical land reforms in the 1980s, redistribution of land to benefit black farmers remained an elusive target, as due to budget constraints the government had no cash to purchase the land owned by white commercial farmers on the open market, and it was prevented from expropriating commercial farms without payment by the Lancaster House Agreement with Britain until April 1990. Moreover, the international financial agencies associated with the structural adjustment programme tended to emphasize the higher productivity of white commercial farms and their crucial contribution to export earnings (Von Blanckenburg, 1994; Anon., 1996a). The decline in public subsidies and in the provision of necessary agricultural inputs in line with structural adjustment programmes means that the gains of land reform made in earlier years are rapidly eroding in several developing countries. In El Salvador, Peru, Honduras and Nicaragua, for example, many production cooperatives established following agrarian reforms are now being dismantled, with members either reverting to individual plots or selling off their plots (Thiesenhusen, 1993; Baumeister, Chapter 3). In Mexico, as a part of the government's commitment to structural adjustment measures, essential provisions for agricultural credit, marketing support and training have been drastically cut, affecting many peasant communities and cooperatives (de Walt et al., 1994).

In the 1980s, key international agencies with a mandate to promote land reform activities, notably the FAO, were mainly involved in carrying out cadastral surveys, improvements in the national land registration systems, and introducing the use of computers for better consolidation of holdings. Naturally, these activities are extremely useful in some countries, but the issues of improved distribution of power and economic resources in rural areas were seen mainly as technological problems. The politically sensitive issue of land redistribution was carefully avoided.

The establishment of private ownership rights to land was considered as the main solution to increasing agricultural productivity and stimulating the regeneration of marketable produce beyond peasants' subsistence needs. Yet various studies and practical experiments illustrate that many of the communal land tenure systems in Africa and parts of Asia and Latin America have the potential to provide strong tenurial security and family welfare. Long-term lease arrangements, combined with state provision of necessary agricultural inputs in other contexts, have helped to improve peasants' income and land productivity, namely in China and Viet Nam (FAO, 1993a). Some of the lease arrangements involving agroforestry schemes in South Asia also have this potential, provided the lease period remains sufficiently long and peasants are allowed to decide how and which food crops to grow in addition to trees.

A dominant trend within the prevailing notion of economic liberalization and private 'entrepreneurship' stimulated by the World Bank, FAO and several multilateral and bilateral agencies in the North is the implementation of 'market-mediated' land reform measures. This approach is currently executed notably in Brazil, Colombia, South Africa, the Philippines and Indonesia. Market-driven land reform agendas function mainly through land registration and titling, especially by increasing credit facilities to purchase land. Although specialists agree that a well functioning land market could sometimes be a source of efficiency gains, it can seldom result in the availability of much land for redistribution to the rural poor (Vogelgesang, 1996; de Janvry, 1997).

Market-assisted land reform programmes are heavily criticized by Southern NGOs. In the Philippines and Indonesia, where market-driven agrarian reforms have recently been attempted, virulent criticisms have been made by local NGOs focusing attention on the negative impacts of the programmes. In the Philippines, market-assisted land reform programmes were launched by the central government under the auspices of the Comprehensive Agrarian Reform Programme (CARP), and in Indonesia they have been implemented by the national government in collaboration with the World Bank and AusAid. In both cases evidence suggests how, instead of benefiting small producers, market-assisted land reform has generally served to tighten the hold of powerful landowners and commercial enterprises backed by the government, and ironically has helped them gain access to even more land through market mechanisms (SENTRA, 1997; Anon., 1997c). In Brazil, the landless labourers' organization Movimento dos Trabalhadores Rurais Sem Terra (MST) has strongly opposed the government's recent market-led land reform programmes, which are financed mainly by the World Bank. MST considers these programmes simply to be a vindictive manoeuvre by the government, landed interests and financial institutions to weaken the organized popular demands for radical land reform in the country (personal observations and discussions with MST activists during a field visit to Parambuco, November 1999).

The state is frequently seen as something of a villain. Most bi- and multilateral agencies have sought to promote the private sector. They have also conceived a greater participation of NGOs in implementing the 'development agenda'. Recent land reform approaches are also influenced by this reasoning. The International Fund for Agricultural Development (IFAD, a UN agency with an exclusive mandate to work with the rural poor in developing countries), for example, has sought to create a major civil society network on land reform covering seven regions and 23 countries.[2] Undoubtedly, the exchange of information and ideas through improved networking has the potential to help civil society organizations and other protagonists to be better informed. However, IFAD has considered the mandate of this network should concentrate on the generation of information showing 'success stories', and has been less keen to support the work of the civil society organizations related to greater advocacy, lobbying and direct action for improved access to land. IFAD seems especially careful not to support groups that directly oppose the government. Furthermore, its rigid institutional framework, designed mainly to fund government-proposed projects, means that it does not have sufficient financial resources to support the work of civil society organizations on a sustained basis.[3] The main point is that international support for strengthening popular local mobilization and action for the land reform process is still insufficient.

As far as NGOs (both international and national) are concerned, the land reform agenda was pursued only timidly throughout the 1980s. Many of them stressed the importance of local populations' access to common property resources, of sustainable farming methods, of the need to recognize the customary rights of indigenous peoples, women's land rights, and so forth, frequently in line with the international debate on the environmental and social crises in developing countries. This gave them international credibility. At the same time, the absence of a strong call for land redistribution helped many NGOs not to come into direct conflict with national and local power structures, including those dominated by large landowners and agro-industrial enterprises.

This seems to have somewhat changed in the 1990s. The establishment of a worldwide network on land reform was mentioned above. The Via Campesina, since its establishment in 1993, has brought together organizations of peasants and small farmers from eight major regions to call for rapid agrarian reforms for food security (Via Campesina, 1998, p.2). Food-First Information and Action Network (FIAN), which asserts the fundamental importance of the human right to food, has sought to mobilize its country and regional members to demand for agrarian reforms (see e.g. Anon., 1997e). The International Union of Food, Agricultural, Hotel, Restaurant, Catering, Tobacco and Allied Workers' Associations, with representation from over 30 small farmers and rural workers' organizations, has sought to promote land reform as one of its main political agendas for its upcoming activities (IUF, 1998). Church-based organizations have also become vocal for agrarian reforms.[4] An example of this is the Food, Land and Hunger Working Group of the Office of the Co-ordinator for Justice, Peace and the Integrity of Creation for the Society of the Divine Word, which interacts with over 100 Catholic orders and is seeking to collect and disseminate information on the transnational ownership of land (Seigel, 1997). Similarly, regional groups such as the Asociacion de Organizaciones Campesinas Centroamericanas para la Cooperación y el Desarrollo (ASOCODE) and the Asian NGO Coalition for Agrarian Reform and Rural Development (ANGOC) have been active in policy advocacy and grassroots actions relating to agrarian reforms. In Africa, too, several of the major agrarian NGOs are active in advocating for land and tenurial reforms. These include the African Organizations Coalition for Food Security and Sustainable Development (AOCFSD), the Agriculture Peasants and Modernization Network (APM), and the National Land Committee (NLC).

Recent examples of national and grassroots organizations involved in land and tenurial reforms are also not lacking. MST in Brazil is currently a prominent case which has been able to mobilize a large number of small farmers and agricultural labourers inside the country and generate a great deal of international support for a radical change in land ownership. In the Philippines, the People's Campaign for Agrarian Reform (AR Now!) brings together 13 major NGOs active in agrarian reform advocacy, networking and farmers' assistance programmes. In Bangladesh, the Association for Land Reform and Development (ALRD) has established an extensive network with 108 NGOs and public interest groups to play a more active role in pushing for agrarian reform. In South Africa, the National Land Committee (a major NGO focusing on land reform and rural reconstruction) brings together 12 associations, rural development committees, rural workers' unions, etc. Similarly, in Venezuela Acción Campesina is linking with some 166 organizations to make networking more effective. In Guatemala, a country marked by extreme land inequality and rural violence, the Coordinación de ONG y Cooperativas (CONGCOOP) has since 1992 congregated 27 national NGOs and cooperatives to press for radical land reform measures and improved agrarian support services.

The ability of 'civil society' organizations, such as those mentioned above, in ultimately producing desirable changes in tenure relations and the improved livelihoods of peasants, is generally more complicated than it might appear on the surface. Their actual strength, weaknesses, internal dynamics and contradictions with external forces need to be assessed more realistically. Indeed, it makes little sense to romanticize the role of civil society organizations when neither the trends nor the outcomes favourable to poor peasants and rural workers are clear. Nevertheless, this may help in the long run to make poorer rural producers aware of their land rights and bring them into wider social movements. Socially just and economically opportune changes in property relations are difficult to come by; and even if they are produced, protecting their gains is frequently difficult.

Scope for land reform

Land reform is defined here to be a significant change in agrarian structure, resulting in increased access to land by the rural poor, as well as a secured tenure for those who actually work on the land. It also includes access to agricultural inputs, markets, services and other needed assistance. Bringing about sweeping land reform encompassing these aspects in different socio-economic contexts is obviously extremely difficult. It requires political commitment and risk on the part of national leadership, combined with a strong popular mobilization in rural areas. Alliances with supportive groups in urban areas and abroad are also crucial.

What is the scope for land reform today, as well as in the foreseeable future? This will to an extent vary from country to country, or even from locality to locality. In addition to the political factor mentioned above, the prospects for land reform are intimately tied to the level of rural demographic concentration, land availability, technological advancement and prevailing systems of property relations. This would also differ between small-cultivator systems, communal land tenure and large commercial holdings operated through hired labourers and contract farmers. What is certain, though, is that given the current gravity of rural poverty and hunger, as well as the necessity to make land reform relevant to the largest number of rural populations dependent on land and other natural resources, there is a clear need to consider broadening the scope of land reform. For present purposes, the concept of land reform is used primarily to encompass access to land, security of land rights and titles, and improvement in production structures.

Access to land

In countries where large holdings persist and fertile land is concentrated in the hands of a few, there would be clear prospects for acquiring new land by the poorer peasants and rural workers when redistributive land reform measures are introduced. This is currently the case in most Latin American countries, southern Africa, and a few Asian countries such as the Philippines. Land redistribution should also include restitution, which is a major part of the present land reform initiatives in southern Africa.[5] In these and many other countries, there are also manifold prospects for lowering the existing land ceilings and distributing different types of cultivated land held by central government, local authorities, corporations and commercial estates to the benefit of the landless. For example, in Bangladesh – a country with the one of the world's highest ratios of people to (cultivated) land – the government, together with NGOs, has been involved since 1984 in a major programme of land reform involving the provision of government land (known as *Khas* land) to a considerable number of landless people (Huda, 1993).

If the goal of land reform programmes should be to provide greater access to land, one must ask about the other possibilities of bringing more land under cultivation and developing other activities supportive of rural livelihoods. This is because cultivated land (the main area included in land reform programmes so far) often constitutes less than 20 per cent of the land area in most developing countries. It frequently makes up around 10 per cent of the land area; for example, China – the world's most populous country with a rising food demand – has less than 11 per cent of its land mass under cultivation (FAO, 1993a). Leaving aside important tracts in protected forests and water bodies, schemes such as small-scale land settlement, forest farming, agro-forestry, extension of cultivation in areas adjacent to settlements, and land reclamation activities could be suitable in various contexts.[6]

Similarly, the protection of access to common property resources is extremely important. Nearly 500 million rural people are believed to be directly dependent on forest resources for their livelihood (Barraclough and Ghimire, 1995). Many more extract food, raise animals, fish, collect wood and medicinal plants, and so forth, on a regular basis. Also, most of these resources are renewable. It is therefore vital that the use and management of rights of common property resource users should be protected and their knowledge valued. In short, land reform initiatives should contribute to improved rural livelihoods, as well as to more sustainable management of common property resources, through active participation of the local people.

Formalization of land rights and entitlements

Although the urgency to provide secured title to tenants and improved working and living conditions to agricultural workers has been stressed in most past land reform programmes, actual achievement has remained elusive. On the contrary, landowners and employers have sought to evict tenants and reduce wages for landless labourers, taking advantage of landless people desperately seeking wage employment as a result of their eviction or land dispossession, as well as to privatize local common property resources available to the rural poor. Indeed, clear titling and guaranteed rights to land resources are essential to many other groups of poorer, weaker rural inhabitants, such as people practising communal land tenure systems (notably in sub-Saharan Africa), swidden farmers, indigenous peoples (believed to be over 200 million), and households using marginal resources found within settlement areas (these areas cover as much as 17 per cent of the settled area in India; Agarwal, 1994). In addition, any comprehensive land reform must include measures to provide equal rights to resources and equal inheritance rights to women, who constitute a major portion of the rural poor.

Improving post-reform production structures and livelihoods

Provision of agricultural extension/training services, credit, loan guarantees, appropriate technology, markets, and other agricultural inputs and services for small farmers, rural workers and other beneficiaries during the post-land reform period is as crucial as providing them with land in the first place. There is a vast difference between developing countries in their production structures, levels of rural economy and social provisioning, but the issue of improvement in post-reform production structures and peasants' livelihoods is frequently neglected in land reform programmes. Land reform beneficiaries may be organized in such production forms as co-operatives, user groups and informal production bodies. The establishment of local land committees or other community organizations may prove highly useful for land improvement and strengthening of sustainable agricultural practices in the wake of land reform or tenurial reorganizations. Regular monitoring of the general living and working conditions of beneficiaries is also important, especially to ensure that they continue to hold their land, that they do not enter into a vicious circle of indebtedness, and that their production potentials are more fully exploited.

OVERVIEW: PROCESSES, ACTORS AND POWER RELATIONS AFFECTING LAND REFORM

Many of the points and issues referred to in the preceding section are taken up and cross-examined in the present volume. It is clear that despite broad agreement amongst bi/multilateral agencies, governments and NGOs on the need to promote land reform, and attempts to undertake a few programme activities, there has been very little research and critical reflection on what exactly defines land reform at the start of the twenty-first century. What is the actual scope of land reform in different contexts? How are current approaches, such as market-driven land reform, tested? What can their protagonists expect in the way of participation and reaction of the pledged beneficiaries? What are the real as well as potential prospects for handling rural poverty and related socio-political marginalization through land reform? What else might be tried? What are the global forces and trends that render peasants' livelihoods more vulnerable? Which are the major institutions and actors obstructing or assisting local mobilization? What recourse and allies can peasants count on? These are some of the basic questions or concerns of any student of land reform and rural social transformation, but answers are difficult to come by, and the literature is scattered. The bulk of the theoretical and analytical findings and analyses that do exist are mostly from the 1960s and 1970s, when land reform was commonly seen as fundamental to equitable rural social development in national and international policy-making circles, albeit with differing interpretations and performance.

About this book

This volume obviously cannot profess to answer all the above questions. Its main emphasis lies in analysing those forces and actors currently shaping discourses and policies on land reform. It examines through multiple lenses (market, social alliances, role of state policies, peasant organizations) how issues of land access, distribution, sustainable use and the like are being played out in rural arenas. It grounds its theoretical discourse in evidence from the field through case studies and presentation of research results, and covers a spectrum of regions from Latin America to Africa, Asia, and the Near East.

The underlying premise of this volume is twofold. Firstly, it contends that there is a need to revisit the discourse on land and tenure issues and re-examine the current land reform approaches and probable outcomes. Secondly, all chapters achieve a clear consensus that for any effective and socially just land reform, the active participation of peasants and their representative organizations is vital in addition to a supportive atmosphere at national and international levels.

This introductory chapter attempts to set the stage for the debate, and briefly discusses why the need for new theoretical and research material on land reform has become so vital today. The volume contains seven more chapters: in the second, Solon Barraclough discusses the role of the state and other actors in land reform. Using case studies from Latin America, he analyses the constraints and configurations under which governments operate, as well as examining what roles other actors (NGOs, international agencies, peasant organizations, landholders, etc.) also play in promoting land reform. Eduardo Baumeister, in Chapter 3, reviews the land reform experiences in Central America. He examines, in particular, the strengths and weaknesses of local initiatives to secure benefits incurred through three decades of reforms, as well as past and pending opportunities and dangers. Case studies focus on El Salvador, Honduras and Nicaragua. Peter Dorner, in the subsequent chapter, shifts our attention to the international arena, looking at the impact of recent strides in technology and globaliza-tion on local-level initiatives in land reform. How have the growing inter-dependence of countries, the rising power of transnationals, and advances in information technology affected the debate on land reform? What are the current openings and constraints under which local-level actors operate? Given the recent surge in interest in market-based land reforms promoted by dominant bi/multilateral institutions, Riad El-Ghonemy, in Chapter 5, adopts a political-economy approach to expose the limitations of these types of policies. Using background material from Egypt and empirical evidence from Brazil, Colombia, the Philippines, South Africa and Malawi, he argues for more politically oriented land redistributive measures in addition to the use of the market mechanism in some circumstances. The following three chapters analyse land reform from the angle of civil society organizations and local-level actors. In Chapter 6, Krishna Ghimire takes a critical look at the crucial role of the legal system in supporting peasants during land reform processes. Case studies from Bangladesh and the Philippines are used to address the potentially beneficial (as well as harm-ful) roles lawyers and legal aid can play in assisting peasants. In Chapter 7, Gerrit Huizer reviews the historical patterns of social mobilizations by peasants and their allies. He analyses eleven case studies to show that socially redistributive land reforms have been contingent on successful peasant mobilization. Set against the background of the Philippine agrarian reform programme, Jose Olano, in Chapter 8, investigates the various attempts made by peasant organizations to manage agrarian conflict. Specific cases are analysed to suggest that peasant organizations need to combine not only formal means, but also informal actions, including the use of their inner strengths and creativity, to resolve problems.

Below, a brief overview is given of the issues and problems evoked by these different chapters. However, the reader must remain aware that separating themes is a superficial task. It heightens academic clarity, but in the real world, as the contributors emphasize, the problems and forces often collide and overlap with each other. The three vital ingredients in land reform: state, market, and civil society, exist in a dynamic agrarian arena, with the lines separating them becoming increasingly blurred.

Local agrarian structure and vulnerability

When one examines the available information on land issues (rates of landlessness, land dispossession, rural poverty, land conflicts, etc.), two initial observations emerge. One, the amount of available data on the current situation (especially since 1990) is greatly lacking, and secondly, what data do exist point to ever-increasing rates of landlessness, growing rural inequalities, increasing frequency of land conflicts, and high levels of malnutrition and food insecurity. For example, between 1980 and 1985, the totally landless population in developing countries rose from 171 million to 180 million (FAO, 1987, p.45). It is possible that some of this growth was due to demographic expansion within the category of the landless population, but clearly the increase in the rate of landlessness is considerably higher than the average population growth in developing countries during that period.

Glaring rural inequalities exist in terms of landholding in many developing countries. In Asia, 37 and 36 per cent of the rural households in the Philippines and Indonesia (Java only) are totally landless. Bangladesh and India have nearly the same proportion of landless people. In Latin America the picture is not much better, with the rates of the total landless being 77 per cent in the Dominican Republic, 41 per cent in El Salvador, 39 per cent in Brazil, and 37 per cent in Mexico. In Africa, there exists a conspicuous land inequality in South Africa and Zimbabwe due to an oppressive colonial legacy. In Egypt 29 per cent of the rural population is totally landless, whilst in Morocco 33 per cent (FAO, 1987; Alamgir and Arora, 1991; Jazairy et al., 1992).

The problem is even more acute when the near-landless population is considered. For example, in India and Bangladesh 55 and 78 per cent of the rural population hold less than 1 ha per household, respectively. In Kenya and Lesotho, nearly one-third of the rural households cultivate less than 1 ha. In Latin America, 60, 41 and 76 per cent of El Salvadorian, Guatemalan and Jamaican rural households operate less than 2 ha each (FAO, 1987; Alamgir and Arora, 1991; Jazairy et al., 1992). Even though the original sources and validity of some of these figures are questionable, the general magnitude of landlessness or near landlessness is quite apparent.

Rural vulnerability is not always entirely related to the lack of access to land. Nevertheless, households that are able to hold land and cultivate it in accordance with their own priorities are likely to face less food insecurity. It is therefore legitimate to articulate for changes in tenurial relations designed to provide more land to the rural poor. This naturally has to be combined with the provision of improved, locally adapted agricultural techniques and support services.

Not all the countries with a high proportion of rural landlessness mentioned above have lacked agrarian reform measures. Mexico and several other Central American countries have seen many radical land legislations in the past decades, but reform processes were frequently weakened by countervailing political forces, and there was little attempt to protect the past gains of land reform such as protection of cooperatives, provision for credits, support to peasant mobilization, and awareness building (see Chapters 2–4). And there are many cases where the land reform measures introduced have not been sufficiently effective to confront the power of the local landed elites and agribusiness: two such examples are Brazil and the Philippines. Brazil is often cited as having one of the highest incidences of rural poverty in Latin America (affecting 73 per cent of the rural population), and with marked rural inequalities whereby 88 per cent of the land lies with the wealthiest 20 per cent of the rural population, while 40 per cent of small farmers retain 1 per cent of the land (IFAD, 1993). Land reform measures introduced so far have not been able to alter this situation. Similarly, in the Philippines after 11 consecutive agrarian reforms, repression by landowners or transnational companies and the lack of extension services and legal land titles to supposed beneficiaries are common. In the province of Central Luzon, upheld as a shining example of agrarian reform success, 70 per cent of rice farmers and 50 per cent of sugar farmers remain landless (Karunan, 1992, p.85). Other figures show that several thousand farmers working as tenants are forced to turn over 60 to 70 per cent of their produce to landowners (Anon., 1996b). Indeed, Olano suggests (Chapter 8) that peasant ownership of total cultivated land area nationwide has not changed, if not declined, despite attempts at agrarian reforms; on the other extreme, large landowners constituting 2 per cent of the landowners controlled 36 per cent of all farmland.

Within rural areas, the lack of access to land and formal title affects different population groups differently. In addition to the direct use of land for food production and income generation, it is often the main source of creating wage employment. A whole range of artisan and petty trading activities are associated with agricultural production, distribution and consumption patterns. In a situation of extreme inequality and lack of access to productive resources, conflicts between poorer production groups may be as acute as between poor peasants and rich farmers. For example, landless households who would have to rely on agricultural wage labour now find themselves competing with small farmers in trying to supplement their meagre farm income through wage labour in the area. In some cases conflicts may take place within a given group; for example, in Zimbabwe any major redistribution of white-owned commercial farms to black farmers may mean the loss of wage employment for an important number of agricultural labourers currently employed by these farms, thereby making them compete with other rural workers for agricultural wage employment available locally. Different groups of rural poor directly compete for natural resources in rangeland areas, water bodies and forests. New, poorer migrants may come into conflict with the traditional resource users or tribal populations.

A growing number of conflicts over land and natural resources are those involving indigenous peoples. The roots of many of these conflicts and tensions can be traced back to colonization, but have intensified with time due to rising external population pressures on land resources and commercial interests. Most conflicts revolve around the protection of customary land rights for indigenous peoples that are often ignored, or recognized on paper only, with specific problematic areas involving conflicts between customary and national laws, and a growing frequency of land conflicts as large tracts of land are appropriated for either commercial use or environmental protection projects such as the establishment of strict nature reserves or parks (Plant, 1993; Ganz, 1996; Ghimire and Pimbert, 1997). Frequently, land utilized by indigenous peoples is being defined as 'vacant' land and made part and parcel of government settlement programmes (or else invaded by poorer squatters). Their land is distributed to smallholders, tenant farmers, migrant workers and others who themselves have lost access to land and are forced to move into forest and tribal areas for survival. Given that indigenous land claims usually lack formal written titles, land can also be easily expropriated by powerful groups. All this has severe livelihood repercussions for indigenous peoples. A World Bank study in 1990 showed that there was a high correlation between poverty levels and ethnic background, with indigenous peoples being disproportionately represented among the poor or at high risk of poverty in Bolivia, Ecuador, Guatemala, Mexico, Peru, India and Bangladesh (World Bank, 1990, p.37).

Another social group that needs to be noted here is rural women, as the majority fall consistently among those most vulnerable and deprived. In all categories of rural poor lacking access to land and its resources – landless, indigenous groups, sharecroppers – women are often doubly penalized, first for belonging to these categories, and secondly because of their gender. It is suggested that since the 1970s the number of women living below the poverty line has increased by 50 per cent, in comparison with 30 per cent for their male counterparts (FAO, 1996a). Despite this high-level poverty and socio-political marginalization amongst women, and despite the over-whelming contribution of women to agriculture and their responsibility for the household (and often national) food security, the majority of poor rural women tend to have access to only marginal and least-productive land, and are the last to benefit from any legal land titles and services provided by land reform programmes (Jazairy et al., 1992, Agarwal, 1994, Gore, 1994, Faruquee and Carey, 1997, El-Ghonemy, Chapter 5). For example, in Kenya, although 98 per cent of women are engaged full-time in farming activities, with 35 per cent of smallholdings run by women, only 5 per cent of Kenyan women own land in their own name (Jazairy et al., 1992; Gore, 1994). In Central America, where only one member of a household can be appointed as the official beneficiary of reform, women are losing access. Thus 6 per cent of beneficiaries are women in Nicaragua, and only 3.8 per cent in Honduras (Jazairy et al., 1992). Baumeister (Chapter 3) suggests that, despite their active contribution – in countries such as Nicaragua and Honduras 20–25 per cent of women are involved in farming activities – women are still culturally and officially seen as non-active economically.

The prevalence of very unjust social and agrarian structures, combined with the lack of off-farm rural employment opportunities, are clear signs of widespread socio-economic marginalization and vulnerability amongst land-poor groups such as agricultural workers, tenants, indigenous peoples and women. Despite wider diffusion of agricultural technology and increased productivity, rural development programmes have produced few concrete results by way of poverty eradication in the absence of desirable agrarian and other needed institutional reforms. Many rural or agricultural development programmes have become increasingly ineffective in recent years, in large part due to liberalization and structural adjustment policies. This has meant a drastic reduction in subsidies, credit and extension services for poorer farmers. Basic food items such as wheat and rice are increasingly imported from rich countries, while at the same time the production of export-oriented cash crops like coffee, bananas and cocoa is encouraged. In any event, a large number of poorer households are lacking the basic production item: land. The recent official change of focus from redistributive land reform programmes to market-assisted ones is that most of the rural poor lack the necessary collateral to secure land or make it productive through continued investment in technology and land improvement (see Chapter 5).

Weakening role of the state

The role of the state is crucial in any land reform programme, not only for practical reasons (carrying out cadastral surveys, promulgating and implementing relevant legislation, providing technical and financial support, etc.), but also because land reform is inherently a political process. Without the implementation by the state of effective, socially just land laws, policies and strategies, land reform remains a dead letter, regardless of donor pressure or popular demand for land by the landless. The provision of vital credit and extension services by the government to land beneficiaries is also important in guaranteeing the sustainability of the whole process. Despite a great deal of scope for an effective state intervention, few national governments have successfully implemented progressive land reform measures. This indicates the political nature of reform, which necessarily involves the appropriation and redistribution of land, often from the powerful landed groups holding significant social, economic and political weight within the state apparatus. Concomitant with this is the fact that upsetting these same actors translates into a loss of political influence or other social, economic favours from large landed families, business owners and other powerful actors for the national political elites. In any event, in many countries the largest landowners themselves are the leading elite groups in power.

Drawing findings from experiences in a number of Latin American countries, Barraclough argues (Chapter 2) that it is precisely when powerful groups holding political power, under pressure from peasant organizations and other sectors of civil society, feel it is essential to adopt land reform measures in favour of the rural poor that changes can effectively occur. Peasant organizations, their supporters and donor policies play an important lobbying and catalytic role, but ultimately their demands have to be institutionalized by the state (Huizer, Chapter 7). The latter can be a source of justice in favour of the rural poor, as well as being the single largest obstacle to their betterment by swinging in favour of the powerful landed elite.

At the same time, current trends of globalization and growing reliance on the market have curtailed the amount of space a state has to manoeuvre. Dorner (Chapter 4) suggests that the nation-state has lost much of its autonomy, and levels of decision-making are increasingly confused with the growing internationalization of trade, the proliferation of transnational companies that defy national boundaries, and the advances in technology that make all this possible. The ability of the state is thus restricted by larger forces that it can only partially control. The days when robust state intervention was seen as important for planning and rural poverty reduction have now passed, in favour of 'minimum government' (Chambers, 1991). Most developing countries have large debts and are tied in some manner to economic reform designed by large lending institutions. As a result, their priorities have clearly shifted from providing basic social welfare services to servicing foreign debt burdens. In certain cases the state is already so weakened, in terms of its ability to manage the economy and play an interlocutor role with organized social groups, that it may not make sense to target an absent state and withdrawn representatives in demanding tenurial reforms and agricultural development. This is further exacerbated by the apparent remoteness of the decision-making centres of foreign-based enterprises and agro-industrial conglomerates that are now extending their control over national domains (Piña, 1998).

Baumeister (Chapter 3), in his discussion of post-reform measures in Central America, draws very similar conclusions. Examining the after-effects of land reform programmes introduced since the 1950s, he shows how governments are presently unable to deliver the necessary services in order to address problems of rural inequality and landlessness. Constrained by civil war and structural adjustment programmes that demand cuts in government subsidies and public-sector spending, the percentage of the national budget allocated to agrarian reform policies is increasingly on the decline in the majority of the Central American countries. This means that original intentions of increasing agricultural production and providing expropriated land to land-poor families have been largely put aside, due to the lack of resources for agricultural development and compensation to large landowners. Instead, beneficiaries are losing access to rural credit facilities, physical capital in the form of land, machinery, irrigation equipment, and technical assistance provided by the state. Large cooperatives in countries such as Nicaragua and El Salvador are being dismantled, with vast tracts of the best arable land being sold to multinationals and powerful national agribusiness groups. Baumeister also notes that beneficiaries have also altered their techniques and systems of production so that farming, cattle and forest resources are used more intensely for consumption and profit purposes, with negative environmental repercussions. The end result, however, does little to mitigate insecurity, as beneficiaries are increasingly losing access to land they had secured under reform. The state, often in close alliance with powerful business interests, is doing little to roll back this process.

The state is by no means a monolithic institution. It does have divergent structures and institutions, as well as individuals with varied interests. Not all states are giving up their economic managerial role to the multilateral agencies and transnational companies. Peasant marginalization and vulnerability do remain a matter of concern for some governments. In any event, all governments are keenly aware of the political consequences of widespread rural discontent and opposition. Progressive political elites, technicians and administrators (who can be found in any state) can play an important role in supporting peasants' demands for land and agricultural support services. In some cases, the state might be quite committed to agrarian reforms (e.g. South Africa, Zimbabwe). In such circumstances, various partnership and joint-action programmes between government agencies and peasant groups, aimed at reducing rural landlessness and poverty, would be conceivable. Importantly, many governments do have agrarian reform policies. The main problem is that they are frequently timid, despite the enormity of landlessness and rural inequalities, and try not to confront the local and national power structures. The usual result has been slow or ineffective implementation of reform measures, unless there is strong popular mobilization for land reform combined at times with outside pressure. How to exert political pressure on the state so that it becomes engaged in comprehensive land reform activities in different contexts is therefore a crucial question. Some of these aspects will be taken up later in discussion of the role of peasants' associations and other civil society organizations in land reform.

Market reliance as the solution?

As indicated above, the utilization of the market mechanism is considered by many bi- and multilateral agencies to be the main remedy for today's rural landlessness and poverty. This is also being proposed with a view to reducing the role of the state in land reform, and goes along perfectly with the market liberalization policies that are being promoted. The establishment of land banks to offer credit to farmers for land purchases, and attempts to improve land records through cadastral surveys, are the two key elements of the present market-based land reform measures. As already noted earlier, these measures have been executed notably in Brazil, Colombia, South Africa, the Philippines and Indonesia, but some elements of market mechanisms are utilized in land transaction and titling in many other countries. In Latin America these include Bolivia, Honduras, El Salvador, Ecuador and, more recently, Guatemala. In Africa, in addition to South Africa, Zimbabwe, Mozambique, Kenya and Uganda have sought to utilize market mechanisms in the formalization of land claims and titling. In Asia, governments have proposed to follow the market-oriented land redistribution approach in Bangladesh, Nepal, Thailand and many others, in addition to the Philippines and Indonesia mentioned above. Northern bilateral bodies and multilateral financial institutions see good prospects for the involvement of civil society organizations, such as local NGOs, in assisting market-based land reform through assisting farmers and the government in identifying land, selection and training of beneficiaries, and loan repayment. This is, for example, the case with a new World Bank/IFAD/FAO project on market-based land reform (focused on Brazil, Colombia, South Africa and the Philippines) which, amongst others, proposes to create a civil society network in these countries (IFAD/World Bank/FAO, 1997).

If peasants are able to obtain land without having to undergo direct confrontation with landowners or the state, all the better. But the reality is that the prospects for making more land available on the market for redistribution are limited in many countries where land is scarce and landholdings amongst larger farmers are already small. The costs of land purchase and titling have proved onerous for small-scale producers everywhere, especially given the uncertain price of many agricultural products. Some scholars argue that any important programme of credit-financed land purchases by the landless could be self-defeating, driving land prices up (Schönleitner, 1997, p.28). Financial support for the post-reform period is usually very limited. At the same time, there are few concrete policy measures that discourage speculators and investors from taking advantage of subsidized land and agricultural services. According to some observers, this policy may instead result in new processes of land concentration: 'Land is often bought by a small group of the "well-to-do", processes of land speculation intensify and land prices increase, often creating (new) insecurities for large groups of the farming population' (Van der Haar and Zoomers, 1998, pp.1–2).

Moreover, gender biases are inherent in most land markets. Lacking access to credit facilities, women have poor purchasing power. Furthermore, even when they can purchase land, it is often controlled by the male members of households (Faruquee and Carey, 1997). Gore (1994) notes that in Kenya, for example, where only a few women have legal land titles in their name, access to land markets, credit facilities and technical assistance services is difficult and an increasing number of women are landless or dependent on men for their tenurial security. Market-assisted land reform measures have so far failed to recognize this problem.

In this volume, El-Ghonemy (Chapter 5) examines market-based land reform from two angles: firstly by analysing the experience of five countries with the strategy (Brazil, Colombia, Kenya, the Philippines and South Africa); and secondly by assessing the impact of privatization measures on communal-based land systems in sub-Saharan Africa (Ivory Coast, Malawi and Uganda). In both instances the many flaws and problems inherent in current market-based land reforms become apparent. He questions whether markets as an economic instrument can be simplistically applied to issues of land and property rights, which are social institutions; and whether most wage-dependent rural landless labourers actually have the means to purchase land in their lifetime (Gordillo de Anda, 1997, p.3).

In the case of sub-Saharan Africa the scenario is particularly distressing, with rising poverty and malnutrition, declining food production levels, and heightened rural inequality. In a previous work El-Ghonemy (1990a, p.162) documented that out of a total number of 2 112 000 holdings in the small-farm sector in Kenya, 83 per cent are less than 2 ha, whereas in the large-farm sector there are 2192 farms with a total area of 2.6 million ha, with 930 being 500 ha or greater. Likewise Bruce and Migot-Adhola (1994) show that the privatization and individualization of customary land tenure has led to increased land concentration, marginalization and landlessness, with the rich siphoning off all the wealth and resources. Evidence suggests that rural credit has rarely been made available to poor peasants, and instead the majority of buyers are high-ranking politicians, businessmen and urban speculators; Gore (1994) draws the same conclusions in his research on sub-Saharan Africa.

Similar problems are highlighted by Baumeister (Chapter 3) in his study on Central America, where market-based land transfers are promoted. The result is that in El Salvador, land is being sold by cooperatives and individual peasants to urban developers; in Honduras it is purchased by large multi-nationals involved in banana production; while in Nicaragua beneficiaries of earlier reform are selling off their land to large landowners engaged in cash-crop production. As evoked earlier, agrarian debt runs rampant and the land market is seen as a way for quick money by the rural poor rather than long-term tenure security.

In the Philippines, many of the beneficiaries have taken credit to buy land extending over a period of 30 years (representing 10–15 per cent of their annual produce), but unstable commodity pricing and the absence of the necessary agricultural extension support has forced many to borrow money from local moneylenders by mortgaging their land already in the provisory entitlement period (Chapter 6).

What does emerge from these observations is that the market can prove a useful instrument only if combined with a greater degree of state inter-vention, NGO participation and peasant mobilization. The state's role is crucial in an attempt to reduce the power of landlords and merchants, to pressure large landowners to relinquish land beyond the permitted average ceiling, to decide on the land price, and to monitor the whole land registra-tion process. Specific attention needs to be given to such weaker social groups as women and agricultural labourers. But to allow a free hand to the landowners and banks to decide on land prices, repayment procedures, crop production patterns, etc. in the name of non-intervention in the mar-ket transaction process would mean the emergence of new inequalities and peasants' further dependence on landlords, banks and grain merchants. The final goal of addressing rural inequalities and insecure livelihoods in a more potent manner is scarcely feasible through this approach. Dorner's response (Chapter 4), with many others, is the need to 'level the playing field' and enforce accountability and responsibility at each level. To do this, new institutional rules and practices need to be devised, rather than just changing the organizations and individuals at play. Ideally, this would mean that those causing most damage would be willing to pay for it and mitigate the costs, while benefits would be easily available to all to share equally.

Popular mobilization for land reform

Wider political mobilization and actions by peasants, their representative organizations and other supportive institutions are key to putting pressure on the government to consider land reform as an important political agenda. This may take the form of an attempt to strengthen internal polit-ical mobilization, self-help groupings, awareness campaigns, training pro-grammes, networking and dissemination of useful information on reform laws and peasants' rights. Direct actions may be organized, such as squatting on landlords' estates, invasion by tenants/sharecroppers to remove crops from landowners' fields, surrounding of officials and landowners to press for lower rents or crop share and increased wages for agricultural labourers and women. These direct actions may be combined with the attempt to influence the mass media for public support, lobbying of political parties, local governments and the bureaucracy, as well as their own mobilization for direct electoral participation aimed at emphasizing their need and aspiration to land. Popular mobilization is crucial not only during the promulgation of reform legislation by the government, but also during the implementation phase, so that powerful landowners do not twist the law in their favour. This process is also important in improving post-reform production structures and local livelihood systems.

Several of the chapters in this volume critically examine the role of grassroots-level mobilization in initiating and sustaining land reform processes. Huizer (Chapter 7) uses a historical lens to argue that peasants are far from passive social forces. Following an extensive discussion of several case studies (including Mexico, Russia, China, Indonesia and Zimbabwe), the author documents the growth of peasant mobilizations, from an unbearable feeling of frustration with the oppressive status quo, to rallying support around a specific cause, to building up the organization to handle longer-term aims of influencing policy-making, and assisting the state in post-reform measures. All this, however, comes from a long process of struggle in the face of opposition by powerful landowners and others who use all tactics to resist peasant demands. The use of force in the form of forced evictions, harassment, physical intimidation and even assassination has been a common experience.

Barraclough draws similar conclusions in Chapter 2. Based on an analysis of the Chilean and other Latin American experiences, he suggests that autonomous peasant movements were difficult to achieve and institutionalize. Many tended to last for a relatively short period; once land had been obtained, many peasants were on their own. The more peasants were socio-economically and ethnically stratified, the more difficult it was to maintain the momentum. Post-reform authoritarian regimes often repressed or co-opted all autonomous peasant organizations.

The support of rural and urban trade unions, NGOs, church groups, academics and public figures is especially crucial in sustaining peasant movements. A few aspects of the importance of legal assistance and support from lawyers and NGOs providing legal and paralegal services are analysed Chapter 6. It seems that even where progressive land reforms and land rights exist in favour of the rural poor, local courts frequently rule in favour of those with social and economic power. The examples illustrated are of Bangladesh and the Philippines. Both countries have legal provisions to provide land to the landless and other marginalized groups, but both countries have dismal records in actual delivery of land and other resources. Seeking alliances with larger NGOs, legal aid clinics, individual lawyers and schoolteachers, peasant groups are now collectively taking cases of wrong-doing to court, and rallying public support for their cause. This type of assistance by external allies is not always easy to secure for peasants with limited resources, based in remote villages. Even though legal and parale-gal organizations are fraught with internal inconsistencies, they are, never-theless, extremely valuable in providing help to peasant groups in the form of knowledge of land legislation, material and financial tools, and overall legal assistance.

External groups, such as NGOs and peasants' organizations, are also effective in conflict mediation. In Chapter 8, Olano highlights this phe-nomenon with the experience of Filipino NGOs and progressive farmers' unions in managing agrarian conflicts. The intervention of the state is not always accessible or impartial. Hence this task often falls to civil society groups. In rural areas their presence is vital, given the escalation of land-based conflicts worldwide.[7] Olano infers that even if the end result is not always the desired one, at least it engages public attention and provides peasants with an opportunity to enlarge their network.

Dorner, in Chapter 4, referring to the recent uprising by the Chiapas peasants in Mexico and their effective use of the Internet to inform their grievances, suggests that new technologies in the area of communication and transportation have given local communities new leverage. This is not the only example. Local peasants' movements such as MST in Brazil, Demokratikong Magbubukid sa Pilipinas in the Philippines, and numerous dynamic peasant movements in India have been able to seize information and also promote their cause on a global scale. A growing number of agrarian NGOs are now developing websites, making television and video documentaries, producing and taking part in radio programmes, and networking with regional and international groups, so that there is cross-fertilization of information and strong solidarity can be built. In this respect, the processes of globalization associated with rapid development and diffusion in information technology may effectively be helping to har-ness their benefits in a productive way for local groups.

CONCLUSIONS

A number of conclusions can be drawn from the preceding discussion. First, land reform is a valid policy option for rural development today, and will continue to be so in the coming decades. Secure access to land is per-haps the best economic and social cushion that a land-poor rural house-hold could expect to have, especially given the increased market pressure in rural areas. Naturally, access to land alone is never sufficient to ensure a decent living; the provision of appropriate agricultural technology and support services such as credit and markets is crucial if agriculture is to continue to prove a viable livelihood alternative for the rural poor. Other

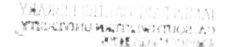

basic needs, such as healthcare, shelter, education and democratic representation, are also important.

Second, there are clear prospects for land reform in terms of the land area that could be made available. Besides the possibility of expropriation of large landholdings for redistribution (restitution in some cases) to the landless in developing countries dominated by bimodal agricultural production systems, there are possibilities for reducing existing land ceilings for large landowners and redistributing excess land to the landless in many other countries, including countries with smallholder agriculture. In addition, there are various other types of cultivated land held under government institutions, parastatal companies, local authorities and private corporations that could be made available for redistribution. In particular, given the current extent of rural poverty and hunger, additional cultivable land should be brought under agriculture through small-scale land settlement, reclamation and extension of cultivation in adjacent forest areas. The local extraction of common property resources, such as forests, water bodies and rangeland, is vital for supplementing crop production. An increased Western environmental lobby to conserve tropical forests and other natural resources in recent years has resulted in a near absence of dialogue and imaginative, socio-ecologically integrated project planning concerning wider land/resource use options, including flexible access to, and use of, common property resources. Both experts and activists on land reform have lacked imagination in this respect, tending to limit the scope of land reform merely to the redistributive policies involving cultivated land, and ignoring the wider prospects of land distribution and use.

Third, it is also evident that land reform measures need to be perceptive and adapted to specific local circumstances. Where land is scarce and average holdings are small, including those of the landed elites, agrarian reforms in such contexts would have to concentrate more on improved tenants' rights and better working conditions for rural workers; fuller use of common property resources; restrictions on land sales; progressive taxes; and peasants' access to subsidized credits and production services. Even in the case of medium-sized and large farms which are mechanized and productive, their subdivision into small plots may result in reduced production in the short run. Large commercial farms may be transformed into worker-managed cooperatives so that production levels remain satisfactory, or their income is better distributed. Granting private title to land may be useful in some circumstances, whilst in others communal land-tenure systems and long-term lease holding may be more appropriate. On the whole, in labour surplus situations, more employment-generating agricultural production systems, rural industrialization and locally grounded livelihood practices need to accompany land reform measures.

Fourth, no sweeping land redistributive measures capable of redressing rural inequality are feasible through the market mechanism as currently called for by major bi/multilateral development agencies. This approach treats land merely as a commodity, while above all it is a social institution. For the majority of the rural poor, land is not only the main source of survival, but also a way of living and maintaining dignity. It is unlikely that there would ever be sufficient land in the market on a voluntary 'willing seller, willing buyer' basis for the majority of the land-aspiring rural poor to gain access to it. Indeed, land markets are highly unfavourable to the poor, while providing further economic opportunities for speculators to grab more land. Even where peasants have been able to acquire land through this mechanism, for most it has been very difficult to obtain the necessary agricultural inputs and services. Market-assisted land reform programmes are launched in tandem with economic adjustment programmes that mean cuts in agricultural subsidies, and in any case poor peasants and the landless are the least favoured groups for credit by formal lending institutions. It is true that increased emphasis on the market mechanism has allowed some governments to evade more radical land reform measures, while rural inequalities and poverty are ever more serious. Comprehensive, yet locally adopted, land redistributive and use measures are the fundamental solutions, but these are frequently politically more risky.

Fifth, strong popular local mobilization and participation during the land reform process are especially indispensable. Without these, the national elites are unlikely to take peasants and their representative organizations seriously, either as allies or as credible opponents to be reckoned with. They may, instead, take donor agencies and landed groups more seriously. Organized demand for land; strong internal political mobilization; direct action to obtain land (e.g. land invasions); active use of electoral means; and wider alliances are key if any sweeping redistributive measures are to be introduced. Beneficiaries need to be actively involved in the land identification, acquisition and titling process if land is to be redistributed in their favour and large landowners are to be unable to circumvent the legislation. Progressive NGOs and other concerned external actors can be the vital allies of peasants, helping them to mobilize public support, provide legal aid, raise awareness, and lobby. They serve as useful intermediaries between local actors and the state institutions or, increasingly, between peasants and donor agencies. But different constraints faced by civil society organizations concerned with the land question should not be forgotten. Many of their attempts are generally small scale, designed to tackle immediate requirements. Their approaches to land reform and rural development are hardly autonomous and consistent, especially given financial dependencies on outside agencies. Nevertheless, whatever limited support these groups are able to provide is crucial for peasants, as there are few reliable outside forces that peasants can count on. One of the positive side-effects of globalization and recent democratic processes has been easier access to information and knowledge about peasants' rights, experiences of other countries, and routes to possible action. NGOs and other civil society organizations are instrumental in widely disseminating information on events in rural areas, such as massive land invasion by the MST in Brazil, mobilization by Chiapas peasants in Mexico, raids of cash-crop plantations in Benin, and land conflicts between rural labourers and landed groups and agribusiness in the Philippines. This has helped peasant sectors to be increasingly aware and alert.

Finally, more research is required on a number of points. As referred to above, there has been a lack of information for the past decade on landlessness, landholding patterns, land consolidation processes and land conflicts. Most of the available information is outdated, and institutions such as the FAO, which had played a leading role in compiling data, have lost interest in recent years. This is explained in part by their increased faith in the market mechanism to alleviate rural poverty, and in part due to their declining compassion for the rural cause. There is little systematic information on how land reform measures introduced earlier are evolving, especially from the point of view of their ability to offer peasants improved living and working conditions. Recent patterns of agrarian change, including the evolution of 'contract farming' (instead of traditional sharecropping), the impact of tenancy liberalization (as seen in Egypt), land dispossession by transnational corporations and national agribusiness, the repressive role of paramilitary forces (e.g. in Colombia, Indonesia, Mexico and the Philippines), and the emerging consequences of market-led land reform need critical examination. There has been little attempt to unravel what the concrete policy options could be in relation to the availability of different types of land in varied socio-ecological contexts. What are the specific measures that could be taken to integrate gender and ethnicity aspects in land reform programmes? How could the more progressive elements within the state and international funding institutions be influenced? What are the recent patterns of grassroots political mobilization and action for land reform, given that rural stratification and conflicts are becoming intense between various producer groups and rural households? How stable is the alliance of peasants with NGOs and other civil society organizations? Information is also lacking on the current role of NGOs and other civil society forces in defending peasants' basic land rights, managing tenurial conflicts, and improving post-reform production structures and livelihoods. These are questions to which attention is needed, but they are not the only ones.

Land reform is not merely providing land from one tenurial group to another. It is about changing power structures and socio-economic relations; it is about ensuring a better livelihood for peasants. Bold political measures, imaginative land-use policies and technical packages that may be envisaged require a great deal of thought, debate, research and trying out of specific proposals in concrete contexts. Betting uniquely on the market mechanism to rectify rural inequality and landlessness in a preconceived manner (without critical inquiry and reflection) is neither realistic nor befitting to a vast number of increasingly impoverished rural poor in the developing world.

CHAPTER TWO

The Role of the State and Other Actors in Land Reform

Solon L. Barraclough

INTRODUCTION: INEQUITABLE AGRARIAN STRUCTURES AND ACTORS

Most of the rural poor in developing countries are landless or nearly land-less, but they usually have some kind of access to agricultural land. They are likely to be full-time or seasonal wage workers, tenants of various types, squatters or smallholders with insufficient land and insecure property rights. The main problem for the rural poor lies in insecure and inequitable terms of access to land and other requisites for decent livelihoods. Many are unable to produce enough to meet their basic needs. Others produce a surplus that is appropriated by landlords, employers, creditors, intermediaries, collectors of fees or taxes, and others. As a result, the rural poor in developing countries are often unable to provide themselves and their families with locally acceptable livelihoods. As they usually have no opportunities for finding better livelihoods elsewhere, and as the state seldom has the capacity to provide them with basic social services or other relief, land reform may be the only viable solution for their acute poverty.

There are many other reasons for undertaking land reforms, depending on each particular situation. Landlords may be consumption-prone and inefficient. Smallholders often use their land and labour more intensively and efficiently than do large-scale producers. Increased demand for consumption goods, inputs and services by land reform beneficiaries can stimulate integrated and more sustainable rural development. Highly concentrated control of land is usually incompatible with democratic processes and institutions. The issues of equity, security and acceptable livelihoods for the rural poor, however, are always fundamental.

Land reform necessarily requires participation by its intended beneficiaries, as well as by the large holders who lose some of their land rights and by the state that, as a minimum, provides the legal framework for reform. As will be seen, there are always many other social actors in bringing about reform and in shaping its subsequent evolution. Sometimes other actors are far more influential than are the landless and near-landless who are supposed to benefit, or the large landowners who stand to lose.

The role of the state in land reform is crucial. This is because the state comprises the institutionalized political organization of society. It articulates and implements public policy as well as adjudicating conflicts. In theory, the state has a monopoly of the legitimate use of coercive force within its territory, together with the responsibility of pursuing 'public good' for all its citizens. Land reform without the state's participation would be a contradiction in terms. How the state participates, to what avail, to whose advantage or detriment, and the roles of other social actors constitute the subject of the present inquiry. But the answers to these questions are quite different for each time and place.

Other potential 'external' supporters of reform could include urban-based labour unions and professionals, nationalist entrepreneurs or military officers, some foreign aid agencies, environmentally or human rights-oriented NGOs, as well as associated political parties. A similar list could be made of potential opponents and co-opters of reforms. Many of the same actors would appear on both lists. It is not very useful to make hypothetical lists, however, before examining who the principal social actors influencing reforms were in concrete situations. They have been somewhat different in each case, but they usually have included both domestic and transnational groups. A few broad patterns are discernible that will be mentioned later.

Dynamics of a few twentieth century Latin American land reforms

A review of the role of the state and of other social actors in several land reform processes in Latin America in recent decades is instructive. It brings out the contradictory pressures on the state from different support groups concerning security of tenure and more equitable access to land which, by definition, are the key issues of land reform. It asks how public policies contributed to or hindered the grassroots mobilization and organization of the rural poor, with the aim of bringing about and consolidating more equitable land tenure arrangements. Who were the beneficiaries and on what terms did they receive better access to land? How were former large owners compensated? What kind of agrarian structure emerged? The state is shown to play a very contradictory role. Moreover, its role can change rapidly with variations in the relative power of different social groups and shifting alliances among them. A review of the roles of major actors in each case helps focus the discussion.

An assessment of several major twentieth century land reforms concluded that each reform process was, to some extent, unique. The actions of different groups of peasants, rural workers and rural elites interacted in very specific historical contexts with those of the state and other domestic and foreign-based actors in shaping outcomes. Ongoing social processes are invariably too complex for reductionist explanations unless they are essentially definitional truisms. In any event, the well known social, economic and administrative arguments commonly advanced in favour of land reforms, or to oppose them, seem to have had rather minor impacts on the political processes determining what actually happened (Barraclough, 1992).

The cases discussed here are from Latin America where I was deeply involved with land reform issues from the late 1950s. Generalizations from these Latin American experiences are supplemented by references to land reforms in a few Asian and African countries.

Mexico

The first major twentieth century land reform occurred in Mexico. Land reform began in several Mexican states soon after 1910, and culminated nationwide in the late 1930s. In 1910, over half the country's agricultural land was held in about 6000 large estates of over 1000 ha each; a few of these estates were over a million hectares in size. These large holdings were controlled by only about 1000 landowning families and corporations. The country's total population was some 16 million, over two-thirds of whom were engaged in agriculture.

Most of the Mexican rural population in 1910 was landless or nearly landless. About half resided within large estates to which they owed onerous labour services, rents or product shares. Nearly all the remainder were in smallholding communities with precarious rights to small parcels of land. There were also several thousand private producers (*rancheros*) with holdings ranging from less than 100 to over 1000 ha. Of course, highly variable land quality and access to water meant that these indicators of size of holdings are at best only a very rough measure of land concentration.

The concentration of land in large estates had increased rapidly in Mexico during the late nineteenth and early twentieth centuries. The estate owners had incorporated many new areas that had previously been legally considered to be communally owned or state-owned lands, as well as some land that had been small, privately owned properties. Communal and other peasant producers would seldom voluntarily sell at any price the land and water rights upon which their livelihoods depended. Unable to purchase the land and water they needed for expansion, the large estate owners acquired it by other means. The state's laws, judiciary, police powers and economic policies were all supportive of the estate owners' agenda. As a result, many peasant communities and smaller private landholders had lost access to some or all of their customary resources during the previous four decades.

Large-scale agriculture in Mexico before the revolution had become increasingly commercialized. Production of sugar, cotton, coffee, cattle and the like for domestic and export markets grew rapidly and benefited from state protection and subsidies. Production of corn, beans and other staples consumed by the poor, on the other hand, had decreased, while growing imports of these foods, principally from the USA, had been actively encouraged. New investments in agro-industry, railroads, other urban and rural infrastructure and mining poured into the country from the USA and Western Europe, but they failed to benefit most of the rural poor. This created a receptive context for the subsequent revolutionary process leading to massive land reform (Herzog, 1960; Hansen, 1971).

The authoritarian Diaz regime had exercised the state's power skilfully and ruthlessly to advance the modernization agenda of wealthy investors and estate owners. The central government forged complex political alliances in each Mexican state and locality that rewarded leaders who cooperated with its programme while eliminating or marginalizing those who did not. The estate owners achieved most of what they wanted, but at the price of having to accept some populist programmes and political leadership embedded in local power structures that included indigenous and *mestizo* communities. This helped to control peasant unrest. High-level technocrats (*los cientificos*) were extremely influential in formulating and administering the state's policies nationally. Execution of the programme on the ground, however, was frequently entrusted to notables and technicians with family and other connections with local communities, as well as with estate owners.

What began as an intra-elite struggle for power accompanied by several minor conflicts was soon transformed into a major social explosion. This was facilitated when competing elite factions sought broader popular support that could reinforce their relative bargaining power. Armed peasants in some states took advantage of a breakdown in central government authority to reclaim communal lands and to occupy haciendas. The peasant uprising was particularly intense in the southern state of Morelos, where indigenous communal traditions were strong and where the recent expansion of large estates into communal areas had been very aggressive, generating many conflicts (Womack, 1969; Warman, 1976). By 1916 peasant armies led by Emiliano Zapata had occupied most of the large estates and redistributed lands to peasant communities that had lost them earlier. In the North, however, where US influences were greatest and where the major challenge to the Diaz regime had originated, indigenous traditions were much weaker. There, peasant demands for return of lost lands tended to be secondary to those for better wages and working conditions, as well as for more equitable opportunities to establish privately owned commercial farms and other opportunities for social and economic advancement (Hansen, 1971).

The 1917 constitution declared the supremacy of the state – representing the public interest – over private property, thus legitimizing the expropriation and redistribution of land. This concession to peasant revolutionary forces and ideals, however, was for the most part implemented only in places where armed peasants had to be pacified. Although a new agrarian reform law was proclaimed in 1922, only about 8 million ha had been legally redistributed by 1934 at the beginning of the Cárdenas administration.

The Cárdenas government was faced with widespread unemployment and declining incomes accompanying the great depression of the 1930s. Its populist coalition mobilized the peasantry as well as urban workers and important middle-class sectors in support of a wide range of social reforms. About two-fifths of Mexico's arable land (some 18 million ha) was expropriated during the 1934 and 1940 period (Hansen, 1971). By 1940, land reform had included about half the country's farm lands and had benefited over half of its rural poor. The land was redistributed to tenants, workers and peasants in communally held *ejidos*. These were communally owned but mostly worked in small parcels by individual families. A few successful, collectively worked *ejido* enterprises also emerged with government support. Most notable among these were the collectively worked cotton-producing *ejidos* in the arid northern Laguna region (Restrepo and Eckstein, 1975; Alcántara Ferrer, 1997).

Usually the beneficiaries of land reforms in Mexico were not required to pay for the land they received, while the former large owners were not compensated. The state assumed the obligation to provide the peasants with credit, technical assistance, marketing and social services. An aim of the insurgent peasant communities, as well as of most progressive reformers in the Cárdenas coalition, was for the *ejidos* to become democratically self-managed by their members and to be as autonomous as possible. This was the rationale for creating an *ejido* bank to serve land reform beneficiaries so that they would not have to compete with better heeled and better educated commercial farmers for scarce public funds for agricultural inputs and services.

Post-Cárdenas regimes presided over an expanding economy and urbanizing society. They continued land expropriation and redistribution, but primarily of poor quality land in response to localized social problems and clientelistic pressures from powerful support groups. The Institutional Revolutionary Party (PRI)-affiliated peasant and labour confederations acted more and more as instruments for social and political control and less as semi-autonomous organizations belonging to their members and representing their interests. The state's virtual monopoly of credit, marketing channels and technical assistance was often used to control and divide the peasantry. Successive PRI regimes after 1940 enabled the country to experience four decades of rapid economic growth and relative internal peace, but the bulk of the peasantry again became increasingly marginalized. In some respects, Mexico's development strategy and the political instruments used to implement it in the 1980s resembled the Diaz regime a century earlier. The differences were fundamental, however, as the country had become predominately urban, relatively industrialized and, except for a few regions such as parts of Chiapas, the rural poor were no longer at the mercy of a traditional rural elite dominated by owners of a few large estates. The land reform, despite all its deficiencies and ambiguities, had made a major contribution to these changes.

Francisco Madero's successful campaign to unseat Diaz at the beginning of the revolution was partly organized and financed with the help of allies in the USA. The US army intervened twice during the revolutionary conflicts but, unlike in Guatemala, Chile and Nicaragua later, the USA did not attempt to stop land reform. In fact, the Roosevelt administration was rather sympathetic during the Cárdenas period.

Several outside actors other than the state, peasants and competing political factions and parties made important contributions in promoting and consolidating land reform. The role of rural school teachers was often crucial for partially literate peasants in articulating their demands and aspirations. A rural teacher drafted the Zapatistas' *Plan de Ayala* which served as a powerful manifesto for the agrarian movement when the revolution began. Dedicated idealistic lawyers, agronomists and many others worked with peasant activists throughout the reform period. Urban-based artists and intellectuals were particularly active during the 1920s and 1930s in support of reform. Labour union support of the peasantry was also frequently decisive in advancing land reform. Many journalists, writers and researchers had an important role in informing public opinion at home and abroad about the nature of the social conflicts behind revolutionary violence. During the Cárdenas period, the league of socialist agronomists provided invaluable technical assistance for many *ejidos* throughout the country, and especially the collective *ejidos*. During the post-war decades, numerous domestic and international NGOs helped peasants with advocacy, research and technical assistance. After 1950, international and bilateral aid agencies also provided some assistance for rural development projects, but on a much less important scale than in many other developing countries.

Bolivia

Land reform in many respects resembled that in Mexico earlier. The 1951–52 Bolivian revolution followed several decades of unstable control of the state by competing oligarchic factions allied with various professional and other emerging new social groups. Backed by powerful militant miners' unions, urban workers, nationalist military officers and some sections of the peasantry, the nationalist revolutionary party (MNR) returned to power in 1952, a decade after it had been forced out by the more traditional factions of the large estate-owning, mining and military oligarchy.

The MNR had made rather vague populist promises of land for the country's severely repressed indigenous peasantry, as well as for the somewhat better-off *cholo* (*mestizo*) rural minority. The *cholos* in rural areas spoke Spanish and had adopted many urban customs which facilitated their roles as intermediaries between the urban-based elite, mostly of European descent, and the indigenous rural majority. Most of the Indians were serfs on large estates, or resided in indigenous communities that had lost their best lands to the estates. Since the colonial period they had been without basic civil rights and deprived of formal education as a matter of state policy. By the mid-twentieth century many had been exposed to new ideas and aspirations through forced labour in the strongly unionized mines, conscription in the army during the costly Chaco war with Paraguay in the 1930s, contact with missionary schools, and diverse other channels.

Following the disruption of traditional state power during the revolution, organized peasants sometimes occupied large estates and burned hacienda buildings in rural areas. In others places, frightened absentee estate owners simply abandoned their rural properties. In 1961, for example, I visited an abandoned large estate near Cochabamba with a Quechua-speaking Peruvian anthropologist. The hacienda buildings were all intact, as were the estate's rather meagre stocks of farm machinery which remained untouched in their sheds. Part of the estate had been reclaimed by a neighbouring indigenous community, while the rest was divided into family-sized plots for self-provisioning by the estate's *peons* and other resident tenants who also retained most of the estate's pastures for their common use. These peasants told us that they had never been visited by a state agrarian official since the revolution 10 years earlier.

The 1953 agrarian reform legislation provided for expropriation of poorly managed large estates and the partial expropriation of other large rural properties for redistribution to the peasantry. In many ways this was merely a legal recognition of a *de facto* land reform process that had already taken place or was well under way. Providing legal titles to land reform beneficiaries did not even commence in most places until the early 1960s, and in some areas it has not yet been completed. The reform was cheap for the state in financial terms because previously the peasants had been mostly farming the same lands in the same ways as afterwards. The main benefits for the peasants were that they no longer had to deliver part of their produce together with their labour services to the representatives of the estate owners, and that they now had greater independence and human dignity.

During the 1950s, large estates that had included more than half of Bolivia's agricultural land, located mostly in the Andean high plains and valleys, were taken over by their tenant residents and nearby communities. Over half the country's rural poor received better access to land. Overall, food production increased during the reform, but marketed food supplies for the cities declined when most peasant producers increased their own consumption. Peasant food production could have increased much more than it did following the reform if state policies had been supportive. The ready availability of highly subsidized cheap food imports from the USA and later from Europe, however, made it unnecessary for the state to pursue a peasant-based development strategy after the revolution and land reform. Most public and private investments in agriculture after the early 1950s were directed towards a few large agro-industrial producers in Bolivia's Amazon region that had been little affected by the land reform.

Peasant organizations were frequently infiltrated and co-opted for political purposes. Those former estate owners who retained part of their properties were often able to reconstruct clientelistic networks. The biggest achievement of the reform was that the country's indigenous majority were, for the first time since the Spanish conquest, legally recognized to be full citizens with formal rights to vote, to basic education, and to relatively secure communal or individual landholdings.

As in Mexico, many other actors influenced the land reform and its aftermath. Peasant organizations, labour unions and the state, however, were the principal protagonists. Bilateral and international aid agencies were active in Bolivia following the land reform. As seen above, sometimes their policies had negative consequences for the peasantry. During the 1980s international and national NGOs became very active in many rural areas. Some of them helped to attenuate the negative impacts for the rural poor of the World Bank/International Monetary Fund-sponsored structural adjustment programme that began in 1985. The number of officially registered NGOs increased from about 100 to over 500 between 1980 and the early 1990s. Some played constructive roles in training, technical assistance and advocacy for peasant causes. Many, however, sponsored small-scale projects in rural communities that had little positive impact, while staff salaries and other NGO operating costs absorbed most of their resources. NGO activities often helped to deflect political opposition to the state's neoliberal policies which prejudiced much of the peasantry. In this way some NGOs helped to legitimize the dominant anti-peasant development strategy.

Guatemala

Social reforms extending minimal legal and political rights to the country's indigenous rural majority began with the Arevelo administration in 1944, following the collapse of the lengthy Ubico dictatorship. These reforms were primarily instigated by middle-class urban sectors, and also by some progressive nationalist elements in the army that had formerly been closely allied with the traditional landowning oligarchy. The large landowners' control of the state had been severely weakened during the Second World War by the loss of its German markets for coffee exports and German investments in coffee production, as well as by the nationalization of many German-owned large coffee estates in response to US pressures.

In 1952 the Arbenz regime, which had been democratically elected, promulgated an agrarian reform. This land reform was motivated in part by a desire of the new administration to modernize the country more rapidly along lines inspired by the experience in Mexico, where many progressive Guatemalans had been exiled during the Ubico regime. Also, the government sought to broaden its popular base by including the mostly indigenous peasant majority among its supporters. Land from large privately and publicly held estates was redistributed to peasant producers in smallhold-ings. The state attempted to provide the peasants with credit, access to markets and technical assistance. Large landowners were compensated with state bonds on the basis of their usually greatly undervalued tax dec-larations. About 40 per cent of the rural poor received land between 1952 and 1954.

This land reform, however, was short-lived. Large areas held by the US-based United Fruit Company were expropriated. This contributed to the US administration's cold-war preoccupation about the possible spread in Latin America of governments with Marxist sympathies. Moreover, the US administration's Secretary of State and its head of the Central Intelligence Agency had close ties with the United Fruit Company. The US government planned and supported a military coup in Guatemala that took place in 1954. A US air force officer told me a decade later that he was sent to Guatemala in 1953 to help prepare the coup. After a year of work he reported that it was ready and would be successful, but that based on his experience in the country he believed overthrowing the reformist Arbenz government would be contrary to US interests. He was rewarded by being transferred immediately to the front lines in the Korean war.

The coup succeeded and the new military regime annulled the land reform. Expropriated lands were returned to the former large estate own-ers. Peasant and worker organizations were severely repressed. In the 1990s about 3 per cent of the owners of agricultural land in Guatemala controlled over two-thirds of the country's agricultural area. Some 90 per cent of the rural population, mostly Indians, were nearly or completely landless. The prolonged bloody civil war after 1954 left over 150 000 killed and many more displaced or exiled.

Peasant militancy had played a much smaller role in the Arbenz reform than it had in those of Mexico and Bolivia. Latent peasant demands and resentment, however, had been an important factor in convincing political leaders that the reform would attract important peasant support. Progres-sive intellectuals, as well as some former military officers (of whom Arbenz was one), were extremely influential in promoting the land reform. So, too, were labour union leaders and professionals including many agronomists and teachers.

After the 1954 military coup, progressive sectors of the Catholic Church as well as several national and international agencies and NGOs de-nounced the abuses suffered by peasants, often at great personal and insti-tutional cost. Many NGOs and international agencies, however, tacitly supported repression of peasant protests. Intervention by the US govern-ment had been decisive in undoing the Arbenz reform and in propping up subsequent repressive regimes. Much later in 1997, the United Nations with US support helped to broker a fragile negotiated peace agreement, but without land reform.

Puerto Rico

In the 1940s Puerto Rico was still a US territory acquired through the Spanish American war nearly half a century earlier. Peasant unrest was endemic in this small, densely populated island. Its agriculture was dominated by corporate large estates producing sugar for the protected US market. In the 1930s nearly three-quarters of the population depended on sugar production directly or indirectly for their livelihoods. As a result, the island had become heavily dependent on US imports for most of its food supplies. The 'New Deal' in the USA greatly influenced US policies in Puerto Rico. New Deal legislation extended US labour and civil rights protection to the island's population, as well as attempting to bring about a more equitable distribution of the island's income. Puerto Rican nationalists were campaigning, often violently, for full independence, while the conservative Puerto Rican republican party wanted full statehood. The US administration supported the popular democratic party, led by Luis Muñoz Marín, in its demands for New Deal-type economic and social reforms together with greater autonomy for the island, but still leaving it associated with the USA and its people as US citizens.

Both the US administration and Muñoz's popular democratic party supported a rather radical land reform in the late 1940s. The big sugar corporations were expropriated (with compensation) and converted into worker-managed proportional-profit farms. In addition, an important portion of the rural population received titles to small plots of land for a house and garden. Political support for these policies in the USA came from labour unions and other progressive allies of the Roosevelt and Truman administrations. Also, the land reform received some support from sugar producers in Hawaii and Louisiana who had to compete with lower-cost Puerto Rican sugar producers in the protected US market.

The land reform contributed to providing Muñoz Marín's party with durable, widespread popular support during and after the island's transition to associated Commonwealth status with the USA in 1950. The proportional-profit farms seldom made profits, however, as sugar production became increasingly non-competitive. Other Caribbean sugar-producing countries such as Cuba were unhampered by US labour laws, and their sugar workers had few possibilities of finding alternative livelihoods. Industrial and other urban job opportunities were expanding in Puerto Rico, and were also available for Puerto Ricans by easy emigration to the USA. The distribution to many rural families of small house and garden plots as a result of the land reform was popular among Puerto Ricans. The rural population increasingly saw its only path to socio-economic advancement to lie with urban employment or emigration to the USA, not in peasant agriculture. When the family had secure title to a parcel of land and house it was much easier for the younger members to seek employment elsewhere.

After the land reform, Puerto Rico continued to depend heavily on food imports and income transfers from the USA. Sugar production fell, as did many other Puerto Rican agricultural exports, while the island became increasingly integrated into the USA. Despite a shrinking agricultural sector, however, the land reform was a resounding political success for its instigators. The island's agricultural production would have declined in any event given the international context, but without the land reform the negative social impacts would have been much more severe.

Cuba

In the 1950s Cuba was even more dependent on sugar exports than Puerto Rico had been in the 1930s. Not only was control of agricultural land largely monopolized by a few domestic and foreign individual and corporate owners, but the escape valves of emigration to the USA and income transfers to the rural poor from the USA were largely closed. Instead of a somewhat socially concerned colonial administration such as that of Puerto Rico in the 1930s and 1940s, the Cuban state had been administered by a series of rather corrupt governments that had inherited power after US occupation forces had left the country four decades earlier.

The Cuban revolutionary forces that triumphed in 1959 counted on broad-based support from peasants, workers, nationalist intellectuals and professionals, as well as many other sectors of Cuban society. Not surprisingly, land reform was a high priority for the Castro-led revolutionary forces. They had been protected and augmented by the peasantry of Oriente for many months before the collapse of the Batista dictatorship.

The first Cuban agrarian reform was mild in comparison to those in Mexico and Bolivia, as only very large holdings were expropriated. When the USA retaliated with a trade embargo, all US-owned property was expropriated. Under a second agrarian reform law, all holdings over 67 ha were taken over by the state. Three-quarters of the country's agricultural land had been expropriated by 1964. Most estates were first turned over to their resident workers as cooperatives, and these were soon converted into state farms. Over a quarter of the agricultural land, however, was held by individual peasant farmers or by smallholders' production cooperatives.

The inclusion of most expropriated land in large state farm units was partly a consequence of the pre-reform agrarian structure. The sugar plantations and many large ranches and other estates were modern, integrated, industrial operating units with heavy investments in machinery, irrigation and other infrastructure. Their workers were not peasant producers, but primarily industrial workers. One state farm I visited in 1972 had recently received modern dairy equipment from Czechoslovakia. Examination of its accounts suggested that worker productivity had not increased as a result of this huge investment. In discussions about this paradox with the farm's administrative council, it turned out that the workers had decided to reduce their work time from one 12 hour-per-day shift to two seven-hour shifts on receipt of the labour-saving modern equipment. This was congruent with industrial worker experiences and aspirations, but not with those of peasant farmers.

Cuban agricultural production declined in the 1960s, but then increased at about the average rate for Latin America during the 1970s and early 1980s. Massive aid from the Soviet bloc had partially been offset by the US embargo, but had been sufficient to support an expanding economy and rising living standards for most Cubans. Extreme rural poverty had virtually been eliminated in Cuba after the land reform. Everyone was entitled to basic food rations as well as to good quality education and health services. After the collapse of the USSR, however, lack of imported inputs such as livestock feed, fuel, chemicals and repair parts caused agricultural production to fall drastically.

In an attempt to improve efficiency and incentives, farmers' markets were again legalized in 1993. Over half the area in state farms was turned over to smaller production cooperatives in what amounted to another land reform. These and other reforms helped stop the decline in production but the situation remained critical, largely due to the country's greatly reduced import capacity accentuated by a tightened US embargo. Dependency on food imports had been over one-third of consumption before the revolution, and increased to over half of consumption by the 1980s. Similar levels of dependency on food imports were registered in most other Caribbean island states in the 1970s and 1980s. In Cuba in 1996 it remained close to 40 per cent of a reduced level of food consumption. This high level of dependency on food imports was a result not of the land reform, but rather of a development strategy that gave a high priority to promoting sugar and a few other exports while neglecting small-scale agriculture.

The state and the rural poor were the primary actors initiating the Cuban land reform. The policies of the ruling party, the USSR and the USA, however, decisively influenced how the land reform evolved. These 'external' actors' policies have in part determined the fluctuations in living levels and productivities of the land reform beneficiaries since 1964.

Venezuela

Land reform in the early 1960s was negotiated by a new democratically elected government that had replaced a prolonged and brutal military dictatorship. The land reform had been preceded by widespread peasant union organization and protests that contributed to the previous authoritarian regime's collapse. A quarter of the country's rural landless received farms of about 10 ha each, that included about one-tenth of the country's agricultural land. Half the land allocated to peasants came from expropriated large estates and half from state-owned public lands.

Venezuela in the early 1960s was in transition from being largely an agriculturally based economy to an urban society whose economy was based primarily on petroleum exports. Income from petroleum enabled the state to minimize opposition to the land reform by granting liberal compensation to the owners of expropriated large estates and by providing liberal credits, infrastructure and services for land reform beneficiaries. I visited expropriated large estates in the 1960s where the owners had deliberately promoted strikes and demands for land by their workers and tenants in order to qualify for expropriation, and thus to receive compensation from the state for their properties at higher-than-market values.

This well financed market-friendly reform, however, was not notably successful either in reducing rural poverty or in stimulating agricultural production. Much of the worst rural poverty was in areas little affected by the land reform. Food security improved for those who gained access to land from the reform, but the land reform's impact was dwarfed by the petroleum boom in the 1960s and 1970s, and later by the collapse of petroleum prices in the 1980s.

Peasant unions allied with political parties seeking peasant support had been principal actors in bringing about this land reform. Other actors included progressive church groups, labour unions, NGOs, many professionals and intellectuals, as well as bilateral and international organizations. Intra-elite competition for power and the relative decline of the influence of large landowners in an increasingly urban- and petroleum-based economy dominated by transnational corporations had greatly facilitated 'a market-friendly land reform'. But the land reform had a rather small socio-economic and political impact on Venezuelan society compared to those in Mexico, Bolivia and Cuba.

Chile

Electoral politics was an important mechanism pushing land reform in Chile from a timid beginning to a radical climax, implying profound modifications in agrarian structure. A counter-reform after 1973 was accompanied by further structural changes. I was deeply involved with Chilean land reform issues from 1959 through 1973, first as a specialist of the Food and Agriculture Organization (FAO) on agrarian policies, and after 1964 as manager of an FAO/UN Development Programme technical assistance project designed to support the Chilean Agrarian Reform Research and Training Institute (ICIRA) which was one of the actors in the reform process. All participant observers have their own interpretations of the roles of various actors, but many of us tend to agree on several key points. What follows, of course, are my own views.

Land ownership in Chile before the land reforms of the 1960s and early 1970s remained highly concentrated in large estates. Over 80 per cent of the country's agricultural land was included in only some 10 000 properties in

1955. The owners of these large estates would have represented only 3 per cent of the total number of rural families (most large estate owners, however, were absentee, living all or part of the time in urban areas), assuming a separate owner for each estate.

The legal concentration of land ownership in Chile in the 1950s was about the same as it had been before land reform in Mexico, Bolivia, Cuba and several other Latin American countries. The quasi-feudal domination by large landowners over the rural population, however, had begun to be eroded seriously in Chile since the early 1920s. Passive resistance to the estate owners' dominance of the countryside was often supplemented by strikes and other forms of overt protest, especially by workers who had returned from temporary labour in the unionized nitrate fields, mines or urban centres.

Under political pressures from unions, middle-class groups and left-leaning parties in 1931, Chile adopted a national labour code inspired by International Labour Organization (ILO) standards. The large landowners' association (SNA) bitterly, and in part successfully, resisted extension of the code's provisions to the rural workforce. Nonetheless, it provided a legal rallying point for rural workers with the help of leftist parties, urban labour unions and other allies to press for greater rights such as protection against arbitrary dismissals, payment in cash for part of their labour services, and reduced hyperexploitation by estate owners of their workers' wives and children, as well as the right to form rural peasant leagues or unions. Occasionally they were successful in resisting estate owners' demands. Outcomes of rural conflicts depended largely on the shifting political alliances of the moment supporting the national government. By the 1950s, despite many vicissitudes in the fortunes of those fighting for greater rights of the rural poor, private land ownership did not imply the same degree of arbitrary power by large estate owners as it had earlier (Affonso et al., 1970; Loveman, 1976).

At the same time, a new class of entrepreneurial farmers was slowly emerging in several agricultural regions. These capitalist farmers often found it more profitable to adopt modern, capital-intensive technologies, to depend largely on a non-resident workforce paid mostly in cash (a dubious benefit for workers, given persistent inflation), and to subdivide large estates into smaller operating units. Some were members of old landowning families, but others were relative newcomers associated with emerging markets and agro-industries. The SNA in the 1950s and 1960s no longer represented only traditional hacienda owners, but also modern commercial farmers who frequently had divergent views about priorities. The latter tended to be less hostile than the former to labour standards and other modifications of traditional arbitrary rights associated with private ownership of large landholdings. Some of these commercial large and medium-sized farmers supported limited land reform aimed at breaking up traditional large quasi-feudal estates.

The Chilean oligarchy since the late nineteenth century had used formal democratic institutions such as popular elections for the presidency and legislature to help resolve many intra-elite conflicts for control of the state's resources and patronage. The electorate was courted by political parties and populist leaders (who often bought their votes). It had been gradually broadened to include large sections of the urban middle and working classes. Until the electoral reform of 1958 introducing the secret ballot for rural voters, however, the landed rural oligarchy could effectively control the votes of its workers, tenants and other clients.

In this context, electoral competition had contributed to significant political and socio-economic gains by urban popular and middle classes, but to a much smaller degree by the rural poor. Mineral exports had been the principal source of foreign exchange since the late nineteenth century. By the early 1950s over two-thirds of the population was classified as being urban. Labour, trade and professional unions had become legal, well organized and influential in the cities and mines. In agriculture, however, workers' unions and other forms of peasant organization remained virtually illegal until the mid-1960s. Public services such as schools and health clinics had penetrated into the countryside very slowly in comparison with their rapid improvement in cities and towns. Nonetheless, they had spread to many rural towns and villages by 1950, which meant that there was increasingly a bureaucratic presence of the central government in rural areas that large landowners found very difficult to control. Strikes and other forms of conflict between estate owners and their labour force, as well as with members of smallholding communities, had surged earlier during the popular front administration of the late 1930s. This eventually led to outlawing of the Communist Party from 1948 to 1958. Repression failed to smother rural strikes and conflicts, however, as the Communists continued underground activities while other leftist parties and affiliated unions agitated and organized more openly in rural areas. Moreover, progressive elements in the Catholic Church in the early 1950s also supported peasants' demands for better wages, working conditions and social services, as well as for more equitable access to land.

The outgoing Ibáñez administration legalized the Communist party again in 1958. It also introduced the rural electoral reform. The subsequent strong showing of the Socialist–Communist coalition in rural areas demonstrated that the large landowners could no longer control the votes of their tenants and workers. The Christian Democrats and the Leftist Popular Action Front (FRAP) had both promised agrarian reform. Moreover, a last-minute populist candidate had barely taken enough votes from the FRAP to deny it a plurality. The election left the propertied classes shaken, as well as many foreign investors and the US embassy, as the other two-thirds had all voted for candidates proposing some kind of land reform.

The first timid legislation towards land reform had been enacted in 1928 following several years of peasant protests and other signs of rural social unrest. An agricultural colonization agency (Caja de Colonización Agrícola) was established with the mission of creating rural settlements of small farmers to absorb unemployed rural workers and others demanding better access to land. The *Caja* was authorized to purchase estates offered for sale in order to subdivide them into family-sized units for sale at an attractive price to settlers, who were to be provided with credit and infrastructure together with technical and marketing assistance. The *Caja* also had legal authority to expropriate certain abandoned or poorly worked large estates, but these powers were not used as it never had sufficient funds to purchase and subdivide more than a fraction of the lands available on the market and lands already held by the state. Following its creation in 1928 until the agrarian reform law of 1962, the *Caja* had settled some 3500 beneficiaries – an average of about 100 colonists per year, many of whom were neither landless nor near-landless.

The Alessandri administration enacted a land reform law in 1962. It enabled the state to expropriate abandoned or poorly managed large estates as well as various other categories of land, such as part of those lands irrigated by publicly financed projects, estates held by public agencies and lands deemed essential to the public interest because of environmental values, and their redistribution in 'economic units' to smallholders. It also permitted partial payment in cash to expropriated owners with deferred payment of the remainder in government bonds, but this provision required a time-consuming constitutional amendment.

The 1962 agrarian reform law did not result in much land reform during the two remaining years of the Alessandri administration. No poorly worked estates were actually expropriated. Estates that were voluntarily sold by their owners usually received prices lower than were asked, but far above tax-assessed values. A few large estates owned by government agencies were also subdivided. Part of these purchased and public agency-held estates were allocated to beneficiaries in 'economic units' estimated to be sufficient for profitable family-operated farms. Some of the land was allocated in larger, medium-sized commercial units, and other areas were allocated to estate workers and tenants in sub-subsistence house-and-garden plots with the new owners still dependent on wage labour for a major portion of their livelihoods.

Of a projected 12 000 beneficiaries from 1962 to 1964, only a few over 1000 actually received land. This led many critical observers, including this author, to qualify it as a 'flowerpot reform'. But critics failed to recognize the importance of the Alessandri reform. It legally institutionalized several fundamental changes in rural power relationships that would be used by the subsequent Christian Democrat administration to implement a much more radical land reform programme. The 1962 law transformed the agricultural colonization agency into an agrarian reform corporation (CORA) with legal powers of expropriation with deferred payments. A parallel agency (Instituto de Desarrollo Agropecuario, INDAP) was created to provide credit and assistance to smallholders who constituted a major portion of the rural poor. Agrarian courts were instituted to resolve conflicts between expropriated estate owners and the state. The Alessandri land reform led to minimal changes in land tenure from 1962 to 1964, but the stage was set for much more profound land reform when the state perceived a political imperative to pursue it.

The principal actors in bringing about this first land reform law included diverse groups of peasants and rural worker activists allied with urban-based labour unions and leftist political parties, as well as progressive sectors of the Catholic Church. A Church-sponsored NGO (Instituto de Promoción Agraria, INPROA) initiated pilot land reform subdivisions on Church lands in 1960. These experiences were incorporated later into the Christian Democrats' reform project.

Fear of defeat in the 1964 election led the governing coalition of right-wing and centrist political parties to take the advocacy of land reform by their competitors very seriously and to try to undermine their popular support by advancing their own proposals. They were helped in this by divisions among estate owners, and even more among their urban-based allies, about the desirability of defending the traditional hacienda system.

Another factor leading to more radical reforms was a change in the US government's policies. The new Kennedy administration in 1960 was alarmed by the initial success of the Cuban revolution and its widespread support in Latin America. It initiated the 'Alliance for Progress' designed to encourage social reforms in Latin America that would help to forestall revolutionary movements. The USA promised important financial aid for reformist programmes, including those of agrarian reform.

The 'Declaration of Punta de Este' launching the Alliance recognized the need to reform 'unjust structures of land tenure and use, with a view to replacing latifundia and dwarf holdings by an equitable system of land tenure so that . . . the land will become for the man who works it the basis of his economic stability, the foundation of his increasing welfare and the guarantee of his freedom and dignity.' This wording was drafted by delegates from Mexico, Venezuela, Bolivia and Brazil, all of whom had experienced or anticipated radical land reforms in their own countries. It had to be approved by all the member governments of the Organization of American States, however, including the USA, revolutionary Cuba, and land-owning oligarchy-dominated states such as Peru. By chance, I was rapporteur for the Commission at Punta del Este drafting this resolution on agrarian reform and can attest to the difficulties in finding an acceptable wording. The declaration did not commit any signatory to concrete action, but it provided a certain international legitimacy for those in member countries advocating land reforms. Also, it held out the incentive of increased US aid. Undoubtedly, these factors played an important role in the Alessandri government's decision to adopt its land reform law of 1962 and later for the more radical Christian Democrat administration law of 1967.

The Christian Democrats headed by Eduardo Frei could gain the 1964 Chilean presidential election only with the support of the centrist and right-wing parties that had constituted the previous Alessandri administration. They had been persuaded to support Frei's candidature despite his promise of radical land and other reforms, because of the high probability that the socialist–communist coalition would win if the right fielded its own candidate. US diplomats and investors played an important role in the political manoeuvres leading to the Christian Democrats' electoral victory in 1964.

The new administration introduced legislation designed to reform the country's land tenure system much more drastically than had been permitted by the Alessandri agrarian reform law. Estates larger than 80 ha equivalent of good irrigated land were subject to expropriation, but their owners could reserve up to 40 ha for themselves. It also introduced a new labour code to facilitate the organization of rural workers' and peasants' unions and to improve labour standards and social services in the countryside. While these laws were being prepared and debated, the government implemented existing legislation fully to advance land reform. The Alessandri agrarian reform law was used to expropriate some 500 large, extensively used, privately owned estates pending approval of the new land reform legislation. Several estates still held by public agencies were designated for agrarian reform programmes. INDAP aggressively encouraged smallholders' cooperatives and associations, providing technical assistance and credit. Labour department inspectors were instructed to enforce regulations on rural estates and to investigate worker and peasant petitions. The police were no longer readily available to break rural strikers or to dismantle agricultural workers' unions at estate owners' requests.

By 1970 over 1300 large estates, including over 3 million ha, had been expropriated benefiting some 20 000 workers and peasants. But this was only one-fifth the number of beneficiaries that had been promised by the Frei administration in its electoral campaign. Moreover, the state had no clear programme concerning the new land tenure structure to emerge from the reform. As a transitional measure, most expropriated estates were jointly administered by representatives of the agrarian reform corporation and by committees elected by their former workers and tenants. These administrative units or *asentamientos* usually coincided with the expropriated estates. After a transition period of about five years, the beneficiary tenants and workers would have the option of receiving legal title to the land as cooperative properties or in individual holdings. Where the workers and tenants were well organized with dynamic leadership, they often had important participation in managing the *asentamientos*. In other expropriated estates, however, CORA functionaries played a dominant role.

The Popular Unity (UP) coalition of socialists, communists and other left-wing parties won a narrow plurality in the 1970 presidential election. Unlike in 1964, the rightist parties and Christian Democrats had both fielded candidates. The UP picked up crucial support in rural areas with its promise for more rapid and radical land reform. The Allende administration, however, did not have a majority in the legislature, which meant that it could not enact new legislation to implement its 'socialist' programme. The government decided to exploit the earlier land reform and labour legislation already in place to the fullest extent possible. The UP coalition vigorously promoted the political mobilization and organization of rural workers and peasants and supported their demands for land. Within two years the government had expropriated nearly all the remaining large estates. In addition, rural union membership, which had already expanded from a few thousand to 140 000 in the 1964–70 period, jumped to 210 000 by 1972.

The Allende administration faced the same dilemma as its predecessor of how to transfer the expropriated land to a socially differentiated and partially mobilized peasantry. The expropriated estates accounted for about 36 per cent of the country's farm land and for 30 per cent of its total agricultural output, but employed only about one-fifth of the entire agricultural workforce. Many of these workers did not reside in the expropriated estates, but in rural communities with insufficient land to provide for self-provisioning. These part-time estate workers and other very smallholders comprised about three-fifths of the agricultural population. Moreover, some residents within the estates farmed small areas temporarily allocated to them as partial payment for their labour on the estate. Many others had no access to land for their own use, and others were sharecroppers or renters of estate lands to produce primarily for the market. Most of the estates had centralized infrastructure such as irrigation systems, buildings and machinery that could not be readily subdivided for the use of family farms. Different categories of estate workers tended to have divergent views about whether the land should be subdivided into family-sized parcels or managed jointly in worker-managed cooperatives. Workers residing elsewhere also wanted to receive land, but estate residents naturally resisted taking in outsiders as beneficiaries. These differences in perceived interests were frequently reinforced by divergent ideological positions taken by political parties and factions within them.

The UP's answer to these conflicts of interest and perceptions was essentially the same as that of the Christian Democrats earlier. The expropriated estates were jointly managed by elected workers' committees together with CORA technicians. These units were called agrarian reform centres (CERAS) instead of *asentamientos*. A few state farms were also created. As before, there were wide differences in the real degree of worker participation. This depended largely on such factors as the degree of peasants' organization and the quality of their leadership, as well as on the capacity of the state bureaucracy. In theory, the CERAS were supposed eventually to evolve into larger decentralized and democratic planning and production units that could absorb many of the rural landless and near-landless not residing within the expropriated estates. This never happened, and it is doubtful that it could have. In any event, the reform process was abruptly halted by the 1973 military coup.

Following the coup, some of the expropriated land was returned to its former owners on the legal basis of irregularities in expropriation procedures. Most of the rest was assigned to individual beneficiaries in family-sized holdings with the obligation to meet annual interest and amortization payments. A large portion of the beneficiaries soon had to sell in the absence of adequate state credits and technical assistance. Nonetheless, the country's agrarian structure had been radically transformed. The large estates had nearly disappeared, while smallholders controlled one-third of the land in contrast to only one-tenth a decade earlier. Medium-sized capitalist farms worked mostly by a non-resident labour force dominated Chilean agrarian structure in the 1980s and 1990s after the counter-reform.

The protests and demands of peasants and other rural workers, supported by labour unions and other urban allies, were principal factors in bringing about land reform in Chile. Only a small minority of the peasantry actively agitated and organized as long as estate owners were able to maintain their monopoly of land ownership and the control of the state's rural institutions, including especially its police powers. This activist minority, however, enjoyed the latent if timorous sympathies of a large proportion of the rural poor. When the state's frequently changing governing coalitions shared power with leftist urban-based parties, however, the rural oligarchy's political power was progressively weakened over nearly five decades, even while it maintained the ownership of most agricultural land. After the 1958 electoral reform, the competition of political parties for support of rural voters became a major mechanism accelerating the land reform process.

Chilean and foreign intellectuals contributed to this land reform process. Many called attention to the inequities of the hacienda system and to pressures resulting in reforms of parallel land systems elsewhere. Several actively collaborated in efforts to organize rural workers, smallholders and the country's remaining indigenous communities. The synergy between intellectual perceptions, research and communication of ideas and information, on the one hand, and praxis on the other, is widely recognized, but disentangling them is virtually impossible.

The UN and other international organizations contributed to the reform process, although their roles were usually marginal compared to those of domestic social actors. The Economic Commission for Latin America and the Caribbean (ECLAC) published several reports in the 1950s calling for land reforms in Latin America in order to remove a major obstacle to national development. The Interamerican Committee for Agricultural Development (ICAD – in Spanish CIDA) released its report *Tenencia de la tierra y desarrollo del sector agrícola – Chile in 1963*. This research was one of seven country case studies I coordinated. It was carried out by national researchers with financial support and technical help from five UN and interamerican organizations (Organization of American States, Inter-American Institute for Agricultural Co-operation, Inter-American Development Bank, ECLAC and FAO). The Chilean report strongly recommended land reform. But these findings would have fallen on deaf ears or been suppressed, as happened in Guatemala and some other countries, if the Chilean political context had not been receptive. In the Chilean case, the report was published by CORA and used politically to show international support for the new land reform programme.

The Chilean Agrarian Reform Research and Training Institute (ICIRA) was supported by FAO/UNDP financial resources and technical assistance. The UN Educational, Scientific and Cultural Organization (UNESCO) and the ILO also cooperated. Its activities illustrate some of the opportunities and limitations for international organization support of land reform. It commenced organizing practical training courses for government extension agents, agrarian officials and peasant organization leaders in 1964. It recruited an outstanding Spanish legal specialist to assist in drafting the Frei administration's agrarian reform law. An exiled former Minister of Labour from Brazil did the same for the new legislation, facilitating and regulating rural labour unions. ICIRA specialists in farm management, cooperatives, credit, social relations, new communications technologies, rural education, irrigation, marketing and various other fields were able to help Chilean teams develop their own programmes. It also served as a coordinating centre for numerous NGO and bilateral technical assistance programmes for land reform. By 1972, ICIRA programmes of technical assistance, training and research were active in support of CORA, INDAP and several other government agencies wherever land reform was being implemented.

After the Pinochet military coup the whole land reform support programme was soon closed down. Many participants were jailed, exiled or worse. The international agencies supporting it simply dropped land reform from their agenda in Chile.

The Kennedy administration in the USA, as seen above, played a key role through the 'Alliance for Progress' in convincing the Chilean government to adopt its 1962 land reform law. This was followed by the more radical Frei administration legislation. The Nixon administration in the USA, however, was overtly hostile to parts of the Frei administration's reform programme that it deemed to be collectivist- or Marxist-oriented. It actively worked to destabilize the Allende government. US support was crucial for the success of the Pinochet-led military coup that terminated the Chilean land reform programme.

Peru

In rural Peru, large estates first established in the sixteenth century still dominated the agrarian structure in the early 1960s in much the same way as in many other parts of Latin America. Large, modern, irrigated plantations in the coastal region producing sugar, rice and a few other commercial crops had a long history of union organization and labour conflicts. Big haciendas controlled most of the highlands. As in Bolivia, the indigenous rural residents were serfs on the highland estates or had been relegated to communities on poorer lands. There were continuous conflicts between estate owners and the largely self-provisioning indigenous communities. Land occupations by *communeros* reclaiming lost territories had become frequent. Most of the highland estates provided low economic returns and were technologically backward. In the eastern valleys descending to the Amazon basin, there were a few relatively profitable large plantations of tea, coffee, cacao and other export crops.

By 1960 the army was engaged in numerous operations against peasant guerrillas in much of the country. A prolonged violent struggle in one of the eastern valleys, La Convención, had led the military government in 1962 to impose a small land reform there. It benefited most of the better-off tenants but practically excluded the majority of the rural poor. Nonetheless, it helped to quell guerrilla activity in the region, at least temporarily. Peasant strikes and land occupations had provoked this mini-reform, but army officers and professionals from the Ministry of Agriculture planned and implemented it. These military and civilian professionals were mostly of middle-class *mestizo* origins with little sympathy for the large landowners, who were mostly of European descent. The large estates were partially expropriated with deferred compensation for their owners. The indigenous tenants with labour obligations to the estates received the units they had been cultivating, while some sub-tenants and other workers received small plots, and others were left landless. This experience was successful in contributing to pacification from the army's viewpoint, and was a prelude to the greater reform later.

Following a brief period of civilian government from 1964 to 1968, the military again took control of the state. It announced a nationalist development programme that included a radical land reform. General Velasco Alverado, the new President, cited the recommendations for land reform of the ICAD report on land tenure and agricultural development in Peru that was published in 1966 by the Pan-American Union, as one of the government's justifications for the planned land reform.

In an interview with four visiting 'land reform specialists' in 1969, General Velasco explained that the principal objective of the reform was to speed up the transition of Peru to a more modern and socially integrated society. He hoped this could be accomplished in Peru without a bloody civil war such as the one that had killed over a million Mexicans in that country's earlier agrarian transition. We questioned whether this could be done by government decree.

The Velasco government expropriated nearly all the large estates in Peru.

These included one-third of the country's land and one-fifth of its farm workforce. An initial attempt to convert expropriated estates into worker-managed cooperatives eventually petered out. Falling prices for agricultural export commodities in the 1970s left most modern, large, capital-intensive units unprofitable. Large-scale, centralized management of traditional highland estates was no more remunerative when carried on by workers' committees and state technicians than it had been before reform. Moreover, neighbouring indigenous communities that were supposed to share the profits of the land reform cooperatives seldom received any, as there were few profits to distribute.

The reform accelerated the disintegration of Peru's quasi-feudal hacienda system. By the 1980s it had been largely replaced by small and medium-sized farm units. The peasant mobilization to form rural unions and cooperatives stimulated by the Velasco government was short-lived once he disappeared. Rural Peru continued to be plagued by guerrilla activities in many regions after the reform. These were associated with continued extreme widespread rural poverty, depressed prices for peasant food crops and a booming Mafia-controlled export market for illegal coca.

In contrast to Chile and several of the other reforms mentioned earlier, professional army officers were key actors in bringing about the reform. These officers were usually of mixed European and indigenous ancestry, and frequently were recruited from the urban middle classes or from rural landowning families who were not part of the traditional oligarchy. Most resented the racial discrimination of the old rural aristocracy. Moreover, counter-insurgency training by the USA had contributed to the spread of many modernization ideals in the armed forces, as well as to a greater appreciation of the social origins of peasant unrest. Unfortunately, US military training had not done the same for ideals of democratic participation and respect for human rights. Without the reform, however, the land issue would have been even more contentious than it was in the 1980s and 1990s.

Nicaragua and El Salvador

The most recent important land reforms in Latin America took place in these two Central American countries during the 1980s. Both were stimulated by revolutionary insurgencies that had generated significant support from peasants and rural workers demanding land or better wages and working conditions. Land ownership in both countries had been highly concentrated, mostly in large export crop-oriented estates. Land ownership was much more skewed in densely populated El Salvador than in land-abundant Nicaragua. In both countries there had been agro-export booms that had disrupted the livelihoods of the peasantry and displaced large numbers from their customary lands. The latest export boom ended in the 1970s, intensifying rural unrest. Also, in both countries there was a long history of peasant insurgency. There had been a bloody peasant massacre in El Salvador in 1932 when the army slaughtered over 20 000 peasants and rural workers who were demanding land and better wages.

In Nicaragua land reform followed the military victory of the Sandinista rebel forces in 1979. Properties of the ousted Somoza dictatorship were seized and initially converted into state enterprises. These confiscated estates included about one-fifth of the country's agricultural land. Many private estate owners were required to make idle land available to landless peasants for self-provisioning at nominal rents, while wages and working conditions were improved under state and union pressures. The reform was extended to include expropriation of other large estates in the early 1980s, as well as to provide titles to squatters and tenants in frontier regions for the land they occupied. If one includes provisional titles granted to squatters on state lands, by 1986 nearly half the agricultural land and half the rural population had been included in the reform. About 12 per cent of the expropriated land was in state farms, the rest in cooperatives or in individual smallholdings.

The Nicaraguan rural workers' federation (ATC), and the small farmers' organization (UNAG) that was created in 1981, played active roles in pushing the land reform. Both were associated with the Sandinista party (FSLN), but enjoyed considerable autonomy in formulating their demands, especially UNAG. Sandinista officials and professionals were, of course, key players. The Centre for Agrarian Reform Research and Studies (CIERA) played a similar role to that of ICIRA in Chile in attempting to monitor the land reform process, to analyse problems and to suggest possible solutions, as well as to communicate its findings to state officials, peasant leaders and the general public.

The land reform process in Nicaragua was necessarily subordinated to the Sandinistas' struggle for political survival in the face of increasingly aggressive US hostility. The USA organized and financed invading insurgent forces (*contras*). It also imposed a strict economic embargo designed to make the economy scream. Both sides competed for support by discontented peasants. This often accelerated land reform initiatives by the government, but the war usually undermined any economic benefits that might have ensued from reform for the peasants.

Foreign and domestic NGOs and solidarity groups were active in support of the reform, but with highly variable effectiveness. Eastern bloc and Western European economic aid helped offset the damage caused by the US embargo and the US-supported 'low intensity' warfare (Barraclough et al., 1988). But it was a losing battle. The Sandinistas gained a democratic election in 1984, but they lost in 1990. A decade of hardship with heavy war casualties, two periods of hyperinflation, the collapse of the Soviet Union, and a well financed campaign by an opposition coalition advised by some of the world's top electoral propaganda specialists had left voters with little hope for a better future unless the US-backed candidate won.

As in the Chilean case, the role of international organizations in support of the land reform was mixed. Most offered some technical assistance and other help, especially in the reform's early stages. IFAD, for example, provided a loan to support a land reform-linked rural development project with the prospect of financing a larger package of similar projects. When the US imposed its embargo, however, IFAD funding abruptly stopped. Agencies such as the World Food Programme, UNDP, UN Children's Fund, FAO and several others continued some assistance programmes, but with many difficulties and hesitations. When the new government in 1991 gave a priority to supporting larger private producers, including transnational investors in agro-industries, international agencies followed the government's lead. Land reform beneficiaries and their cooperatives found themselves virtually without access to credit, technical assistance or good markets after 1990, although a few NGOs valiantly continued to try to help them. Some agrarian reform cooperatives have survived with NGO help, but others disintegrated. Many indebted land reform beneficiaries lost their land, but land ownership remains far more equitable than it was before the reform.

In El Salvador, the 1980 land reform law followed a military coup in 1979 by progressive officers. The USA strongly supported this land reform; in fact it was drafted with the help of US advisers and imposed on a reluctant oligarchy under US pressure. The USA hoped the land reform would help pacify the rebellious countryside. Some 400 large estates (over 500 ha each), including one-fourth of the country's agricultural land, were expropriated and assigned to their workers as production cooperatives. On average, cooperative members had rights to land amounting to about 8 ha each. These beneficiaries, however, made up only 7 per cent of the agricultural labour force.

The second phase of the reform that would have expropriated land in 12 000 estates of from 150 to 500 ha each (55 per cent of all farm land) was never implemented due to opposition from the traditional oligarchy and changing US priorities. Phase III provided land titles for poor tenants. Some 65 000 small tenants became 'owners', often at the expense of other small proprietors rather than large land owners. These beneficiaries received an average of 1.5 ha each of mostly poor quality land. The land reform had benefited less than one-fifth of the rural labour force and included a little over a quarter of the agricultural area (Barraclough and Scott, 1987).

The land reform cooperatives were burdened with heavy debts for the assessed value of the land, machinery, infrastructure and operating capital they received. The government's espousal of neoliberal policies after the mid-1980s, combined with deteriorating terms of trade, left most of the cooperatives insolvent. If they were subdivided among their members the debt would be equally non-payable, as it would be apportioned among their ex-members. Most of the rural population remained landless or near landless. The peace process implied that many thousands of former government soldiers and ex-guerrilla fighters were seeking land and employment, as in Nicaragua after 1990. In El Salvador, however, remittances from migrants to the USA, together with substantial new foreign investments and liberal US economic aid, helped to generate an expanding economy. Even so, access to land remained a serious and highly conflictive issue. Without the land reform, however, the peace agreement would probably have been delayed much longer than it was.

THE PRINCIPAL ACTORS IN RECENT LAND REFORMS

As seen from the cases discussed above, each agrarian reform process was different. Experiences with land reforms in other parts of the world merely reinforce this conclusion. Nevertheless, a few broad generalizations are possible.

Contradictory role of the state

In every Latin American case where significant land redistribution benefiting the rural poor took place, the state played a decisive role. The state had also been instrumental in preventing land reform earlier, and in deforming it later to the advantage of non-poor social groups. The state's role was different in each stage of a country's land reform process, as well as from one country to another. It depended on a host of internal and external factors. The agrarian structure before reform, the nature of the state and of its principal support groups, the degrees of peasant and rural worker mobilization and organization, and the terms of insertion of the country into the global system were only a few of the important factors. These and many other factors must be taken into account in order to explain why these land reforms succeeded at least partially and temporarily. Similarly, they help explain why no significant land reforms have yet taken place in countries such as Brazil, and many others where land concentration, rural poverty and exploitation of the peasantry were every bit as bad as in the cases summarized above.

In Mexico, Bolivia, Cuba and Nicaragua, land reform accompanied social revolutions in which insurgent political forces seized state power with wide popular support. The social forces driving these revolutions varied. Peasant insurrections for restitution of lost lands and protesting against abuses by quasi-feudal landlords were decisive in initiating land reforms in Mexico and Bolivia, as well as contributing to post-revolutionary land reform in Cuba and Nicaragua. All of these peasant struggles for land were linked with urban-based middle-class nationalist and anti-imperialist movements. They were also fuelled by struggles for control of state power among competing elites. But the nationalist element was much stronger in relatively developed Cuba than in pauperized Bolivia, where resentment of centuries of racial discrimination was a powerful force in mobilizing the peasantry.

These observations about land reforms accompanying social revolutions are consistent with the processes leading to two of the most massive revolutionary land reforms of the mid-twentieth century, those in China and Viet Nam. In China the success of the Communist revolution largely hinged on the impotency of the nationalist government to resist the Japanese invasion, and its inability to respond to peasants' demands after Japan's subsequent defeat in the Second World War. Peasant movements had provided the major social forces fuelling the Communist uprising that had commenced in the 1920s. The Chinese land reform after the victory of Maoist armies in 1949 was the most profound and extensive in history (Shillinglaw, 1974). In Viet Nam, land reform cannot be explained without reference to the replacement of the French colonial power by Japan and the subsequent return of the French. Following the French colonial army's defeat, the South Vietnamese state was supported by the Americans, only to be defeated by the North Vietnamese Communists. The North Vietnamese state had mobilized the peasantry around its demands for land (Luu, 1982).

One must be extremely cautious, however, about generalizations that analyse revolutionary land reforms in one category and non-revolutionary reforms in another. The overlapping and contradictions within each of these categories overshadow their superficial similarities. Non-revolutionary land reforms shared numerous characteristics with the revolutionary ones mentioned above. A common ingredient of all was peasant organization and struggle for more equitable and secure access to land.

Of the Latin American cases, electoral politics were important in bringing about land reforms in Guatemala, Puerto Rico, Venezuela and Chile. But within these countries each process was different. The Guatemalan government's electoral support in 1950 came mainly from urban voters as most peasants still could not vote, but the Arbenz administration regarded them as potential supporters for future elections. The 1952 land reform was instigated by a democratically elected government. It was quickly reversed by a US-backed military coup. Puerto Rico was a US possession at the time of its land reform. The reform was initiated by both the elected colonial government that had sought popular electoral support from rural workers and peasants, and by the US-appointed governor. The Puerto Rican advocates of land reform had been encouraged by the US authorities administering the island for diverse ideological, political and economic reasons. Venezuela's elected government, like that of Guatemala in 1944, had replaced a repressive authoritarian dictatorship. In Venezuela the dictator had in part been deposed by pressure from peasant union activists. Its limited 'market-friendly' land reform, however, was facilitated by ample state revenues from petroleum exports. In Chile, multiparty competition for rural votes played a decisive role in placing land reform on the political agenda. The reform was stopped by a US-supported military coup.

Authoritarian military juntas had initiated serious land reforms in Peru and El Salvador. In both cases, pacification of guerrilla insurgencies with widespread peasant support had been a major objective of the state in espousing land reform.

Principal actors in the post-Second World War land reform processes in Asia carried out by authoritarian governments included the military and an organized peasantry, which was consistent with the Latin American cases summarized above. Two of the most successful state-directed non-revolutionary land reforms after the Second World War took place in South Korea and Taiwan. Both had been Japanese colonies for over four decades: South Korea was occupied by the US army, and Taiwan by Chinese nationalist forces with US help.

The reform in South Korea had been inspired in part by fear that the Communists who took power in North Korea with the help of the USSR after Japan's defeat would be able to mobilize peasant support in the South. Moreover, the South Korean post-war government had been anti-colonial, having few ties with local landlords who had often cooperated with the Japanese. A very drastic land reform was implemented with US help. Land owned by Japanese colonists was distributed to former tenants and workers. A ceiling on all individual holdings throughout the country was set at 3 ha of good crop land, and land in excess of this ceiling was distributed to former tenants. Rents were fixed at low levels for cultivators who did not become landowners. It is often forgotten, however, that there had been a long history of peasant organization and protest around land issues during Japanese colonial rule.

In Taiwan, the Chinese nationalist government with important US help moved to the island after its 1949 defeat on the mainland. It had no obligations to Taiwanese landlords, and many of its members blamed the failure to implement land reform in mainland China for its defeat by the communists. Also, the government wanted to avoid strengthening a Taiwanese rich-farmer class that might have aspirations to form a Taiwanese state separate from China (Pearse, 1980). It promptly initiated a drastic land reform. The reform received important financial and technical assistance from the US government. In any case, as in South Korea, it was primarily a tenancy reform. It provided secure property rights on a very egalitarian basis to former renters and sharecroppers with very low limits set for the amount of land that could be controlled by an individual owner.

In each case, the state's role in land reform was crucial. It sometimes promoted reform, sometimes prevented it, and sometimes reversed it, and sometimes diverted it to benefit other groups than the rural poor. The state always had some scope for autonomous policies, but the space available for changing long-established property relations was extremely circumscribed except in exceptional circumstances. A primary mission of the state was usually to protect the status quo in this respect, as it traditionally derived its power primarily from support of the propertied classes. The changes in state policies leading to or accompanying land reform can be explained *ex post* by the emergence of new influential social actors such as organized peasants and workers together with powerful allies in other sectors of society, but this explanation can easily become tautological. It has limited *ex ante* predictive value because so many other factors intervene that there are inevitably great uncertainties. The same is true of explanations emphasizing the extreme dependency of developing countries within the world capitalist system, although, as was seen, foreign interventions often played decisive roles in initiating or stopping reforms.

The main operational conclusion of our review of the state's role is that land reforms occur only when dominant groups among those wielding state power perceive a political imperative to adopt a popularly based development strategy that requires active support from important sectors of the rural poor. The political mobilization and organization of the rural landless and near-landless is a necessary condition for land reform; but it is not a sufficient one. Poor peasants and rural workers will require powerful allies in other sectors of society, and frequently also from abroad, in order to bring about a more equitable distribution of land.

Peasant organizations

In every case where significant land reforms occurred, protests and demands by organized peasant producers and rural workers made crucial contributions to bringing them about. Peasant activists who initially agitated and organized to bring about reform were usually only a small minority among the rural poor, especially in repressive contexts, but they enjoyed wide covert and passive support. It was possible for widely different groups of the rural poor to unite in protests against the monopolization of land and abusive treatment by landlords and their allies. The large landowners could always persuade some of their tenants and workers to oppose reform through the use of patronage and threats of reprisals, but this was ineffective in the face of widespread discontent and other processes weakening their control over state policies.

Relatively autonomous and democratic participation by organized peasants in implementing land reform, however, was much more difficult to achieve and institutionalize. Even where it was approached it could rarely be maintained for long periods. It was much more difficult for the rural poor to remain united once land became available through reform. How it should be allocated and to whom, as well as how it should be managed and by whom, were inevitably conflictive issues. The more socially differentiated the rural poor were along socio-economic and ethnic lines, the more contentious these issues became. Rural elites faced similar difficulties of internal divisions in maintaining a united front against land reform, but this did not make democratic participation by potential beneficiaries any easier once a reform process was under way. Several of these problems were emphasized when discussing the Chilean and other Latin American experiences earlier.

When reform was administered by the state's bureaucracy, or by a political party on which a weak state largely depended, the issue of democratic peasant participation frequently became acute. State and party officials were often as prone to use patronage and petty corruption to divide peasant organizations for their own ends as were private estate owners and managers or representatives of private corporations. The Mexican case, especially after 1940, is a good example.

These difficulties in approaching and institutionalizing democratic peasant participation in land reforms help to explain why the reforms seldom met the utopian expectations of some of their advocates. This does not detract from the substantial social gains for the rural poor associated with very imperfect land reforms. One has to ask what would have happened if the reforms had never taken place. This is a counterfactual question that can never be definitively answered, but exploring it is instructive. In any event, it is extremely naive to assume that similar abuses would not have arisen if the reform process had been administered by 'civil society' organizations such as NGOs.

Peasant organizations and mobilization were an essential ingredient of all the reforms reviewed above. NGOs, international organizations and others attempting to bring about land reform should recognize this fact. They should also keep in mind that democratic and reasonably autonomous peasant organizations are necessary for institutionalizing reform and preventing it from being diverted to the benefit of others. This is an even more difficult challenge.

The large landholders

As was to be expected, most large landowners resisted land reform in every case examined, although in diverse degrees and by many different methods. Without large landowner resistance, land reform would not be a controversial political issue. Where landlords maintained quasi-feudal social relationships with the rural poor, as in most of Latin America, conflicts inevitably arose with the penetration of market forces (potential profits for some groups from selling and buying in expanding national and transnational markets). Commercialization led to changes in production patterns and technologies. These, in turn, contributed to new social differentiations, to the appropriation of many of the traditional land rights of the poor by large landowners or other outsiders, and to opportunities for some peasants and workers to obtain cash incomes from the sale of natural resources, products and labour if they could get rid of their customary obligations to landed elites. The 1960 revolt of peasant producers with labour obligations to large tea, coffee and cocoa producers in La Convención, Peru is a good example of these latter conflicts, while the demands of indigenous communities for restitution of lost lands in Mexico and Bolivia illustrates the former.

Where some large producers found it profitable to adopt modern, capital-intensive technologies, they had less need for a large resident workforce. Instead, it was more profitable to recruit seasonal workers, while taking for their own commercial use the land previously allocated to resident tenants in return for labour services and part of their produce to the estate. This process was particularly evident in central Chile in the 1950s, and helped create a context favourable for land reform. Similar processes leading to conflicting goals among large landowners were noted in all the cases reviewed above. Moreover, several large landowners became convinced intellectually of the need for land reform. Travel and education sometimes led to an appreciation of historical processes affecting agrarian structures that could be better understood by progressive estate owners, who stood to lose traditional prerogatives by reform, than by urban intellectuals.

Such contradictions among estate owners were reflected by divisions within large landholders' organizations and associations, such as the SNA in Chile. They were seldom able to present a united front when political pressures for land reform mounted. Moreover, to the degree that urbanization and industrialization proceeded, landholding oligarchies became relatively less influential in national affairs. Many diversified their assets and activities to other sectors such as industry, finance and commerce, while retaining a near-monopoly of agricultural land in one or several rural localities. This helped them maintain their power at local levels. It also diluted their political clout nationally when faced with growing demands for land reform, as they had to take into account their own and their urban allies' frequently contradictory non-agricultural interests.

The processes associated with increasing marketization, technological modernization and social differentiation affected both landowning elites and the rural poor in many contradictory ways. Based on the evidence from the cases reviewed above, they accelerated land reforms in some contexts and retarded them in others. It would be a mistake to conclude that 'globalization' in the late twentieth century has left land reform an anachronism. On the contrary, in many developing countries land tenure issues are becoming increasingly acute in the face of growing social polarization, widespread poverty and the absence of alternative employment opportunities for the rural poor. The many divergent interests among the rural poor make their struggle for land reform difficult. The increasingly divergent interests among landholding elites, however, present new opportunities for bringing about land reforms that could benefit the rural landless and near landless.

Political parties

Political parties played a prominent role in the land reforms reviewed above. This is to be expected in what is primarily a political process. Their roles varied widely, however, in different political systems. In formally demo-cratic states with functioning multiparty systems immediately before and during land reform, competition for the votes of the rural poor and others who might benefit from a redistribution of rights to land was important in placing land reform high on the political agenda. This was especially the case with the reforms in Puerto Rico, Venezuela and Chile. Political parties openly competed for popular electoral support by promising land reform. They often actively promoted peasant and rural worker organizations with political goals. In this they were helped by urban-based labour unions affili-ated or allied with political parties. Land reform laws were enacted by elected legislatures after open debate and many compromises with diverse parties and factions. The Chilean case in the 1960s and early 1970s was a good example.

In more authoritarian political systems, open party competition for popu-lar support was outlawed or severely constrained. Nonetheless, political parties invariably played a role. If genuine opposition parties were out-lawed, which was frequently the case, leftist parties still agitated and organ-ized clandestinely. This usually increased pressures on the regime to support some kind of land reform measures. Moreover, authoritarian mili-tary regimes were often far from monolithic. Competing factions among their officers frequently sought populist support, which sometimes led them to undertake rather radical land reforms. This was notably the case with the 1969 Velasco Alverado regime in Peru, the 1979 military junta in El Salvador, and the Chinese nationalist government's reform in Taiwan.

Regimes that came to power as a result of popularly based revolutionary movements, such as those that emerged in Mexico, Bolivia, Nicaragua, Cuba, China and Viet Nam, were politically committed to radical land reforms. They needed to consolidate their popular support in the country-side. These regimes' commitments to the aspirations and welfare of the rural poor were constrained and diluted by competing social forces and priorities once the revolutionary party was firmly in control, but the revo-lutionary political party was invariably a leading actor both in carrying out land reform and in its subsequent evolution.

Effective land reforms have never been primarily technocratic exercises. Their realization always required the active participation of political parties or surrogate political organizations. A non-political land reform would be an oxymoron – a contradiction in terms.

NGOs

Non-governmental organizations constitute an extremely mixed assort-ment of social actors. Their name suggests not what they are, but what they are not. They are commonly considered to be non-state and not-for-profit organizations with the aim of advancing particular social, cultural or eco-nomic interests. What they are and what they do in practice obviously depends on specific historical circumstances, as does the content of the complementary concept of 'civil society'. The dividing lines between NGOs and state-controlled or state-sponsored organizations, as well as between civil society and the state or the market, tend to be exceedingly blurred in practice. For the purpose of assessing NGOs' roles in land reforms, we are especially interested in those NGOs ostensibly dedicated to improving the welfare of the rural poor and promoting other aspects of sustainable rural development.

In some contexts, peasants' associations, large landowners' societies, cooperatives, workers' unions, religious and professional organizations, consumers' societies and the like are considered to be NGOs, while in others they may be regarded by critics as being agents of the state or of the market. Special attention is paid here to self-proclaimed national and international 'charities' and similar NGOs supposedly dedicated to social development, environmental protection and other humanitarian goals.

Such NGOs were active in all the land reforms mentioned earlier. Their roles tended to be peripheral to those of the state, political parties and popularly based non-state organizations such as peasants' associations and rural workers' unions. NGOs, however, were sometimes able to play important catalytic roles. They contributed through advocacy as well as with technical and material support for popularly based movements and organizations involved in land reform. The league of socialist agronomists in Mexico made important contributions to the initial success of several collective *ejidos*, for example. INPROA's experience in transforming church-owned estates into peasants' cooperatives provided an important input into the Christian Democrat administration's agrarian reform in Chile. During the Pinochet dictatorship, NGOs often played a vital role in Chile by providing some assistance to land reform beneficiaries that had been virtually abandoned by the state agencies previously helping them. NGO activities proliferated in post-land-reform Bolivia, Nicaragua and El Salvador. But the contribution of NGOs was by no means always positive or effective for the rural poor.

When the state was actively attempting to implement or guide popularly based land reforms – as in Mexico in the 1930s, Bolivia and Guatemala in the early 1950s, Cuba and Venezuela in the early 1960s, Chile and Peru in the late 1960s/early 1970s, and Nicaragua in the early 1980s – it was relatively easy for NGOs to contribute to these programmes. National NGOs were able to mobilize locally available capacities of students, technicians, professionals, researchers and many others to provide technical assistance, legal aid, training courses and other resources in support of reform processes. They complemented and supplemented the efforts of grassroots organizations and state agencies. International NGOs were able to do the same by working through state agencies, local NGOs and peasant-based organizations. Also they often brought badly needed material help and technical expertise from abroad, as well as helping to inform governments and public opinion in their home countries about the reforms' aims, accomplishments and difficulties.

During such conflictive and often chaotic land reform processes, there were always some NGOs attempting to slow or reverse state-supported land reform programmes. Frequently they were financed by sources at home or abroad that were opposed to reforming established land tenure systems for the benefit of the rural poor. They often shared political and ideological orientations with traditional landed elites, or with would-be modernizing elites hoping to replace them but that were marginalized by the actual changes taking place. To the extent that the state was able to maintain a reasonably coherent, popularly based programme, their disruptive initiatives could be subordinated to the land reform process. Sometimes they called attention to abuses and weaknesses in state-supported programmes that were subsequently corrected. Frequently, however, such NGOs strengthened counter-reform movements. These NGOs often contributed to the weakening or replacement of regimes committed to improving the livelihoods of the rural poor as rapidly as possible through land reform and complementary policies.

In situations where state policies were overtly hostile to land reform, or at best contradictory and ambivalent with regard to the needs and aspirations of the rural poor, NGOs with sincere humanitarian and sustainable development goals faced other dilemmas. The state did not perceive peasants or the rural landless as crucial supporters, but was extremely sensitive to the demands of large landholders who constituted a major support group. Should NGOs vigorously advocate land reform at the risk of being expelled from rural areas and of exposing the popularly based organizations with which they worked to possibly fatal reprisals? Or should they accept the agrarian structure in which they had to operate and try to deliver technical assistance, credit, health and educational services to a few groups in need of them, knowing full well that their limited resources and their political impotence could make little difference for most of the poor unless the agrarian structure was reformed? Should they concentrate their scant resources on local-level micro-projects of relief and income generation that could possibly show positive results for a few beneficiaries? Or should they use their limited resources to support peasants' and workers' organizations as well as to publicize problems of human rights abuses, corruption, and exploitation by landlords, merchants and state officials? Was not there a danger that by helping only a few of the poor this could reduce the militancy of broad-based peasant and landless worker movements by dividing them? If a small minority of the poor with NGO help could benefit within the existing land tenure system, would not many others conclude that their principal problem was not due to exploitative institutions and elite biased policies but to insufficient aid and charity? Moreover, in conflictive and socially polarized contexts, would not the bulk of NGO resources be diverted to strengthen the power of local landed elites through appropriation and redistribution along clientelistic lines?

Each situation was different. NGOs' courses of action largely depended on their assessments of present possibilities and future prospects. Sometimes NGOs made significant contributions towards increasing the awareness of peasants' organizations, influential sectors of public opinion, political leaders and sympathetic state officials of the need for land reform and the possibilities of bringing it about. Often their efforts may have inadvertently weakened peasants' and workers' movements pressing for institutional and policy reforms, and sometimes exposed them to brutal reprisals. Much depended on the dedication, skill and courage of well intentioned NGOs as well as on the context. And much depended on chance.

NGOs operate under many constraints that inevitably influence their judgement about priorities and possibilities. In the first place, they depend on host-country governments for their legitimacy. National NGOs require legal status in order to operate openly and to enjoy possible tax privileges. International NGOs have to obtain government approval even to enter the country. Obviously, NGOs cannot operate as if the state does not exist.

They are dependent on donors for all or part of their resources. Much of their financing comes from other NGOs, private or public corporations and from government agencies, as well as from individuals who support their causes. In the case of many international NGOs, an increasing part of their resources in recent years has come directly or indirectly from their home-country governments, although this varies greatly from one to another. Moreover, most require tax-exempt status in order to survive. NGOs cannot be oblivious to the desires and perceptions of their donors. Competition among NGOs for donations keeps them sensitive to donors' perceived priorities.

NGOs ought to be accountable to the groups they are supposedly serving. Few NGOs, however, have formal mechanisms making them accountable to their clients if these are the rural poor. Occasional internal or external evaluations are common, but the evaluators seldom include representatives of intended beneficiaries. Instead, their accountability to clients, like those of business enterprises to customers, is informally enforced by competition among NGOs. In poor countries the number of potential clients far exceeds the supply of services offered by socially oriented NGOs. Nevertheless, competing NGOs have frequently divided rural communities and peasant organizations in their quest for poor clients and attractive projects in order to justify their activities to donors. I have seen this in Bolivia, for example.

In view of these constraints, one can better appreciate the dedicated and highly professional contributions many NGOs have been able to make in support of social and humanitarian causes. They have often played crucial roles in movements aimed at approaching more socially and ecologically sustainable styles of development. But their capacity is limited. They can sometimes contribute to the emergence of social forces leading to popularly based institutional and policy reforms. They cannot be expected to be substitutes for a democratic political system accountable to its participants. Only states have the potential to deal effectively with mass poverty in a world of plenty.

International organizations

International organizations and agencies associated with the UN system are in some ways in a uniquely advantageous position for promoting land reforms in developing countries. The UN Charter and its subsequent Declarations of Human Rights and of Economic and Social Rights helped legitimize discussion of land reform issues in international fora. The same was true for numerous other resolutions and declarations, some of them referring explicitly to land tenure issues adopted by the UN General Assembly, and by several of the other organizations that are part of the UN system, such as FAO and the ILO. These statements of principle or intent provided internationally recognized rallying points for peasant organizations and others in many countries with repressive regimes beholden to large landowner supporters. They had no enforceable legal authority, but they frequently boosted the moral and political credibility of those advocating reform. As mentioned earlier, the Punta del Este declaration on land reform adopted by the Organization of American States, for example, helped to place agrarian issues high on the political agenda in several Latin American states during the 1960s.

Several international organizations have sponsored research that helped call attention to the need for land reform. As mentioned earlier, ECLAC published studies in the 1950s analysing agrarian problems in Latin America that had considerable influence in later debates. The ILO and the old League of Nations had sponsored research on the importance of agrarian problems as early as the late 1920s, R.H. Tawney's *Land and Labour in China* (Tawney, 1932) being an outstanding example. The ICAD studies of land tenure issues in Latin America mentioned above were sponsored by five international organizations and were influential in shaping later debates in the region. FAO published several documents showing the need for agrarian reforms based on research it had carried out or sponsored. In the 1960s and 1970s it organized, with the ILO and the UN, international agrarian reform conferences which produced strong resolutions on land reform.

International organizations have provided useful technical assistance in many countries carrying out land reforms. FAO sent a highly qualified Mexican expert to Bolivia in the 1950s to advise the government on land reform issues based on the Mexican experience. After the 1950s, FAO, ILO, UNESCO and several other international agencies offered technical assistance to member governments undertaking land reform programmes. This assistance tended to be particularly effective when aimed at helping government agencies to establish research and training institutions with the active participation of peasants' cooperatives and unions.

The international organizations, like most NGOs, however, were invariably extremely sensitive to the political context in which they operated. When the government was no longer interested in pursuing agrarian reform objectives, they usually withdrew their support for peasants' unions and cooperatives that had been pressing for land reform and had been among the beneficiaries of earlier programmes. International agencies tended to measure their success or failure principally by what governments of the day wanted. They often failed to insist that they also had an obligation to tailor their assistance to be congruent with international conventions and resolutions concerning human rights and sustainable development.

This was particularly the case with the international financial institutions. These adopted strong anti-poverty and environmental protection rhetoric, but they argued that their neoliberal policies would best promote economic growth and hence lead to sustainable development. This ignored the fact that the social and ecological problems they hoped to solve through more rapid economic growth had been largely generated by the pattern of economic growth that had been taking place. This style of development was unlikely to become sustainable without popularly based institutional changes such as land reform. To the extent that they have recognized this dilemma, they have tended to advocate 'market friendly' land reforms. As was seen earlier, this fails to offer a solution and could easily make the situation worse for many of the rural poor.

International organizations such as FAO and IFAD have not responded more imaginatively to the current rural livelihood and ecological crisis in developing countries than have the Bretton Woods Institutions. This can be explained by the constraints mentioned earlier. Many of their member countries and of their own secretariats have produced lucid analyses of agrarian problems. Nonetheless, their policies for dealing with them remain timid, ineffective and confined to minor variations on those being advocated by the 'Washington Consensus'. This situation is unlikely to improve unless powerful social forces can somehow be generated in both developed and developing countries, leading to a strong and democratic UN that is accountable to all the world's peoples, including the poor.

CONCLUSION: THE NEED FOR FLEXIBLE APPROACHES TO LAND REFORM

A land tenure system is a subset of social relations. It specifies the rights and duties of diverse stakeholders in their access to land and to its potential benefits. The dichotomy between public and private property is dangerously misleading. Formal land tenure rules that fail to recognize this complexity of land tenure are unrealistic and ahistorical.

Nineteenth-century apologists of Western capitalism advanced the notion that land was merely another commercial commodity, like coal or textiles. They rationalized the myth of unlimited rights of landowners to use and abuse their properties and to evict at will tenants, workers and other users. The rights of customary users were legally extinguished, although in practice this was seldom fully achieved without violent conflict and multiple exceptions. The Communist manifesto reinforced wide acceptance of the dichotomy between public and private property as its qualifications of 'bourgoise property' and 'presently existing private property' were usually forgotten. In rich, industrialized countries, private property rights to land are increasingly restricted through zoning regulations, rights of eminent domain, land use and environmental protection rules, subsidies, differential taxes, protection of tenants' and workers' rights and multiple other mechanisms. The fiction that a corporate entity controlling land, no matter how large, is legally the same as a person, no matter how poor and powerless, weakens many initiatives to enforce social obligations associated with land ownership and use.

Land reform is primarily an issue of basic human rights. It implies access to land and its benefits on more equitable and secure terms for all of those who physically work it and primarily depend upon it for their livelihoods. In unjust agrarian structures, this implies redistributing land rights to benefit the landless and near-landless at the expense of large landholders and others who appropriated most of its benefits before reform.

Once the validity of these concepts of land tenure and land reform are understood, it becomes easier to devise ways to bring about land reform. What land reform implies in practice always depends on the context and particular circumstances, but the basic principles remain the same. In developing countries, land reform usually involves expropriating large holdings and redistributing them as individual family holdings or as worker-managed cooperatives, but there are many variations and sequences depending on the situation. Where customary common property regimes are still vigorous, reform might mean secure tenure and restitution of lost lands. In some cases land reform goals could be approached without redistributing land, but this is highly unlikely in poor countries. What is fundamental is that the beneficiaries participate actively and democratically in the process, and that all of those needing access to the land for their livelihoods are included. At the same time, the basic rights of communities, unborn generations and other legitimate stakeholders have to be protected.

Progressive NGOs and committed international organizations can play important roles as catalysts in helping grassroots peasant and landless movements to organize and press their demands for land. They can help through research focused on the livelihood and sustainable development problems of the rural poor. They can provide valuable technical assistance, material resources and legal aid. They can facilitate the use of modern communication technologies by peasants and others struggling for reform. They can publicize violations of socio-economic and human rights, corruption and other abuses suffered by the poor. They can advance land reforms through advocacy at all levels.

But their roles will always be auxiliary to what must be fundamentally a domestic political process. The main actors in bringing about and consolidating genuine land reform must always include the landless and near-landless, together with their political allies and the state. Well intentioned NGOs and international organizations can help. They can also hinder if they fail to take into account the complex social dynamics that land reform implies.

CHAPTER THREE

Peasant Initiatives in Land Reform in Central America[1]

Eduardo Baumeister

INTRODUCTION

Towards the end of the 1970s, the Central American countries were the most rural and agrarian in Latin America. They were rural in terms of the proportion of rural to national population; and they were agrarian because of the importance that both agricultural production and export had for their economies. Land was concentrated in a few hands, and the workforce was mostly composed of paid and semi-paid labourers. In the 1990s, even though agriculture remained a significant sector for both the economy and the population, its importance as an employment generator and in exports decreased, partly due to increasing urbanization. For example, in El Salvador, Nicaragua and Honduras (the three case study countries in this chapter) 290 000 rural families – approximately 23 per cent of all rural families – obtained access to land (Tables 3.1–3.3). In the 1990s, land sale reduced the number of beneficiaries in the three countries.

By the end of the 1980s, peasant beneficiaries of the agrarian reform adopted strategies within two basic lines. On the one hand, some strategies were intended to modify state promotion policies and the internal organization of beneficiary groups. On the other hand, especially in the 1990s, strategies were directed to partially or totally defend the land obtained during the agrarian reform; to find new production technologies; to introduce new forms of recognition for familial work; and to promote other agricultural and

Table 3.1 Importance of agrarian reform in Latin America

Country	Percentage of held land	Percentage of rural families
Nicaragua (1997)	28	35
El Salvador (1997)	24	24
Honduras (1997)	13	13
Mexico (1970)	42	50
Bolivia (1970)	18	39
Peru (1976)	42	25
Chile (1973)	40	20

Sources: Honduras: Ruben, 1997; El Salvador: World Bank, 1997b; Shaw, 1997; Nicaragua: Baumeister, 1998.

Table 3.2   Composition of the reformed sector in Honduras (1990–95)

Sector	No. of members (000s)	%	Area (000 ha)	%	Area/beneficiary
Beneficiaries of agrarian reform	60.0	12.8	426.2	12.8	7.1
Land settlements	40.0	8.6	234.4	7.0	5.9
Associative enterprises	3.0	0.6	17.0	0.5	5.7
Cooperatives	16.8	3.6	174.8	5.3	10.4

Sources: total number of beneficiaries and area allocated from Posas (1996, p.33), based on data from INA (1994); number of participants and area allocated to settlements, cooperatives and peasant associative enterprises calculated on the basis of Posas (1996) and Ruben (1997).

Table 3.3   Beneficiaries of agrarian reforms according to the socio-political phases of the process in El Salvador and Nicaragua

Phases	El Salvador (000s)	%	Nicaragua (000s)	%
Initial project	37.0	32.5	27.2	24.3
Counter-insurgent 'concessions'	47.0	41.2	37.0	33.0
'Peace'	30.0	26.3	47.8	42.7
Total	114.0	100	112.0	100

Note: El Salvador: the three phases correspond to Phase I and Phase III or 'Finata', that affected the land of small tenants and was designed by R. Prosterman; and the Programa de Transferencia de Tierras agreed after the Peace of 1992 which favoured the demobilized troops of the National Army and the Frente Farabundo Martí de Liberación Nacional. Nicaragua: 'initial project' includes the beneficiaries of the reform (individuals and cooperatives) between 1979 and 1984; 'concessions' encompasses the period 1985–90 when the Sandinista administration made its policies more flexible by handing over more land to cooperatives and individuals – land that between 1979 and 1984 was part of government-owned estates; 'peace' refers to the period post-1990 when demobilized individuals and ex-workers of the state enterprises benefited (includes traditional tenants from ex-government estates or from estates bought for the purpose of the reform after 1990).

Sources: El Salvador: PERA, 1991; Nicaragua: UNAG/FENACOOP, 1989.

forest activities using more sustainable methods. Unfortunately, these efforts were accompanied by important losses in the process of access to land that resulted in massive sales of land throughout the 1990s.

We shall begin by conceptualizing from a comparative perspective the different stages of land reform processes up to the post-reform period in El Salvador, Nicaragua and Honduras. We can identify four basic and distinctive stages inherent to all three cases, particularly in El Salvador and Nicaragua. Factors that need to be taken into account for the analysis include the pressure exerted by changes in the correlation of forces at the government level, and peasants' demands expressed in political–military confrontations and civil wars or resource utilization and low agricultural productivity. We shall summarize the common aspects of agrarian reforms in the three countries, weaknesses in the implementation process, and links with the post-reform stage. We shall also analyse the fact that, despite having obtained great political and state support, the initial stages of the agrarian reforms had a low social impact in terms of the size of the rural population covered. This was the case in El Salvador and Nicaragua, in particular, where the central motivation was to create relatively large, capital-intensive production units focused on agricultural export activities. We shall then discuss different survival strategies chosen by beneficiaries of the reforms, indicating both strong and weak points. Finally, we shall give a balance of the initiatives and draw some conclusions regarding the future of these processes.

STAGES, COMMON ASPECTS AND IMPACTS OF AGRARIAN REFORMS IN CENTRAL AMERICA

Stages

Agrarian reforms in Central America can be divided into four stages. The first stage covers the 1970s in Honduras, Phase I in El Salvador,[2] and the period 1979–84 in Nicaragua. During this period, proposals were given considerable attention, state support was relatively high, and many important projects were implemented.

The second stage was characterized by a change in the direction of the agrarian reform process itself. In order to stop the insurgent pressure in rural areas, the government sought the direct support of small producers and landless peasants. This stage comprises Phase III in El Salvador, and the period of state allocation of land and partial flexibility of the cooperative model in Nicaragua. In Honduras, this stage was marked by the decline of the agrarian reform from the early 1980s onwards, and concern for the titling of national land or areas covered by the agrarian reform. This matter remained unaltered up to 1998, despite little progress being achieved in the titling of national land.[3] As there was no internal insurgent danger as in the past, the decline in agrarian reform has been the result of a conservative turn in development policies.

The third stage applies mostly to El Salvador and Nicaragua, and we shall refer to it as 'Peace Agreements and Agrarian Reform'. Agrarian reform was used as an instrument for the social 're-insertion' of ex-combatants from both regular and insurgent armies. During the first and second stages, the political objective was to isolate peasants from the influence of the insurgent rebel forces and to build a social structure less inclined towards armed protest and the radical questioning of the existing order, but this changed during the third stage. Instead, during this period the rebels themselves, together with their closest support base, were the main beneficiaries of land distribution. Simultaneously, the state's focus on development of the agrarian sector – very much present in the first two stages – diminished.

The fourth stage extends up to 1998 and is marked by the almost total disappearance of agrarian reform from the government's agenda[4] – marked by a neoliberal approach, especially after 1990. The government withdrew as a dealer or financier of agricultural production, elaborated land privatization policies, and encouraged the formation of land markets, the titling of holdings and the fragmentation of collectively owned land. It is within this context that the main beneficiary groups will elucidate their different responses to face the new situation.

Common aspects of agrarian reforms in Central America during the 1970s–1990s

Agrarian reforms in Nicaragua and El Salvador encompassed nearly a quarter and one-third, respectively, of the total cultivated land area, and one-third of rural families benefited from the distribution of land (Table 3.1). They are among the most relevant agrarian reforms in the twentieth century. Even though the amount of land affected by the reform was lower than in the Mexican, Peruvian or Chilean reforms, the quality of land was relatively better in Central America. This can be corroborated by looking at the agricultural exports of the Central American countries. In Nicaragua in the 1980s, the reformed sector covered nearly 30 per cent of the agricultural production for export, adding both the state sector and the co-operative sector's productions. In El Salvador the reformed sector reached 11 per cent of the national production of coffee, 40 per cent of sugarcane, and almost 50 per cent of cotton production (PERA, 1991). In Honduras the reformed sector achieved between 40 and 50 per cent of the production of bananas, sugarcane and African palm (Posas, 1996).

Prevalence of the initiatives of state bureaucracies

Despite people's mobilization and pressure to gain greater access to land and increase their incomes, it was the state which shaped both the initiatives and the forms of agrarian reforms, deciding on the specific properties to be included in the redistribution and organization of workers in the reform process. Technical and military *cadres*, together with political leaders, decided the processes incorporating interests as diverse as the intensification of productive modernization, the containment of popular pressure, and the mobilizations of peasants to 'threaten' traditional proprietors, both local large landowners and multinational companies.[5]

Agrarian reform, as it is usually understood, requires both strong state intervention and autonomy from the classes of rural landowners affected by government actions. This high level of autonomy of state bureaucracies also applied to the mobilized and beneficiary popular groups of the reform. In the context of this 'double' autonomy, the technocratic or ideological views supported by the reformist middle stratum (whether revolutionary or counter-revolutionary) became significantly important. And during the first stage, the result was the existence of relatively large production units with a collectivist commercial approach and strong technical and bureaucratic control.[6]

Socio-political changes before the development of agrarian reform policies

Honduras and El Salvador experienced changes in the political control of their governments, allowing the active participation of the military's reformist factions. In El Salvador, important sectors of the Christian Democracy were also incorporated. In Nicaragua, a revolutionary change took place after the military defeat of the Somocista dynasty.

In Honduras and El Salvador, there was a significant degree of peasant mobilization propelled mostly by the leftist sectors, radical Christian groups or the more traditional factions of the trade unions. Peasants occupied large estates, fought for improved wages, or tried to recuperate national, municipal or village common lands formerly appropriated by large landowners. Paradoxically, it was in Honduras, where there were no subsequent revolutionary uprisings, that the intensity of land occupation was considered to be the highest in Latin America. During the 1970s peasant mobilization was at its peak. The most common path followed was the coordinated appropriation of land on a large scale before sowing time in the rainy season (Posas, 1981; Brockett, 1990).

In Honduras, and especially in El Salvador, the political–military alliance that launched the agrarian reform conceived it both as an instrument for agrarian modernization that would include the popular sectors, and as a control mechanism for potential insurgent groups. In the case of Nicaragua, this emerged towards the mid-1980s when the agrarian reform was used in war zones as an instrument to gather forces and counteract the influence of the counter-revolutionary alliance over the peasants.

Modernization, collectivism and strong state intervention

The three country studies analysed attempted to combine productive modernization, a certain degree of collectivism and strong state control on property assets, productive organization, commercialization control, credit facilities, technical assistance and development plans.

During the agrarian reform's phase of maximum expansion, the focus was on activities related to agricultural export and agro-industries (coffee, sugar refineries, cotton processing, slaughterhouses, processing of fruits that provide oil, etc.): coffee, sugarcane and cotton in El Salvador; African palm and bananas in Honduras, and sugarcane, coffee, cotton and cattle in Nicaragua. However, most beneficiaries concentrated on activities related to basic grains, obtaining lower levels of capitalization than those who focused on agricultural exports.

The operating pattern of most state-run (Nicaragua) or associative (El Salvador and Honduras) production units originated during the reforms developed into the 'plantation' type of organization.

Characteristics of the beneficiaries

In El Salvador and Nicaragua, the main beneficiaries during the principal stage of reform were permanent or seasonal paid workers from expropriated estates. In Honduras, they created or rehabilitated estates using ex-banana workers or semi-proletarian sectors as a base.

Structural imbalance in the reformed sector

Although the three countries achieved a relatively significant economic growth during the 1980s, particularly in agricultural exports, the proportion of the rural population benefiting from the reform was relatively low. In Nicaragua in 1984–85, for example, direct beneficiaries of the reform who received land represented only 11.7 per cent of the total of rural families, based on data provided in this chapter and on a 1985 estimate of the number of rural families (FLACSO, 1995). Phase I of the Agrarian Reform in the early 1980s in El Salvador encompassed only 7 per cent of rural families.[7] This low population coverage led to a rather limited socio-political effect on the stabilization of rural areas.

Socio-political transactions and policy changes

During the second stage, the processes of land reform in the three countries experienced a change of direction from the initial proposal. For instance, in Nicaragua the amount of state-owned land given to individual peasants and cooperatives increased, while in El Salvador tenants became owners. In Honduras, the turning point was marked by the titling of national land and the encouragement of small peasant groups working individually.

El Salvador entered this second stage after Phase II, proposing to deal with properties ranging from 100 to 500 ha. But it was postponed indefinitely. In April 1980, the law for Phase III of the Agrarian Reform – 'land-to-the-tiller' – was promulgated. It had the direct support of Roy Prosterman, an American adviser who had formerly worked in Viet Nam in the same field.[8] However, a serious mistake in the diagnosis showed that the small tenants benefiting from Phase III rented their land to other smaller land-holders who happened to be their relatives in many cases (Deere, 1985, p.67). On the other hand, many tenants were expelled from their plots before they could actually be beneficiaries of this phase. In Nicaragua during the second half of the 1980s, the government gave state land to cooperatives and individual peasants, abandoned the allocation of new land, and encouraged the titling of national land. In Honduras in the early 1970s, the government decreased the amount of land it distributed, and focused on titling national land in the hands of small and medium sized producers. During the 1990s, as the state reduced its support to the cooperative movement, a massive sale of productive land acquired through the reform took place. This time the 'beneficiaries' were the multinational companies and large national producers and agribusiness groups.

Land reform and the pacification of insurgent forces

In El Salvador and Nicaragua, agrarian reforms took place within the context of an internal war in which the government fought the insurgent forces supported by peasant sectors (Frente Farabundo Martí de Liberación Nacional in El Salvador and Resistencia Nicaragüense in Nicaragua). As a consequence of the peace agreements signed in Nicaragua in 1989–90 and El Salvador in 1992, governments used the reform to pacify demobilized armies and the insurgents' rural support base. In both cases these groups represented a significant proportion of the total number of beneficiaries. During this period, production units – individual plots assigned as collective land – did not receive the technical and credit support given to production units in the first stage (Table 3.3). As in other cases of land reform in the twentieth century, land redistribution was used as a political instrument to handle the unsatisfied peasantry, regardless of the state's idea of agricultural development for the betterment of the rural people. In these particular cases, the distribution of land constituted 'political concessions' to the ex-insurgents who retained important rural support. This demonstrated the strong relationship between agrarian reform, peasants' land demands and national politics. This phase evolved at the rise of neoliberal ideologies and public policies opposed to encouraging peasants' movements for greater access to land. This, in conjunction with the unpromising economic conditions, left a great number of potential beneficiaries in a very fragile situation. For many, access to new land became increasingly difficult.

High mobility among cooperative members

A study carried out in El Salvador (Strasma, 1985) on five cooperatives, with an average of 550 ha and 110 permanent members, concluded that total membership declined by 23 per cent over a period of a few years. From the initial number of members, 47.5 per cent left the cooperative for reasons such as expulsion, voluntary resignation, long absences, death, and retirement due to old age. A similar study in Nicaragua (Vaessen, 1997) established that only 56 per cent of cooperative members in 1997 were founding members. A study in Honduras (Ruben, 1997, p.195) pointed out that 29 per cent of cooperative members in the department of Comayagua had changed between 1990 and 1995.

Factors not taken into account when designing agrarian reforms

Many factors were not taken into account when designing the type of production unit required for agrarian reforms. These units were commercial enterprises, collectively or state owned, capital-intensive, and related to agro-industries and agricultural export.

Low levels of legalization and institutionalization

As in all agrarian reforms in Latin America, although beneficiaries were given provisional titles after the land was occupied, the process of legalization was usually not completed. In Nicaragua, the most radical of the three case studies, the confiscation of land did not result in the immediate transfer of land plots to state jurisdiction, in the first place, and to the new landholders – state enterprises, cooperatives or individuals – later. In general, this had important consequences after 1990 when many beneficiaries discovered that the registers had not been changed and their land plots were still in the names of the previous owners.

Policies on agrarian reform took little care to develop markets for beneficiaries in regard to commercialization of their products. The state acted as an intermediary between producers from the reformed sector. It became responsible for dealing with both national and international markets through the government agencies concerned for the commercialization of basic grains and the nationalization of foreign trade. However, after the state abandoned its interventionist approach, the vulnerability of the reformed sector was evident as soon as it had to face the 'real' market. This continued during the post-reform period characterized by neoliberal policies.

Increasing urbanization

Another factor not taken into account during the distribution of land was the importance that urbanization would have in Central America a few years later. A significant proportion of land under agrarian reform in El Salvador, and to a lesser degree in Nicaragua, has become attractive for non-agricultural uses such as urban housing plots or tourist development. In Nicaragua, this has been demonstrated by Managua's suburban growth due to residential expansion and on the Pacific coast due to growth in tourism.

Rural sources of income and livelihood

Agrarian reforms and agricultural policies in the 1970s and 1980s were designed on the assumption that the income of a rural family basically came from agricultural production for self-consumption, permanent or seasonal paid agricultural work, and the sale of agricultural produce. All major agrarian reforms, with both individual and collective allocation of land, focused on handing over land to incorporate a higher proportion of the familial workforce available so that rural structural unemployment would be reduced. In time, this would contribute to the increase of real salaries in the agricultural sector and improve income distribution. In practice, the income of rural families had a more complex composition and included diverse non-agricultural sources such as handicrafts, construction, petty trading, services, and international migrations that were gradually having more weight in rural incomes.

By focusing exclusively on agricultural production, the reforms left aside possibilities for supporting other activities. They did not value the diversification of allotment gardens or provision of areas for growing trees (for firewood, construction, fencing, etc.). The value of these activities for self-consumption or sale was seldom considered important.

State 'tutelage' as a permanent process

The strategies designed for the three agrarian reform processes responded to the governments' overall view of general and permanent state intervention, unlike other agrarian reforms in which they were transitory structures. This tendency was observed in both the Sandinista (Nicaragua) and the Christian Democrat (El Salvador) administrations in which banking and foreign trade were nationalized while agrarian reform was taking place. In El Salvador, the support that these initiatives gained from the conservative Reagan and Bush administrations were essentially related to the counter-insurgent strategy.

In Honduras the degree of intervention was more limited in relation to the extent of the reformed sector. Different state development agencies were perceived as central actors in the investment and organizational process of the new productive sectors. This was also reinforced as the agrarian reform greatly influenced the production of important products such as African palm, sugarcane and bananas.

Peculiarities of Central American agrarian reforms

Agro-export-oriented countries with national control of the production process

In most Latin American countries (Mexico, Bolivia, Chile, Peru, Venezuela – except Cuba), where there were relatively profound agrarian reforms, economic activities related to foreign trade and capital formation had a strong oil and mining component. The singularity of the Central American cases lies with the fact that these countries' exports were exclusively composed of agricultural products. Particularly in Mexico and Peru, agricultural exports were important, but the relative weight of these products on foreign trade and investments was much lower than in the Central American cases.

While in El Salvador and Nicaragua the production process was subject to national control, in Cuba it was based on a plantation enclave economy with a direct presence of foreign capital in the production of export products. Honduras partly had a plantation economy, especially in the northern region, specializing in the production of African palm and banana.

The differences in the dominant export products (agricultural or non-agricultural) and the direct presence of capital influenced the formation of alliances and the degree of opposition on behalf of the landowning classes towards the agrarian reform.

Agrarian reform as part of a wider political conflict

Agrarian reforms took place due to internal political conditions marked by military and political coalitions. In the three cases, the armed forces – independently from the significant ideological distances between the military reformers in Honduras, the counter-insurgent forces supported by the USA in El Salvador, or the most prominent actors in the revolutionary initiative in Nicaragua – supported the agrarian reforms and participated in the appropriation of land, creating the first structures for the new production units.

In El Salvador and Nicaragua, the reform processes had various implications. They had the potential to bring about a radical change in their economic systems as well as the possibility to expand the experience to the rest of Central America. In the national-reformist cases of Mexico, Bolivia, Peru and even Chile in the 1970s, agrarian reform was linked to transformation of the traditional real estate system and elimination of forced labour, *medierias* (sharecroppers), tenancies with labour service obligations, and cash rentals. They also intended to transform cotton and sugarcane plantations on the Peruvian coast or cotton in Mexico into state enterprises or production cooperatives. In any case, despite the violence used in the implementation process (e.g. Mexico or Bolivia) and the radical ideologies that shaped the reforms (e.g. Chile or Peru), the most serious implications for the system's global change took place in Central America during the 1980s.

Although there were certain elements of economic development in the policies that surrounded the agrarian reforms in Nicaragua and El Salvador, these policies essentially contained broader political and ideological elements that surpassed the agrarian issue.[9] Rural areas saw the emergence of many political forces which sought broader alliances to face the adverse national and international political and economic situations in addition to agricultural problems.

The ideological component in the conformation of a new social fabric in rural areas

A common element in the three cases and the rest of Latin America was the establishment of associative or state-owned collective enterprises with strong technical services, and the generalized intervention of engineers and technicians. The ideological goals transcended the more short-term political goals and combined with commercial models based on scale economies. The introduction of technical packages was meant to substantially increase the product both per surface unit and per worker. They also expected to create a new social fabric in which social conflict, prevalent in the past, would diminish. They did not attempt to widen the middle rural sectors, but instead focused on the cooperative members.

The ideological influence is a way to explain one of the paradoxes of agrarian reform in Central America, and probably in many other Latin American cases. The reform was expected to change property relations as well as the organization of the production process by creating collectively owned and organized cooperatives.

PEASANT INITIATIVES AND CENTRAL AMERICAN AGRARIAN REFORMS

Strategy No. 1: sale and lease of land

In the three country case studies, the first strategy adopted by an important number of beneficiaries was the total or partial sale of land, as soon as neoliberal legislation allowed it. How do we conceptualize this strategy that often meant the disappearance of beneficiary groups and the return to paid work? For a better understanding of this situation, it is necessary to look at a number of factors. In the first place, the state had the power to authorize possible transfers. Secondly, most beneficiary groups had very precarious titles over their lands. Finally, until the end of the 1980s, the state provided credits to those groups who owned good land and/or were located in export producing areas, making it possible to keep payment records for the associates' work in each collective group as quasi-paid agricultural workers. Towards the end of the 1980s and the beginning of the 1990s, the situation changed. Together with liberalization in land sales, the state withdrew its credit support and stopped providing facilities for the commercialization of agricultural products. A significant part of the reformed sector entered a state of collective 'anomaly', leading to the sale of land. There are other factors that require close scrutiny:

■ Massive land sales and labourers' attitudes: some groups sold their land and stopped being individual or collective producers. This happened in the north of Honduras where beneficiaries sold their land to banana companies (Funez and Ruben, 1993). This situation made evident one of the inherent problems of the collective commercial model of agrarian reform: the prevalence of a wage worker's mentality which would make the peasant sell his/her land for a quick profit as soon as the legal or quasi-legal situation allowed it.

- Differentiated sales according to beneficiary types: in cases as in Nicaragua, many beneficiaries who had been given land after the demobilization of troops sold their land in order to return to their place of origin. In this case, the sale of land did not mean the total loss of access to land, as many may have used the money they obtained to purchase land in their place of origin or in agricultural frontier areas. A study carried out by Fernández in Rio Blanco, Nicaragua shows that demobilized beneficiaries sold 63 per cent of their land between 1990 and 1996. On the other hand, settlers who had been in the area for years as previous estate labourers sold 25 per cent of the land received from the agrarian reform (Table 4 of Fernández, 1997).

- Sale of land for non-agricultural purposes: especially in El Salvador, agricultural land has been sought for non-agricultural purposes with the growing urbanization and high population density of the country. The price of land has risen, and there is more pressure on cooperatives to sell their land. Some of these new, non-agricultural uses include construction of urban or peri-urban houses, offshore assembling plants, and tourist development. A recent study carried out by Childress (1997) shows that, according to the agricultural lease value for basic grains, the price of the land should have been 8870 colones (approximately US$1000) instead of 20 000 colones per hectare (US$2300), 2.3 times higher than the former value. The author, based on a study of 1500 producers, points out that the decisive factor in the land price rise beyond strictly agricultural parameters relies on the current possibility of using agricultural land for urban purposes. The valuation of 14 cooperatives authorized to sell their land has assigned an average price of US$12 000 per hectare at 1997 prices (including existing improvements, standing crops, etc.) (ISTA, 1997). The problem faced by many cooperatives in El Salvador deepened in 1998. About 85 per cent of the debt incurred since 1980 has been cancelled, making the rest of the debt payable in 12 years. This will convert them into quasi-proprietors, conferring on them the possibility of acting freely in the land markets. This added to increasing pressure on the members to sell their plots partially or totally. It also led to booming prices and the decline of agriculture as a means of gaining livelihoods or foreign currency.

- Land lease: in the three country case studies, a fraction of the cooperatives – with both individual and collective work – have leased their lands to other agricultural workers when they lacked working capital. A study on El Salvador established that 25 per cent of a total of 50 collectively owned cooperatives leased part of their lands (Figure 50 of CONFRAS, 1997). In Honduras, many cooperatives leased their land to companies based in areas producing sugarcane or non-traditional crops such as melon (Cruz and Muñoz, 1997). In Nicaragua, different observers and qualified informers point out that a great number of cooperatives in pasture areas leased their land temporarily to private cattle ranchers.

Implications

The sale, purchase and lease of land – sometimes on an informal basis – remained a widespread phenomenon among small and medium-sized farmers (Salgado, 1994; Nitaplan, 1995). The agrarian reform intended to freeze these processes, and at its peak it managed to do so. However, in the context of the process of liberalization and withdrawal of state support, these practices generalized among the beneficiaries of the reformed sector. Estimates suggest that the number of beneficiaries in the three countries reached 289 000 and land given amounted to 2.5 million ha, of which 1.6 million ha were in Nicaragua. By the end of the 1990s, the number of beneficiaries who still retained the land received from the reform or inherited is lower than indicated above. Important factors leading to this decrease include the 'wage worker's attitude' rather than a cooperativist one; the poor quality of the land received; and the unfavourable location of the plots (especially for demobilized soldiers or peasants displaced by the armed conflict). Some cooperatives and peasants' groups sold their lands in order to pay bank or agrarian debts or to make new investments in their plots, and continued working the remaining land under individual or mixed modalities of tenure and production organization. Simultaneously, some groups leased their plots as they lacked the working capital to exploit their lands.

An exogenous factor that contributed to the reduction in the number of beneficiaries who kept their land was the demand on land for non-agricultural uses, such as urbanization, tourism and tax-free zones. Consequently, the group of beneficiaries who survived had less land that, in turn, was exploited intensively when modes of production changed.

The balance of this process of land sale has significantly reduced the amount of land originally provided to the peasant sector, and in the mid-term it could greatly decrease the achievements of the initial processes of agrarian reform.

Strategy No. 2: semi-collectivization, division of land in collective areas and modes of capitalization

The second strategy observed was the individualization and division of formerly collectively owned land. A 1993 field study in Nicaragua established that 70 per cent of collective cooperatives had parcelled out their land

(Matus et al., 1993). Another study, centred on the Department of Leon and based on a sample of 62 cooperatives, showed that 13 cooperatives were still working collectively, 16 were working the land individually but sharing some services collectively, and 33 were operating on a totally individual basis (Vaessen, 1997). A study carried out in El Salvador showed that in 42 per cent of cooperatives with collective land tenure, the ones that generated more profit were those operating individually (CONFRAS, 1997). A survey carried out among beneficiaries of the reformed sector in Honduras pointed out that 58 per cent preferred collective land titling, while 32 per cent preferred the individual form and 10 per cent a mixed one (Chavez and Childress, 1994). A previous enquiry in the north of the country in the 1980s had shown that, in practice, semi-collective production organization prevailed, with only 26 per cent of the beneficiaries remaining in their cooperatives (Land Tenure Center, 1989).

The result was the strengthening of individual or mixed forms of production organization and/or management of services, such as commercialization of products and access to credit. These individual or mixed management forms allow a higher degree of non-remunerated familial work, stimulate fixed investments, fencing, fruit and wood tree plantations, and increased cattle herds or small coffee plantations. Collective forms are maintained especially in plantation areas related to prevailing agro-industrial activities such as African palm or sugarcane.

Strategy No. 3: changes in production systems

Many beneficiaries radically changed the production systems and techniques they used, shifting from schemes of productivity specialization inspired in the first green revolution to measures where agriculture, stock breeding and forestry were more intensively combined for both sale and family consumption. This significant change is related to the adoption of more individualized methods of production within the cooperatives. The new alternative forms of soil conservation, water retention and fertilization constituted important factors for Central American producers in the 1990s: they saved working capital as they reduced the amount of industrial inputs, and allowed a greater utilization of the producer and his/her family's workforce, in part subutilized in the previous collective schemes.

This change was of great relevance, as the agrarian reform model applied in Central America was deeply influenced by green revolution schemes. This approach relied on the belief that, in conjunction with access to land, beneficiaries should have access to mechanization, improved seeds, chemical fertilizers and insecticides, and productive specialization. Access to these production means would be possible through state bank credits and the commercialization of crops by state-run marketing companies.

This model was deep-rooted in peasant leadership, in particular in the agrarian reform areas. As very few groups actually had access to these technological packages in an integral manner, from the peasants' point of view this model was the one they had to aspire to.

Access to chemical inputs became difficult for wide sectors of small and medium-sized producers when structural adjustment programmes were introduced. On the one hand, the devaluation of local currencies in relation to the US dollar to stimulate exports resulted in a price rise in imported products (fertilizers and insecticides) which increased their relative prices in respect to goods for the internal market (e.g. basic grains). On the other hand, the significant reduction in credit made access to technological packages associated with the green revolution more difficult.

Within this context it is relevant to look at the strategies proposed by the Programa de Campesino a Campesino (PCAC) carried out by the Small Farmers' Organization (UNAG) in Nicaragua since the 1980s, and recently extended to the rest of Central America by the Asociación de Organizaciones Campesinas Centroamericana para la Cooperación y el Desarrollo (ASOCODE). The PCAC focused on promoting activities related to soil conservation, water retention, organic fertilization (e.g. manure, green manure, agro-forestry) and organic pesticides. Training is provided by workshops, and field demonstrations are carried out by peasant promoters supported by a small number of technicians with a facilitating and coordinating role in the different initiatives both nationally and regionally. Approximately 75 per cent of the promoters are men.

In the beginning, this programme rapidly proliferated among small-scale, traditional farmers on hillside land, leaving aside cooperatives with intensive use of external inputs. However, the programme expanded to other beneficiary sectors of the reform, especially to those cooperatives that had been massively divided, and reached two-thirds of Nicaraguan municipalities. Interestingly, 48 per cent of the PCAC promoters were reform beneficiaries and have occupied managerial positions in cooperatives or cooperative unions (Baumeister, 1996).

Although the PCAC has extended to an important proportion of the country, the segment of producers who have actually employed more sustainable technologies is still rather limited. Despite this, there have been noticeable achievements in terms of the reduction of production costs, increased yields per surface unit, and improved soil conservation and water retention. This programme has not only provided producers with an alternative to the chemical and technological packages, but also introduced more sustainable means for the conservation of natural resources. Simultaneously, it has proposed a more integral vision regarding peasant holdings, combining yearly and permanent crops, fruit and wood trees, living fences, allotment gardens for self-consumption, agriculture and livestock. This is a very different vision from that promoted by the paradigm of productive specialization prevailing at the end of the 1970s and the beginning of the 1980s.

An obstacle faced by the programme was the fact that the ideas of the green revolution were deeply established in the cooperative movement. For those interested in managerial reconversion to increase competitiveness and expand to different markets, non-intensive technologies in 'modern' inputs looked like a symbol of backwardness. On the other hand, for those who owned flat land and had been using tractors and green revolution technologies for the past 30 years, these alternative methods are not readily available yet, or at least not on the same scale as for producers of the reformed sector in poor capitalization conditions.

Technologies more readily available among groups linked to peasants' unions and development NGOs suit relatively small plots on work-intensive hillside land where the workforce has a certain level of training, making it possible to carry out different activities (agriculture, livestock, forestry). The use of these technologies will eventually lead to the increase of production per surface unit and decrease the subutilization of the familial work force.[10]

Strategy No. 4: women as organizers, producers and income generators

Peasant women in Central America have been practically invisible in the debate concerning agricultural production. Traditionally, they were perceived as part of the non-active economic population. This 'invisibility' was reflected during the agrarian reform when the number of women who actually had direct access to land was low. In fact, women in Honduras represent only 3.8 per cent of the beneficiaries of the agrarian reform. In Nicaragua the number reached 9.4 per cent, and in El Salvador approximately 11 per cent (de Zeeuw et al., 1997).

Recent studies show that censuses underestimate female participation, notably in the economically active rural population. For instance, in Nicaragua, El Salvador and Honduras official estimates indicate that the proportion of women participating in economic activities represents 12, 12 and 6 per cent, respectively (Chiriboga et al., 1995). More in-depth surveys have revealed a higher percentage of women, raising the previous figures to 20/25 per cent for Nicaragua, 29/35 per cent for El Salvador, and 20/25 per cent for Honduras (Chiriboga et al., 1995).

Most peasant women cultivate small plots of land around their houses where they grow fruit and vegetables as well as other basic food. These products are mostly for self-consumption and help to improve the family's diet. They also constitute an important source of income.

The growing valorization of women as producers and income generators can be observed in the greater organization of rural women. Particularly in Honduras, organizations such as Consejo para el Desarrollo Integral de la Mujer Rural have achieved relevant positions in the coordinating bodies of the organized peasant movement, such as Consejo Coordinador de Organizaciones Campesinas de Honduras. In 1997 in Nicaragua, the Federación de

Productoras Agropecuarias, previously part of UNAG, achieved autonomous status, providing women producers with credit and commercialization services, especially in the north of the country (Anon., 1998a). Approximately 38 per cent of producers participating in alternative technology initiatives are women (UNAG, 1997, p.41). The importance gained by women as producers can be explained by the consequences of the armed conflict that left many homes without a male head. The significance of the allotment gardens run by women for self-consumption and supplementary income also contributed to the process. Although this tendency is still incipient in Central America, the proliferation of more integral visions to other organizations close to the interests of the beneficiaries of reform will make evident the benefits of the more active roles that women can play in the organization of local initiatives.

Strategy No. 5: articulation process with private entrepreneurs

In Honduras and El Salvador, and to a lesser degree in Nicaragua, beneficiaries often associated with agro-industrial entrepreneurs. Peasant groups provided land and labour, while the entrepreneurs facilitated credit, technical assistance, processing and commercialization (for a recent review of this modality in Honduras see Cruz and Muñoz, 1997). This is observable in the cultivation of sugarcane and commercial fruit and vegetables in the principal valleys of Honduras. In El Salvador, coffee and sugarcane producers of the reformed sector found their financing sources in private sugar refineries or coffee plantations linked to private banks (personal observation, July–August 1997).

This strategy reflects many aspects of the current situation of the reformed sector. Firstly, the peasant groups who manage to become involved in this type of partnership are those who own relatively good quality land and are able to produce highly marketable products for both domestic and foreign markets. They are not the weakest groups in terms of the type of resources they control.

Secondly, this alternative emerges partly due to the absence of two other articulation options. The oldest option is related to the original agrarian reform model in which the state and its agencies played all the roles that are currently performed by private entrepreneurs. The prevailing view within the state was of promoting the cooperative sector rather than business and accumulation that logically prevails in the private sector. The second option, which in some cases failed or did not exist, is centred around peasant unions. Since the end of the 1980s and through the 1990s, they have been actively involved in financing, commercialization and industrial processing. Examples are Empresa Cooperativa de Productores Agropecuarios (ECODEPA) in Nicaragua and Sociedad de Cooperativas Cafetaleras de la Reforma Agraria (SOCRA) in El Salvador.[11]

Due to massive withdrawal of the state in the three countries and the deficiencies of the cooperative movement, producers had to take more risky initiatives. The strategies of some private companies have sought 'alliances' with producers from the reformed sector just to acquire their land. For instance, in Honduras an agro-industrial company in the valley of Comayagua which buys vegetables from the local producers and provides technical assistance to them has tried to buy the cooperatives' land (personal communication with an economic adviser of the Programa para la Consolidación de la Reforma Agraria en Comayagua, Tegucigalpa, August 1997). Apart from this, agreements with private entrepreneurs have often pushed producers to monoculture, with the consequent deterioration of soil fertility, especially when using chemicals on a large scale.

Elements inherent to this type of scheme include a reduction in decision margins for small producers, and the fact that the enterprises' perceptions of their profits or losses in the agreement will drive contract agricultural models.

In Honduras in the early 1990s, when the land war for banana plantations began, multinational companies bought large quantities of land from the reformed-sector cooperatives. The companies sought to produce the bananas themselves, as there was a struggle among the different transnational companies for control of the market. At this stage, they considered that contract agriculture was dangerous for their interests as it allowed producers to choose among the different international commercial firms, leaving them in a disadvantaged position (Funez and Ruben, 1993, pp.74–80). The situation in El Salvador was different. Interests in coffee plantations mainly focused on processing and commercialization rather than on direct production. However, the possibility of losing land in credit transactions with private companies was always present. In synthesis, this strategy should be considered as a defence mechanism due to the lack of feasible alternatives generated within the productive sector itself.

Strategy No. 6: direct presence of the productive sector in commercialization, agro-industry and financing

In the early 1990s, especially in Nicaragua and El Salvador, the idea emerged of transforming peasant organizations into union-enterprise organizations. They intended to add a strong economic component to the more traditional roles of the unions in order to counterbalance the withdrawal of the state as a promoter and to keep the organizations independent of the state's policies. Leading organizations included UNAG and Unión Nacional de Productores Autogestionarios in Nicaragua; and in El Salvador, Confederación de Asociaciones Cooperativas de El Salvador, Confederación de Federaciones de la Reforma Agraria de El Salvador (CONFRAS) and Alianza Democrática Campesina.[12] These strategies, propelled by the most prominent unions in the reformed sector such as CONFRAS (El Salvador) and UNAG/-

ECODEPA (Nicaragua), had the aim of participating in agro-industry, and the commercialization and financing of agricultural production and export. In Honduras, the initiative was carried out by the palm-producing cooperatives.

However, a significant number of these initiatives inherited many of the negative aspects of the government's management, such as low managerial capacity, corruption in resource management, political use of economical instruments, and populism. This translated into losses in commercial operations, low return in credits given to grassroots groups, bankruptcy and liquidation of existing assets. Since the 1970s in these three countries, more experiences have failed than succeeded. Some unions have failed or are operating under precarious conditions. For instance, ECODEPA failed commercially and was liquidated in 1996; SOCRA is in a very fragile situation; Cooperativa de la Palma Africana (COPALMA) has reduced its base of cooperatives and is deeply in debt (Anon., 1998b).

Perspectives for the future

Several 'original sins' remained from the unionist and economic structures of the reformed sector which prevented them from facing changes in the economic, political and state scenarios at national and international levels. Historically, peasant organizations – especially those originating during the reform – have played an intermediary role. During the most active periods of reform processes, organizations which were closely linked to political parties, religious organizations and state structures acted as intermediaries between the state and grassroots peasant groups. More recently, they have mediated between international agencies for cooperation (multilateral, bilateral and, in particular, NGOs from the North) and their grassroots structures. The emphasis on mediation weakened their role as representatives. The second negative aspect lay in the way in which many national federations, confederations and unions were constituted: they developed in a top-down fashion, beginning first at the national level.

Both the emphasis on mediation and the institutional distance within the national levels and grassroots organizations have been obstacles to the creation of more representative institutions capable of maintaining a stable channel of communication from bottom to top. Two concrete obstacles emerged from this situation.

- Unions are not able to survive on their members' contributions. There are no membership fees and, due to withdrawal of state support, they depend on the support given by Northern NGOs. In the past few years this financial aid has been progressively reduced, leaving the most important peasant unions in a difficult situation.
- Credit plans developed by the unions, as well as agro-industrial and commercial initiatives, were perceived by grassroots groups as support

projects (i.e. similar to those the state had promoted in its more de-
velopmentalist phases). As a result, there were important unresolved
payments of credits, it was expected that prices paid by unions would
be more favourable than those offered by the traditional private sector, and the productive infrastructure installed was neglected.

There was thus a lack of involvement in productive projects and a populist
attitude towards the resources they received. In the current economic and
political context, the only way to reverse these negative tendencies, suffered by the peasantry in general and the reformed sector in particular, is
by a deep ideological and conceptual renovation.

The rural population in Central America is increasingly involved in multiple occupations and diverse sources of income. They range from work in
allotment gardens for self-consumption, to remittances obtained from
international markets, market-oriented agricultural activities, forest production for both self-consumption and sale, paid work in the surrounding
area, non-agricultural, commercial activities, etc. Therefore there is a need
for a more integral agrarian vision.

Peasant economies must look further than agriculture. There are possibilities such as participating in environmental initiatives through forest
activities supported by Northern NGOs, or the contribution to the maintenance of urban centres due to growing problems regarding water, elec-
tricity and solid waste. Therefore the current scenario is clearly
overwhelming, and goes beyond what is usually called 'the agrarian issue'.
Nowadays it encompasses problems that are related to natural resources,
environmental management and urban development, at both national
and international levels. Hence this new context opens opportunities for
wider and more complex alliances.

It is necessary to appreciate the advantages of more sustainable technologies in terms of water and soil conservation, as well as the benefits of
using alternative fertilizers and pesticides. Close articulation among agriculture, livestock, forestry and artisan fishing has to be recognized in order
to achieve a conceptual renovation that will lead to a new approach
towards 'modernization' and 'progress' for peasant economies in this type
of country.

Similarly, collective action in all its different forms – ranging from claims
to the local authorities to the possibility of exporting high value goods to
the Northern markets via solidarity markets or traditional channels of commercialization – need new organizational structures. Reorganization
should start at the local level and then expand geographically in order to
reverse the traditional approach of top-down initiatives. If the verticalism
and populism present in the agrarian reform processes are not overcome, it
will be difficult to develop more effective and sustainable collective actions.

There is a need for more evolutionist development models, less centred
in political alliances. The conceptual renovation presumes the revaloriza-

tion of political alliances with political parties or governmental agencies. It is evident that peasants' groups originating during the agrarian reform and having problems legalizing their land will still need political alliances to manage catchment areas, build rural roads or other infrastructure, or design laws favourable to agriculture.

This intense lobbying, and the possibilities of alliances in order to obtain resources, should be regarded as complementary to the alternative strategies emerging from the sector. These are the promotion of alternative technologies, the development of local financing and commercialization sources, and articulated programmes to improve the standard of living of the rural population through an intensive use of local resources.

CHAPTER FOUR

Technology and Globalization: Modern-Era Constraints on Local Initiatives for Land Reform

Peter Dorner[1]

Land tenure reform is not a modern phenomenon, nor has reform been confined to developing nations. But recent technological and institutional changes have brought about unprecedented shifts in the options for socio-economic and political action. These changes have, at times, affected the possibilities for effective political and economic action at local and even national levels – actions necessary to implement and preserve the benefits of past reforms or to introduce new reform measures. And, of course, there remains the imbalance of political power and influence within many nation states, which has been and remains the primary deterrent to actions required for equal distribution of resources and opportunities.

The first section of this chapter outlines some of the major land reforms of the twentieth century, with a note on the earlier transformation of European feudalism. Next, some possible sources of political action (at the international, national and local levels) are considered for the initiation and implementation of reforms. The third section examines the globalization of markets and economies, and the negative effects this new order can have – especially on local initiatives dealing with land tenure reforms. The final section suggests some prospective national and international institutional innovations to level the economic playing field; this is followed by the chapter's conclusions.

HISTORICAL LANDMARKS

The European feudal system of several centuries ago is today an anachronism. Although comprising political, social and economic institutions, it was fundamentally an agrarian system built on the control of land. Eventually that system conflicted with the evolving goal of creating strong nation states, proved ill-equipped to respond to the requirements of expanding markets and too inflexible to accommodate the increased use of capital, and failed to meet the needs of human beings' evolving self-conception.

Yet despite its inadequacies, injustices and rigidities by present standards, the feudal system was an adaptation to the times. Growing out of a crumbling and disintegrating world empire, it organized people according to strict class structures with mutual obligations between classes, thereby assuring some degree of cohesion, internal harmony and security from potential enemies external to the feudal manor. But feudal structure was inconsistent with the requirements of changing from an agrarian system to an industrial society. The various attempts at reforming these agrarian systems, and their eventual transformation, define major landmarks in the economic history of the European states. Feudal land tenure systems and peasants' struggle for land rights were key factors in the French Revolution.

The history of the USA is not devoid of the land reform experience. The American Civil War was a conflict over land as well as slavery (Conrad and Meyer, 1964). The Homestead Act of 1862, which provided full title to 160 acres of public land after five years of residence and evidence of improvements, was passed only after many years of debate. The southern states were threatened by a free-land policy because it undermined the slavery system, which was the foundation for cotton production on plantations. There were not enough votes in both houses of Congress to pass the Homestead Act until the southern states seceded over the slavery issue (Edwards, 1940). The failure to follow through with land reform after the Civil War has cast a century-long shadow over race relations and the economic opportunities of black Americans. The slaves were free, but they did not have the independent economic opportunities that could have been theirs had land reform been carried out (Geisler and Popper, 1984).

Russian collectivization may not have provided the individual incentives or decision-making freedom that family farms did; however, the Russian planners' major concern was rapid industrialization. Russian agriculture was producing a substantial export surplus when collectivization policy was implemented, and a key requirement was to free up labour in agriculture and provide it to the new factories. In addition, the state had to 'squeeze' some of the surplus production from the agricultural sector in order to provide relatively cheap food for the growing population in the industrial sector. And collectivization of agriculture was perhaps necessary to ensure party control over the economic system and prevent decentralized political developments. The collective system functioned to achieve these ends (Dorner and Kanel, 1971, p.41–42; see also Nichols, 1964; Owen, 1966).

The recent dismantling of the Soviet Union has created some of the most significant changes since the Russian revolution. The Soviet system of land tenure was never totally static – but recent changes in Russia have been momentous. Indeed, the country's land tenure system has been the object of policy manipulation for most of the twentieth century.

Another example of land tenure policies with various extensions and modifications during the twentieth century is found in Mexico. The constitution of 1917, preceded by years of bloody revolution that left one million dead, declared that all land was owned by the nation. The state had the right to transmit land to individuals in the form of private property, but always retained the right to expropriate the land whenever deemed necessary for public use. Yet, due to fragmented political forces following the revolution, major land distribution did not take place until Cardenas's rule in the 1930s. During his six-year regime, almost 18 million ha were distributed to over 800 000 peasants. This exceeded the amount of land granted by all his predecessors.

In prior regimes distribution was primarily of individual plots to each *ejido* member; however, faced with the need to expropriate large, irrigated haciendas while preserving their productivity, Cardenas created collective *ejidos* – although, over time, most of these *ejidos* were decollectivized, with the land again being operated as small individual units.

The 1960s, under the presidency of Gustavo Diaz Ordaz, witnessed a major redistribution of land. About 25 million ha were distributed, but only 10 per cent of this land was arable. Furthermore, agricultural policies encouraged exports. This, combined with unfavourable terms of trade for agricultural products, led in the 1970s to a sharp decline in basic food crop production and a dramatic increase in export crop production, especially fruits and vegetables (Dorner, 1992, p.39–40; see also Otero, 1989).

Mexico, along with other Latin American nations, has suffered in recent years from the massive international debts accumulated during the 1970s, followed by the economic depression of the 1980s. Partly as a reaction to these hard times, new conditions have evolved that have led to 'the end of agrarian reform in Mexico' (de Walt et al., 1994).

In 1990 and 1991, the Mexican government implemented a number of major changes, including (i) elimination of most food and agricultural input subsidies and food price controls; (ii) opening of markets, including elimination of most tariffs and allowing private enterprises to import food and feed; and (iii) privatization of credit and technical assistance. While these were significant measures designed to insert Mexico and its agriculture into the global community (Gordillo de Anda, 1990), they were only a prelude to the most far-reaching institutional change for rural Mexico since the Revolution – the rewriting of Article 27 of the 1917 Mexican Constitution.

This Article was the institutional response to the demands of '*tierra y libertad*' (land and liberty) shouted on the battlefields by peasant insurgents during the Mexican Revolution. The new provisions of rewritten Article 27 were approved by both houses of Congress and by the legislatures of all 31 states, and became part of the Mexican Constitution in January 1992.

The key provisions of the new agrarian codes are: (i) the government has declared an end to the redistribution of land; (ii) land rights disputes are to be settled by decentralized, autonomous agrarian tribunals; (iii) *ejidatarios* will now have the legal right to sell, rent, sharecrop or mortgage their land; (iv) *ejidatarios* will no longer have to continue working their land to retain control over land rights; and (v) *ejidatarios* can now enter into joint ventures and contracts with private entrepreneurs, including foreign investors whose participation will be limited to 49 per cent of equity capital (de Walt et al., 1994, p.2; see also Cornelius, 1992, pp.3–4).

Following the Second World War, major land reforms were carried out in Japan, Taiwan and South Korea. All things considered, conditions were quite favourable for such activity in these countries. In Japan the decision to implement a fundamental land reform was essentially made by the US occupation forces in the aftermath of Japan's defeat in the Second World War. In Taiwan the exiled government from the mainland, having seen the consequences of an alienated peasantry and lacking a major stake in land ownership in Taiwan, was anxious to win the support of tenant farmers. Additionally, in both Taiwan and South Korea, US influence was very significant (Dorner and Thiesenhusen, 1990; Dorner, 1992).

Although they have had much impact on US thinking about land reform, transformations of agrarian structures in Japan, Taiwan and South Korea were unique in many ways and did not warrant the expectation that the same formula could be exported to other countries. In addition to the unique circumstances with respect to political power arrangements, there were other features favourable to these reforms. The pre-reform land tenure system in these countries is best characterized as a structure of small-operatorship tenancy units. The main target of reform was irrigated rice lands, where there was a long tradition of farmer organizations. The organizations were strengthened by the reforms and played a key role in the transition and in helping the reform's beneficiaries. The reforms basically consisted of cutting the tie between tenants and their landlords – abolishing the rent collection and control system – and the tenants already had a background of relatively independent entrepreneurial activity (Dorner, 1992, p.6; see also Hayami and Ruttan, 1971; Kikuchi and Hayami, 1978).

There was a long tradition of intensive agriculture on small operating units farmed by tenants. By the late 1940s to the early 1950s, commercial fertilizer, improved seed varieties and other scientific practices were rapidly being adopted. The additional post-reform incentives created for tenant producers by freeing them from rents (as well as a strong demand and, slightly later, favourable cost/price ratio) resulted in very progressive agriculture. While not all these results can be attributed to the reforms, their impact was undeniable. However, the assumption that similar results would be forthcoming from Latin American reforms was not warranted. The Asian unimodal system stood in sharp contrast to the dualistic farmsize structure prevailing in most of Latin America (Dorner, 1992, p.7).

The agrarian reform that affected the most people occurred on the Chinese mainland shortly after the end of the Second World War. Initial reforms in the early 1950s were followed later in that decade by complete collectivization and communization of agriculture, a system that prevailed for over 20 years (Dorner and Thiesenhusen, 1990). But since the early 1980s, collective agricultural production has been largely abandoned (as in other areas; see Thiesenhusen, 1989; Melmed-Sanjak and Carter, 1991). The People's Republic of China has established the 'production responsibility system' and essentially returned to individual farming (Dorner, 1992, p.53). This change was followed by a substantial boost in agricultural productivity.

There were several major reforms in Latin America before 1960. Mexico has already been mentioned. Bolivia had a revolution in 1952, followed by substantial reforms. The Arbenz government in Guatemala distributed land to 100 000 families in 1953, only to have the process reversed by a US-backed counter-revolution (Dorner, 1992, p.32; see also Chonchol, 1989, p.8). Cuba's revolution in the late 1950s also led to massive reforms in line with the communist model. After the formation of the Alliance for Progress in 1961, which encouraged programmes of comprehensive agrarian reform, most countries in South and Central America passed specific agrarian reform legislation. Several countries in the region, such as Chile, Peru, Nicaragua and El Salvador, carried out substantial reforms from the 1960s through the 1980s. But the optimistic results posited were seldom realized.

In discussing the Latin American land reforms, Thiesenhusen concludes:

> *Although the agricultural sector was more 'modernized' after the reforms, most of the change occurred in the non-reformed sector and benefited those who were not peasants (although the reforms in Nicaragua and El Salvador are too new to apply this judgement). The region's agrarian reforms, many of them limited to begin with, included built-in features that were inequitable. Furthermore, most reforms were not supported with much credit or technology transfer to beneficiaries. In other instances, they were neutralized by policies that channelled expenditures away from farming in the reformed sector and/or drove down prices for goods produced there. And the context of economic populism surrounding some agrarian reform efforts caused help for the poor to dissipate in bursts of inflation, which had an especially devastating impact on non-beneficiaries. In general, government took away by stealth what it had given with a flourish (Thiesenhusen, 1995, p.xi).*

In most countries of Latin America, the prevailing patterns of land ownership and land use are still wasteful and hard to justify. Modernization of farming, proceeding rapidly, has not solved the problem of extensive land use co-existing with substantial agricultural underemployment. Land reforms of the past are unravelling with neoliberalism and free trade; land reforms of the future must cope with rural–urban and international migration, pressure from indigenous groups and protection of the environment, all complicating factors.

One could go on to list land reforms – some substantial, some quite modest – in other countries such as Egypt, Tanzania and the Philippines. But the purpose here is not to give an exhaustive list of countries where some type of land reform has been implemented during the past century (feudal European reform, of course, came much earlier), but rather to illustrate the universal concern with these agrarian, institutional issues. I have also tried to show the various means by which land reforms have been brought about over the past several centuries.

INTERNATIONAL, NATIONAL AND LOCAL INITIATIVES

Most of the major reforms noted above came after political uprisings and revolution, often followed by authoritarian power (sometimes led by the military; and if not led by a military figure, then the military was at least in full support of such an authoritarian power structure). Extensive reforms carried out under a system of democratic institutions are quite rare.

The action, influence and support of land reform programmes from outside, by another nation, has been widespread. The influence of the USA in Japan, Taiwan and Korea was referred to above. The USA was unable or unwilling to wield that same influence in Viet Nam or the Philippines. Also, US efforts in Latin America, while yielding considerable outcomes in a few areas, never matched the sought-after results. Other nations also tried, with varying degrees of success, to instigate and influence the land reform programmes of other states.

Sweden used its diplomatic and foreign assistance missions in Haile Selassie's Ethiopia to cajole and advise the government to undertake land reform for both domestic and foreign policy reasons. French and British experts tried to convert a variety of communal land systems to Western freehold models throughout their African colonies, before and after independence, thinking that private landholding systems would encourage agricultural productivity by introducing new incentives to farmers. Soviet, Chinese and Israeli officials have used their own approaches to land ownership in order to inspire reforms in many newly independent countries. The specialized agencies of the United Nations and other international organizations, including the Food and Agriculture Organization of the UN (FAO) and the World Bank, have held conferences, offered technical assistance and used various forms of leverage and pressure in Asia, Africa and Latin America to encourage land policies that their experts consider more efficient or more equitable than the existing systems (Montgomery, 1984, pp.3–4).

At times, major land reforms begin as political initiatives and action at the local level. The main thrust of peasant collective action has been land invasion, sometimes out of sheer desperation, sometimes as a means of pressuring the government, or simply as a means of defying the government's inaction. In the case of peasant organizations, one must distinguish between those whose origins and purposes are focused on the struggle for land and fighting for their rights, and those created primarily to perform economic functions.

Peasant collective action in the fight for land was more significant in Latin America's earlier reforms – those of Mexico, Bolivia and Venezuela, for example. However, there were certainly active peasant organizations that made a difference in the Honduran reforms and, to a lesser extent, in the Dominican Republic and El Salvador. In general, the efforts of peasant organizations in Latin America were primarily to gain political power and/or to convince those in power to meet their demands for land.

Organizations created to serve economic functions, such as collective action for obtaining credit, marketing produce, or purchasing inputs and supplies, were not common. This stands in sharp contrast to the farmers' organizations in East Asian reforms, which served as critical partners of government in promoting agricultural research, extension services, farm credit, input and product marketing, and the like (Dorner, 1992, p.52). The difference between Latin America and East Asia is not surprising given the contrasting nature of tenure patterns – the dominant, large-scale latifundia in Latin America versus a preponderance of small, individual (tenant/owner) operatorships in East Asia.

Operating peasant farmers have, through their various forms of organization (economic and political), provided critical supportive action for the implementation of land reforms. Likewise, they have joined together in some post-reform efforts to reshape the organizational structures established by the reforms. The most common case, perhaps, is the move toward individualizing operations initially created as some form of collective/production cooperative, as was the case in Peru, Mexico and the Dominican Republic, among others (Carter and Kanel, 1985; Thiesenhusen, 1989).

A wide range of non-governmental organizations (NGOs) from outside have also often worked with counterparts in the nation carrying out reforms.

Trade unions, church groups and relief agencies have dispatched both technical and popular missions abroad to influence, advise and offer support to agrarian and urban reformers. In land policy disputes in Central and South America, the ultimate influence of OXFAM or AIFLD may be slight, but the impulse to be there persists (Montgomery, 1984, p.4).

Local collective action before and after will remain crucial to the support of meaningful land reforms. However, it must be re-emphasized that major land reforms cannot be carried forward without action and institutional change at the national level as well. The following section explores the hypothesis that local (and sometimes national) action has become more constrained due to a variety of developments over the past 20–30 years.

OBSTACLES TO EFFECTIVE ACTION

During the course of the twentieth century, changes in the conditions of agricultural life were unique and momentous. Early on, a family needed little to provide for its subsistence beyond a parcel of land and the simplest of tools. But subsistence farming is becoming less and less viable: it is next to impossible to barter excess potatoes for the raw materials of other life-sustaining necessities. The market is now all important; all items vital to life are becoming monetarized. Markets penetrate and govern many aspects of life, in even the remotest rural areas. And if they have not yet done so, it is only a matter of time before they do.

The technological revolution in farming (and 'revolution' is not an over-statement of this phenomenon) totally transformed the conditions under which it is carried out. Technology requires increasing attention to and reliance on markets – local and extended. Technology and markets demand new institutional rules and procedures, locally, nationally and internationally.

These developments have led to the increasing globalization of a food system in which the interests and power of other nations, as well as of multinational corporations, penetrate deeply into life and decisions at the local level (Korten, 1995). All these developments have made action and initiatives by local communities and interest groups increasingly difficult.

While all countries import some food, most also export several specific commodities: the quantity of agricultural products moving in international trade is astounding. In 1990, over 200 million metric tons of grain and soy-beans were shipped to international markets – over 11 per cent of total world production (IFPRI, 1995).

One of the most significant phenomena of the past 30 years has been glob-alization: growing ties, linkages and interdependencies among and between nations the world over. It has been developing gradually, but with increasing acceleration over the past 30–35 years. Although we live in a world of increas-ing economic interdependence, most of our institutions remain national and geared to addressing issues internal to the nation state.

All economies, even those of the largest nations that were essentially self-sufficient a generation or two ago, are today highly dependent on interna-tional trade. A corollary of this increased trade is that national economies are less amenable to direction by domestic economic policies, making life increasingly difficult for national legislators and executives. People demand action to improve their economic situation, but the actions neces-sary are only partially under the control of national officials. Furthermore, local initiatives can rarely be fruitful without support from a higher level (Dorner, 1997, p.39).

G. Edward Schuh argues that from the mid-1960s onwards:

have been a period in which the economic integration of the international economy has far outdistanced its political integration. In fact, we have witnessed a successive breakdown and growing irrelevance of international institutions at the very time that our respective economies have become increasingly integrated. Domestic eco-nomic policies have less and less relevance in today's world and do little more than create suspicion and lack of confidence in national governments since their policies do less and less what they say they will (Schuh, 1985, p.16).

And Harlan Cleveland concludes:

No nation controls even that central symbol of national independence, the value of its money; inflation and recession are both transnational (Cleveland, 1985).

Keith Griffin suggests:

> *Globalization is eroding national sovereignty. Improvements in transport and communications have shortened distances, saved time, reduced transportation costs and destroyed the natural protection that once insulated national economies from one another. It no longer is possible for countries to pursue independent economic policies and to ignore economic forces operating at a global level (Griffin, 1996, p.119).*

Perhaps the closest we have come to a really transnational institution with power to enforce its decisions is the increasingly complex multinational corporation. Although they have been much criticized for some of their practices, often appropriately so, it is almost impossible to conceive of the world economy functioning without them. These multinationals account for more than one-fifth of total world production. World trade in many commodities is dominated by multinationals, and a large part of registered international trade represents their internal transactions. With cheap and rapid transportation and instant electronic communication, multinationals can quickly shift capital, technology and management all over the world (Dorner, 1997, pp.39–40). Is it any wonder that national policies do 'less and less' of what they say they will?

Massive technological changes and a growing emphasis on market capitalism leading to complex interrelations and interdependencies in a new globalization of economic activity are certainly among the key features making local action and initiatives more difficult and frequently less effective.

> *The turn toward liberal democracy and the search for individual freedom have been preceded or accompanied by a worldwide shift in favour of market forces and private enterprise in the management and organization of the economy. The origin of this latest burst in economic liberalism may be traced to the crisis experienced by industrial countries in the aftermath of the sharp increases in the price of oil during the 1970s; but the new doctrine has since attracted an ever-increasing number of adherents in countries around the world, including the communist regimes of East and South-East Asia (Ghai and Hewitt de Alcántara, 1994, p.4).*

But there are additional international institutional developments that may have devastating effects – for example, international trade agreements. I refer specifically to the North American Free Trade Agreement (NAFTA) and the General Agreement on Tariffs and Trade (GATT).

I wish to be clear that this is not a treatise against freer trade. I do not see these agreements as some kind of conspiracy against particular groups of producers or consumers. And I believe that these treaties have many positive features to recommend them. Nevertheless, in this complex and interwoven global economy, some areas may feel major negative consequences as these agreements are implemented.

The poor peasants in the Mexican state of Chiapas apparently anticipated such negative consequences when they declared their revolution on the very day that NAFTA went into effect:

> On January 1, 1994, the day that the North American Free Trade Agreement (NAFTA) took effect, the Mexican government and economic elite came face to face with its old nemesis, an armed rebellion of campesinos whose rallying cry was land, justice and democracy. 'Don't forget us', the rebels were saying, 'you depend on us for your political and economic stability. We have not gone away during the past 75 years of post-revolutionary governments, and we will not go away with neoliberalism and free trade' (Barry, 1995, p.3).

Calling NAFTA a death sentence for the people of Chiapas, some 4000 Indians launched an armed rebellion against the Mexican government (Korten, 1995, pp.293–294). Their battle cry – '*Basta!*' (Enough!) – was picked up by popular movements all across Mexico and resonated around the world.

A recent study of NAFTA's impact on peasant corn producers suggests that the development of infrastructure for transport, marketing and commerce is needed to facilitate:

> . . . either the modernization of corn production to reach higher yields or the diversification into non-traditional fruits, vegetables, or field crops. Yet economic restructuring has removed the essential government services of credit, technical assistance, insurance, marketing and agricultural advising precisely at the time when peasants need such services to diversify and modernize their production (Collier, 1994, p.151).

But one can also sympathize with the actions of the Mexican government. Mexico faced a financial crisis in the mid-1990s when the monetary system was in deep trouble and major international financial assistance was required to overcome these conditions. The International Monetary Fund (IMF), along with US loans, provided the help needed to overcome the crisis. But the IMF (as in the assistance offered to the financially troubled South-East and East Asian countries) imposes stringent requirements for major restructuring of a government's economic policies. Such refocused national economic policies frequently create hardships for the average citizen, with some groups enduring more pain than others.

Thus while the current rules and procedures of the global economy often restrict potentially successful initiatives of local groups, national governmental leaders may also, at times, find major restrictions imposed on the scope and focus of economic policy initiatives they might wish to consider.

Still another factor that may restrict successful local actions and initiatives is the increased diversity of economic interests within such areas. This may make it more difficult to achieve the community cohesiveness required for concerted efforts to rally behind one particular interest. I again refer to the writing of Dharam Ghai and Cynthia Hewitt de Alcántara:

Deepening poverty and associated migratory trends also pose serious challenges to community solidarity in the majority of Third World and former socialist countries, as well as in China. Agrarian communities, which have provided the primary framework for local cooperation in developing countries, are being torn apart by contradictory forces associated with globalization and recession: both the increased pace of modernization of the past few decades, and the subsequent withdrawal of many new forms of support on which local people were coming to depend, have left rural communities disorganized and vulnerable. The loss of population, as people try to make a living outside the community, has converted the more remote villages and towns of some Third World countries into hollow shells, and has sharply reduced the ability of the remaining inhabitants to farm or to protect the natural environment (Ghai and Hewitt de Alcántara, 1994, p.13; see also Hewitt de Alcántara, 1994, p.13).

Yet another example from Mexico is taken from a study of the Puebla Project, located on the central plateau of the state of Puebla. The project was initiated in 1967 by the International Corn and Wheat Improvement Center (CIMMYT) and the Mexican government. The key objective of the project was to develop strategies for increasing corn yields on lands operated by small producers under rainfed conditions. But, writes Miguel Sanchez Hernandez:

The diverse types of people in rural communities (poor peasants, middle peasants, rich peasants, landless, small merchants, politicians, artisans, etc.) could react so differently to any organizational process that it would be difficult to put them all together in the same bag (Sanchez Hernandez, 1987, p.66).

In Latin America, at least, this appears to be a general phenomenon. In data compiled by de Janvry and Sadoulet, it appears:

. . . likely that as much as two thirds of the farm households across Latin America derive more than half of their income from off-farm sources – principally wages from employment both in agriculture and in a wide variety of other activities, many of which are linked to agriculture through forward, backward, and final consumption linkages. At the same time, the share of the rural, economically active population working in non-agricultural activities has also increased very rapidly and reached percentages such as 23 in Brazil, 16 in Ecuador, 41 in Costa Rica and 42 in Mexico (de Janvry and Sadoulet, 1989, pp.1209–1210).

It is evident that rural and urban labour markets have become more integrated. Fewer agricultural workers are recruited from among the rural landless and those on very small farms, while more come from households based in rural towns or in cities. The above statistics are especially impressive given the fact that the data are from a decade ago.

There is an additional national institutional issue involved in the question of local initiatives and their effectiveness. And a useful way to think about institutions, suggests Kanel,

> *. . . is to regard them as concerning rules and not, primarily, organizations. Institu-*
> *tions define the roles and status of the actors in the economy, and they define the*
> *rules of the game that the actors can use in relations among themselves and in their*
> *relations with nature (Kanel, 1988, p.427).*

Institutions consist of rules defining for individuals their rights and privileges, responsibilities and obligations, as well as their exposure to the protected rights and activities of others. John R. Commons defined institutions
as 'collective action in restraint, liberation, and expansion of individual
action'. And, according to Commons, a working rule

> *. . . tells what the individual must or must not do (compulsion or duty), what*
> *they may do without interference from other individuals (permission or liberty),*
> *what they can do with the aid of the collective power (capacity or right), and*
> *what they cannot expect the collective power to do in their behalf (incapacity or*
> *exposure). In short, the working rules of associations or governments, when*
> *looked at from the private standpoint of the individual, are the source of his*
> *rights, duties and liberties, as well as his exposures to the protected liberties of*
> *other individuals (Commons, 1957, p.6; for further elaboration of these ideas see*
> *also Kanel, 1974, 1985).*

These rules function at different levels of the economy and society, and at
times there may be conflicts between the rules at the higher levels of government and the need and desire to institute certain actions at local level.
This issue became very clear and obvious in Russia after the central government passed land privatization legislation in the early 1990s. Individual farmers were given the option to obtain land and farm on their own
individual farm unit, or to form partnerships with some of their farmer
colleagues, or to form joint stock companies, or to continue farming
more-or-less as they had been under the collective Kolkhoz or the state
farm Sovkhoz. But at least in the early period following the establishment
of such options (my first-hand knowledge is from work in Russia in 1994),
most farmers chose to continue farming as they had done before this
'paper privatization' took place. A number of comprehensive surveys
clearly showed that the new owners' preferences were to keep the large
production units intact. This was especially the case on those state or collective farms regarded as the more successful operations.

It is quite understandable that many did not wish to leave the current
system and 'go on their own', where rules and procedures were unclear
and untested. Furthermore, collectivization in Russia and the former
Soviet Union had been the norm for so many years, most people had no
experience or memory of an earlier system. People who might have experienced farming on their own and under a different set of institutional
rules would now be of an age where they would not be among the current
workforce.

But there were other obstacles, mainly of an institutional nature. For example, the lack of surveying infrastructure made it impossible to provide individual land titles within any reasonable time schedule. The titles could be challenged because of their ambiguous legal status. Institutional rules and procedures and the physical infrastructure for providing mortgage and production credit, purchasing small quantities of inputs, or selling small quantities of outputs, simply did not exist. All movement of inputs and outputs continued to be geared to the top-down service structure of large collectives. Likewise, farm machinery and building structures were all designed for large production units. Local initiatives were very difficult until changes were introduced at the top and throughout the regional structures, and down to those of the lower governmental echelons, the '*oblast*' and the '*raion*'.

Significant transformation of this system depends on developing a clear, consistent and widely accepted order of rules and procedures, with legally defined and enforceable rights, duties and prohibitions. Certain physical infrastructural facilities must also be provided. Widely available technical assistance and educational programmes are required: (i) to provide individuals with the multiple skills required in farming, many of which are not likely to be learned under a system of large-scale farming with a more specialized labour force; and (ii) to provide the necessary information to get everyone on track and knowledgeable about the new system. Without such changes, mainly at upper levels of government, the prospects of local-level initiatives for transforming such a system are minimal.

PROSPECTIVE INSTITUTIONAL INNOVATIONS TO LEVEL THE PLAYING FIELD

What are the causal elements underlying the problems discussed above? Technology! True, technological developments have played a major role in the globalization of national economies. But can we turn back the clock on technology? Can we turn our back to it and withdraw financing to curtail its development? This is virtually impossible in today's world, and it would hardly be a wise move if it were possible. Technology is largely the result of previous scientific inquiry. We cannot shut down the inquisitiveness of the human mind. The technological genie cannot be put back into the lamp. This is not to say that all things made possible by modern science are also good and should be encouraged and developed. It may, at times, be necessary to curtail or prevent the widespread use and commercialization of selected technological possibilities. But it is a fact that technology and globalization are here to stay.

Technology is, after all, the creation of the human intellect. To try to shut it down would be to deny our own humanity. What we need to do is to use that same creative intelligence to formulate new rules and procedures so that we can reap the positive effects of technology, but at the same time reduce and reallocate as needed the costs and ill effects of that technology and the globalization to which it gives rise.

What about the expanding emphasis on international trade? Here again, building walls around nation states would negatively affect large segments of the population in all countries. And it would not only, or even primarily, be the well-to-do who would suffer from such actions. Likewise, trying to eliminate the multinationals, the IMF or the World Bank would not result in any positive achievements, even if it were possible. But again, and this point must be emphasized, this does not mean that these organizations should be free to continue to carry out their important functions under current rules. We must create new rules to govern the behaviour of these powerful international actors.

True, it is very difficult to prescribe 'specific solutions' for these problems. There is a growing need for a more widely shared awareness of the difficulties outlined, and a critical need for some restructuring of institutions at both international and national levels. Since the 1980s there has been a constant exhortation of the benefits of private enterprise, market forces and competition. Free markets are wonderful if the economy has the right characteristics for them to operate effectively. But market forces are subject to manipulation and control by those with the economic and political power to do so. When resources and opportunities are widely and equitably distributed, most economic activity is best left to individual, private initiative and market forces. But this is not the case where a skewed distribution makes self-help impossible for a large and desperately poor proportion of the society.

In their research focusing on these issues, Carter and Barham point out:

> In general terms . . . laissez faire *does not present a level playing field to small farmers in the context of agro-export boom. More specifically . . . (a) the direction taken by agrarian growth is shaped by farm size biases which arise in the production or marketing of export crops that differentially advantage one class of producers over another; and (b) the importance and strength of these class biases are shaped by the initial distribution of land wealth in the local economy (Carter and Barham, 1996, p.1138; see also Carter et al., 1995).*

Thus, while advocating free markets and open competition can be relevant and fruitful where the economic playing field is level, the clear reality is that it is not – either internationally, as among nation states, or nationally, as between different sectors and/or groups of producers. And while the IMF and the World Bank have been very helpful in the 'bail-out' of nations in major economic distress, the 'strings' attached (the actions required of the nation state in 'exchange' for the massive financial assistance provided) have frequently intensified inequalities within the nation so served.

The rules and procedures of these international agencies must be reviewed so that the strings attached apply also to internal policy measures with respect to the impact alternative measures may have on the poorest and most disadvantaged in the society. The continuing rebellion in the Mexican state of Chiapas is not only over a concern with the impact of freer trade under NAFTA and with the end of agrarian reform following the government's actions in 1992. Nor are all the underlying causes of this rebellion related to these international factors. Nevertheless, these factors do add to the burdens borne by poor rural people. And an additional reaction by the people of Chiapas was likely, due to the negative consequences of the mandated restructuring undertaken to ameliorate the financial crisis of the mid-1990s. Recent demonstrations reported in South Korea and Indonesia have basically the same origin.

But of equal (or perhaps even greater) significance to additional rules and procedures for these international agencies with respect to requirements imposed on nations in time of crisis, there is a desperate need for new and enforceable rules and procedures to be observed and followed by the giant multinational corporations. In most cases these large corporations have fewer high-level rules to abide by than their own. By contracting for and assuring a market for produce worldwide, their decisions can influence in a basic way the land use and tenure relations in vast rural areas. And because they frequently have little or no competition, they are quite free to set prices and conditions favourable to their own best interests. '. . . these institutions have become too big, too distant, and too captive of special interests' (Korten, 1995, p.294).

The fact of the matter is that these large conglomerates do not experience (let alone pay for) the damages and costs that their actions may inflict on innocent people throughout the world. Just as there is a need for stricter rules for internalizing costs of environmental damage and destruction, so there is an urgent need for rules and procedures to internalize some of these 'hidden costs' borne to a great extent by the poor people in countries throughout the world. In a succinct summary of these issues, Barraclough et al. note:

> There are now some 37 000 transnational parent corporations with 200 000 affiliates worldwide. Their annual sales in 1992 were 5.5 trillion dollars and many were financially more powerful than most of the national economies with which they were dealing (UNRISD, 1995). They controlled about 70 per cent of world trade. These transnationals now enjoy freedom without responsibility. Some kind of international code setting minimum social and environmental standards for transnational investors, producers and traders seems at least as logical as the quality standards already widely applied to fruit and other commodities entering world markets, or to the accounting standards already required of international banks (Barraclough et al., 1997, p.103).

If such additional and enforceable rules at the international level were available, they would also provide more flexibility and incentives for national governments to be more responsive to pressures and petitions from the demands of their citizens. Nevertheless, national governments must bear the prime responsibility for development, or the lack of it, within their nation. And national leaders must confront the powerful forces that may be opposed to a more equitable system of production and distribution – especially as they relate to land tenure restructuring and reform. It is only as national governments create the will and ability to confront these barriers that local initiatives will realize their full potential. Local collective action may be able to achieve some advances without such a reshuffling of power at the top, but without decisive action at the national level it will always be limited. The only exception is if such local initiatives spread geographically and result in an overthrow of the current government. And that is certainly not a course for outsiders to suggest or advocate.

Although I have been presenting the case for increasing the opportunities for local action and initiatives, one must also acknowledge the limits of action at this level. Technology has made it impossible to solve some problems and to deal with many issues in the modern world at the local level. A look at technology evolution in the area of transportation will illustrate this point. In the days before the automobile, the major sources of power and transport in farming were horses and oxen. Local communities set the rules governing the issues arising with this level of technology. It was not likely that horses or oxen would be used to travel outside the boundaries of localized jurisdictions.

But with the coming of the automobile, a plethora of conflicting local rules resulted as the automobile could be used to cross a number of jurisdictional boundaries. Roads could not be constructed without dealing with other jurisdictions about this matter. Roads had to go somewhere. Other localities had to be involved and negotiations had to take place. Vehicles and drivers had to be licensed and registered. The handling of a potentially dangerous fuel had to be regulated. The safe use of this powerful horseless carriage required a new set of institutions and the involvement of a larger, higher-up-the-scale political unit to formulate new rules to provide regional or nationwide uniformity. The airplane created still more complex problems, and commercial air traffic today would not be possible without at least minimal international rules – for example a common language for international air traffic controllers and a coordinated system of safety and security procedures (Dorner, 1986, pp.14–15).

Modern technology has shifted decision-making and rule-making to ever higher levels – local, state, regional, national and, increasingly, international. Ours is a world, says Harlan Cleveland:

. . . where science, which has always been transnational, keeps inventing inherently global technologies – for weather observation, military reconnaissance, telecommunications, data processing, resource sensing, and orbital industry. As a result . . . we find ourselves moving beyond concepts of national ownership, sovereignty and citizenship to ideas such as the global commons, the international monitoring of global risks, and 'the common heritage of mankind' (Cleveland, 1985).

I should also refer to a case in my own country, the USA. Institutions at the state and local levels have, at times, failed to protect equally the individual rights guaranteed by our federal constitution. The issue of and struggle over racial equality in the past could not be resolved until they came to be governed by national rather than state or local laws. Likewise, it seems to me, the security and equitable functioning of institutions dealing with land markets, credit and property relations cannot be left solely to local jurisdictions. There must be major inputs and rules of action that are formulated and enforceable at the national level.

We live in a world vastly different from what it was 75 or even 25 years ago. Technology has been a fundamental force behind these momentous changes. Local communities have lost some authority and prospects for productive action, but new technologies in the areas of communication and transportation, among others, have also given local communities new leverage. Nevertheless, in this new and increasingly interdependent global economy and society, new rules at the international and national levels are required to provide additional leverage for the nation state with respect to some areas of policy, but especially to re-empower governmental units at the local and regional levels.

CONCLUSION

In recent years there has been much emphasis on privatization and market solutions. This has certainly been true in the USA, but it is a more general phenomenon. There has been a growing mistrust of government, especially at the national and international levels (Nye et al., 1997). But in general, such prescriptions work to the disadvantage of the poorest and least powerful sectors of the economy and the population. It has also frequently had a debilitating effect on local groups and organizations, and the actions they might wish to take to improve their conditions.

National governments simply cannot negate their responsibilities by denying them and assuming the problems will be solved elsewhere. Local action can be fruitful only if and when the appropriate actions are introduced at higher levels of government. But the issue goes beyond the national level to the international level.

There are two major areas of concern: (i) the restructuring requirements imposed in exchange for financial bail-outs by the IMF, the World Bank and nations contributing to such assistance. This is not to deny that rather severe measures may be needed under certain circumstances. But it is too often the case that those suffering most of the negative consequences of such restructuring are the poor and the near-poor. And this consequence is related to the second area of concern: (ii) the growing urgency for new international rules and enforceable guidelines for actions by the large transnational corporations. Their capacity to move in and out of specific areas and spread the costs of their actions in a random manner, without accountability, must be curtailed.

This is not to condemn all actions of the IMF, nor to suggest that the multinationals should be denied prospects of operating transnationally. But responsible action would dictate that the consequences of action taken by the most powerful international entities be carefully scrutinized and that the negative effects of such actions be shared by those most able to pay for them – and that, likewise, the positive consequences of actions taken by these powerful actors be widely available and shared by the poorer segments of society. These are critical areas for the development and enforcement of international rules of action (that is, for international institutions). Addressing some of these same issues, Griffin and Khan note:

> While it is unrealistic to expect that stabilization can be painless for everyone, the evidence suggests that it is possible to combine stabilization with protection of the poor and preservation of human development achievements (Griffin and Khan, 1992, p.96).

There is one caveat. As suggested earlier, local communities must be given the freedom to act on local problems, but to make such local action possible and productive may indeed require changes in the rules of action (or institutions) at the national level. But these rules at the national level may also, at times, need to proscribe certain actions at the local level. This is required to avoid possible chaotic conditions (contradictory regulations from one community to the next, for example, which could greatly interfere with and restrict movement of goods and people within the nation), and to maintain philosophical, legal and socio-economic consistency between local actions and regional and/or national goals.

It is all too simple to say 'let the market take over, let the local community do it, let local people take charge and solve their own problems', etc. But this denies responsibility that must be shouldered at higher levels – national and international – and it is appropriate to emphasize the international. Griffin explains it this way:

> Unilateral action, slowly but surely, is likely to give way to global collective action. This, in turn, will require strengthening, reforming and in some cases reconstructing global institutions which are democratic and can act in the global public interest (Griffin, 1996, p.120).

Only if responsibility is seriously embraced at each level can there be fruit-ful, harmonious and widely accepted actions and consequences. This is not an easy prescription to follow. And it is especially difficult when dealing such a controversial issue as land reform. Yet issues must be dealt with in this way. The alternatives are either no solution to such vexing problems – and risking a prospective revolt by the otherwise powerless masses – or some selective but key-issue partial solutions with the potential to evolve into more general solutions.

CHAPTER FIVE

The Political Economy of Market-Based Land Reform

M. Riad El-Ghonemy

INTRODUCTION

Perhaps no other policy issue is more susceptible to shifts in ideology and the balance of political power than the transfer of land property rights. The controversy seems to arise from changing the roles of the state and the market in this transfer and, in turn, the distribution of income and opportunities for progress. This chapter examines empirical evidence from developing countries that reveals such ideological shifts – in terms of theoretical construction, development strategies and common-sense beliefs about fairness, caring for the poor, the economics of resource use and the nature of rural people's motives and social values.

Since the end of the Second World War, we have witnessed two contrasting shifts with regard to these roles. The first occurred between the late 1940s and the early 1980s, which I call the decades of the poor peasants and the golden age of genuine land reform. During this period, leaders of most developing countries found it necessary, after gaining independence, to redress past wrongdoings, including colonial land tenure policy. When we look back over that period, it now seems that reforms were evoked out of deep dissatisfaction with the abject poverty, gross inequalities and social instability resulting from colonial policies. Since these countries' economies were fundamentally agrarian and their populations overwhelmingly rural, different types of agrarian reforms (with varied scope and pace of implementation) were instituted. Yet they shared a broad aim: a rapid reduction in poverty and inequalities, combined with emancipation of the peasants from the erstwhile political power of landlords and the monopolies of the latter in land and labour markets.

The nature of changing rural development strategy

In 1979 at the World Conference on Agrarian Reform and Rural Development, governments committed themselves to equitable distribution of land through its 'redistribution with speed' and to systematic monitoring of progress in poverty reduction. They also undertook 'to eliminate severe under-nutrition by the year 2000' (WCARRD, 1979). Alas, this unanimous commitment and enthusiasm was short-lived. Since the early 1980s there has been a sudden shift away from government-implemented redistributive land reform (RLR) toward reliance on the formal credit market and on landed property transfer, freely negotiated in the open market (referred to as land market reform, LMR). By that time, most developing countries were heavily indebted to rich industrial countries which were, themselves, experiencing prolonged economic recession. Western creditors wanted to recover debts and refused to make new loans to the indebted countries unless they signed agreements with the International Monetary Fund (IMF) and the World Bank for debt recovery linked with time-limited market liberalization.[1] Known as economic policy reforms or structural adjustment programme packages, their conditionalities require that adjusting governments should not regulate the working of the market, including the land market. In advocating these policy reforms, rich creditors and aid-giving international organizations (which pretend to be neutral policy advisers and whose influential economists pose as value-free social scientists) state with authority that 'the market' is the most effective land distribution mechanism and 'vehicle for the reduction of unequal patterns of distribution' (see 'Land: the shift to the market' in FAO, 1995).

Accordingly, the pro-social transformation and anti-poverty RLR policy has been suddenly eclipsed and condemned for delaying rural betterment. In devising policy prescriptions that are tightly bound up with aid and debt relief, international aid agencies and donor countries have propagated in their policy packages, a technical programme of agricultural credit and legal procedures for land transactions based on the dominance of a private sector free from price control by the state. The prescribers' views about LMR have become so interwoven with the structural adjustment policy package as to be identified with it. Accordingly, poor peasants and landless workers wishing to purchase a piece of land have to search for a willing seller, negotiate the sale price of land, compete with speculators and rich landowners to secure credit, and even bid at land sale auctions. From what we know of countries' limited experience, there is no novelty in the emphasis on market forces. On the contrary, in the implementation of RLR government-fixed prices have co-existed in varying degrees with market-determined prices of land lease and purchase, as well as the price of money (interest rates) in what is known as the parallel market. Even in socialist economies (such as Tito's Yugoslavia, or China's household responsibilities system since 1979), while means of production were socially owned and major development decisions centrally planned, day-to-day operations were left to individual households and market forces in a system that Oskar Lange called 'market socialism'. This flexibility refutes fears that RLR is rigid, inhibiting the land market from adjusting to realities.

What is more significant in the propagation of LMR is the shift in development objectives and in the ordering of means and ends. Whereas RLR gives high priority to the rapid reduction of poverty in rural areas, combined with the development of the abilities of beneficiaries, sponsors of

LMR accord priority to economic efficiency in the market-determined allocation of resources in order to realize export-led agricultural growth. Toward this end, LMR policy supports the freedom of the producer and of capitalists in the accumulation of land and income, irrespective of adverse distributional consequences and effects on the well-being of the poor. Although the advocates of this approach express concern over increasing poverty, they predict its eventual reduction by a sustained all-round rise in average real income per head. Equitable distribution of growth benefits is not a clear development objective. Seeing land market reform only in narrow economic terms as an end in itself represents a setback in the progress made since the 1950s, both in development thinking and in the realization of equitable rural development.

Being obliged to obey the IMF in implementing currency devaluation and budget cuts, policy-makers adopting the *laissez-faire* land policy (LMR) as part of an economic liberalization policy do not seem concerned about the effects of cuts in government spending on health, education, social security or public investment in rural road construction and irrigation expansion. They expect that these services will be provided by the private sector. Regardless of the merits of enhancing the role of the private sector, the complementarity in raising the capabilities of the rural poor between securing access to land, on the one hand, and agricultural growth, public investment in improvement in health and education systems, on the other, should be the focus of the liberalization of the rural economy. Poor peasants and landless workers – who account for a large proportion of rural people – cannot afford the market-determined prices of human necessities that result from the conversion of health and education from essential public services to marketable commodities.

Why focus on political economy?

The discipline of political economy as a branch of social science enables us to understand the nature and significance of these interconnected components of rural development. It is based on the premise that the economics of agrarian structures cannot be separated from the politics and social organization of the economy within a historical context. The elements in the social organization determining land property and land-use rights include inheritance arrangements, religion, political ideology and bureaucracy, as well as the law, rules and customary arrangements. For example, religion provides the moral foundations that determine whether practices in market transactions are fair or exploitative, as well as God-given inheritance rules, particularly in Islam. Whereas these values and institutional arrangements are considered important in the discipline of political economy, and help us to understand the morality of market reform, they are habitually disregarded by economists, especially the followers of neoclassical economics. By ignoring fairness in wealth distribution and these elements of social organization, conventional economists concentrate on resource efficiency and assert that what a person owns and earns should solely be determined by the market, not by governments or other non-market arrangements.

Some key concepts

For the purpose of this study three distinctions are made in the definition of key terms. The first is between market and non-market land transactions. The former comprise land-lease market and land-purchase market transactions, in which the terms of transactions are negotiated and agreed between the two parties, then registered for enforcement by law. By 'non-market land transactions' is meant government-administered land ownership transfers, rental values and sale price of land. It means also the transfer of *private* land ownership and use rights by the legislative power of the state, inheritance, inter-family marriage, and extortion by virtue of political power and official status, as well as the granting of *public* land under concessional arrangements.

The second distinction is between 'redistributive land reform' and 'agrarian reform'. The former, which has already been briefly described, means the distribution of privately owned land from large landowners to landless workers, agricultural and poorer peasants already cultivating the land as tenants or sharecroppers (referred to as beneficiaries hereafter). As a development strategy, RLR is a manifestation of political will and a strong demonstration of commitment by the country's leadership to rapidly reduce rural poverty and the vast inequalities in rural wealth and opportunities. This strategy views the redistribution of land as a redistribution of purchasing power and opportunities for rural peoples' progress. Redistributive land reform is also viewed as a public action to remedy market failure, by way of breaking monopoly power in land, labour and credit markets. 'Agrarian reform', on the other hand, embraces a wider scope of institutional and technical changes associated with access to land, including one or more of the following: distribution of public land for land settlement schemes; registration of land titles; tenancy regulations; consolidation of fragmented holdings; and so forth.

The third distinction is between the two expected beneficiary groups: landless workers and poor peasants. The former are hired agricultural workers, who do not own, rent or crop-share any area of land. They may own a few animals and supplement their agricultural wage earnings by working occasionally in non-farm activities. Poor peasants, on the other hand, own or rent small areas of land and use family labour for farming their landholding and keeping animals. They usually do not hire outside workers, except in peak seasons. These characteristics of traditional peasants were succinctly phrased 'efficient and poor' by the winner of the Nobel Prize in economics, Theodore Schultz (1964, p.38).

Organization of this chapter

The next section of this chapter presents some of the principal relationships influencing secure access to land, indicating that the subject of land reform deserves to be treated seriously and honestly. It also examines some of the elements of land policy choice that determine who benefits. The purpose is to show that policy should emerge from country-specific situations, and not from an imported ideology serving short-term political motives and prescribing almost identical rural development strategies for poor countries, taking them all along a unique path. This will be followed by a review of empirical experience in the implementation of both RLR and LMR. This empirical approach combines a narrative of institutional arrangements with a quantitative assessment. The chapter next examines the prospects for improving the situation of disadvantaged groups in rural areas and, finally, draws some conclusions.

BASIC PRINCIPLES: ACCESS TO LAND AND POLICY CHOICE

Apart from ideological and political motives, the general proposition is that greater access to land is positively linked to investment and production incentives. It also expands the employment of family farm labour and provides security against hunger and the risk of poverty. These issues are considered in the following sections.

Access to land

Throughout the recorded history of the now developing countries, land has been viewed not solely as a factor of production but as a unique social amenity: a secure form of holding wealth and gaining social and political advantages and family food security. Irrespective of their occupations, most people strive to own a piece of (increasingly scarce) crop land or to expand their existing holdings. Unlike other productive assets, land held individually or communally for a long time is almost sacred and, except in distress-sale situations, it is preserved as a family or tribal heritable bond, that is, a non-marketable family asset. It is thus absurd to view land in a narrow economic sense as a commodity or a factor of production, like a sack of fertilizer, and to analyse the land market exactly like the fertilizer market. However, this is done in LMR rural development policy prescription and analysis. The absurdity of this view was established nearly half a century ago by Arthur Lewis, the 1979 Nobel Prize Laureate in economics (Lewis, 1963, p.91). In the rest of this chapter I shall appeal to common sense, arguing that 'land' and the 'land market' have special socio-political aspects that require a different mode of analysis.

With increasing *direct* demand for access to land and a *derivative* demand for food, in addition to a growing agricultural population, including rising numbers of landless workers, land policy debate has gained importance. Prominent among the debatable issues are farm size and the intensification of land and labour use; environmental considerations of the conservation of soil fertility and grazing areas for the benefit of future generations; the individualization or the preservation of custom-based communal ownership and land-use practices; and the costs of borrowing money for the purchase of land and complementary productive inputs. Because of space limitations, some of these issues are only briefly examined.

Productivity

There has been concern that production would be disrupted by the division of large farms into small family farms through RLR. The arguments are about the economics of the break-up of large, privately owned estates for redistribution as small family holdings. Ideology apart, and despite the controversy over the Western criteria used in judging the productivity of agricultural land in developing countries, the results of rigorous field studies tell us that the productivity of land and labour decline as farm size increases. Inefficiency of resource use in large farms is particularly manifested in sparsely populated countries by widespread absenteeism, underemployment of farm resources, and increasing costs of hiring and supervising labour. Efficient utilization of labour per unit of land (measured as person-days per year and the number of working people per unit of output) tends to be lower in large estates than in smallholdings.

Cost of borrowing

Because they are central elements of LMR, access to and the cost of formal (institutional) credit are linked to property rights in land and to land productivity. According to empirical evidence and common sense, the rate of interest (the cost of borrowing) is negatively related to both the size of landholding and its productive capacity. The larger the size of landholding and the higher its profitability, the lower is the rate of interest, and *vice versa*.

Because loans entail risks to the lender, landless workers and small tenants face serious barriers to entering the credit market. Moneylenders and formal credit institutions consider it highly risky to lend to these asset-poor people. (In a private property market economy, creditors require collateral, the value of which could be claimed in the event of default.) Such potential borrowers are further disadvantaged by being charged higher rates of interest and by bearing high transaction costs (transportation costs, bribing clerks in the credit bank, etc.) relative to the small size of the loans they seek. Except in group lending for production support, a large section of the rural population is denied the opportunity to purchase land and, in turn, to invest. This also deprives the economy of higher potential output. In addition, small tenants face other transaction costs in leasing through the auctioning of land. In the auction, a rich middle-man can meet the financial requirements to outbid poorer competitors for leasing a large area of land, and subleasing it in small units to small tenants at rates higher than those paid to the landlord or landlord's agent.

Evidence suggests that, for these reasons, transaction costs are disproportionately high for small farmers compared to larger farmers. There is also evidence that the market-lending probability is extremely low, approaching a zero chance of securing credit for landless workers who wish to climb the land tenure ladder (from hired worker to tenant to owner). Furthermore, Muslim farming people are constrained by their belief in the immorality of mortgage arrangements. The Koran says that those who live on usury shall rise up before Allah (God) like men whom Satan has made evil by his touch, for they claim that usury is like trade. But Allah permitted trading and prohibited usury (*riba*).[2] In the moral dictates of Islam, while there is a consensus on the prohibition of usury, *riba* being considered as a fundamental sin, there are diverse interpretations concerning morality and immorality of borrowing terms, for example, the payment at a later date of pre-fixed interest on a loan for the purchase of land (a thorough review of these interpretations is given in the work of the present Sheikh of al-Azhar, Mohammad Tantawy, 1992).

Policy choice and the balance of political power

Whether by parliamentary majority or by oligarchy, the choice of land property transfer policy is a product of a number of elements: (i) the initial situation of the rural economy, particularly the extent of landlessness, poverty and inequality; (ii) the lobbying strength of interest groups and the configuration of the political power structure; (iii) the commitment of policy-makers to speedy poverty reduction; (iv) the form of government (parliamentary majority or oligarchy) in which the balance between class interests and the regime's interests are weighted; (v) the resources available for policy implementation, including budgetary allocations, administrative capabilities and technical skills of civil servants; and (vi) the extent of influence and pressure exerted by foreign agents with disguised ideological motives regarding land tenure and equity issues. Examples of this last factor include the perennial influence of the multinational enterprises in the Philippines, and the post-1980 alliance of Western rich donors and the World Bank/IMF in their policy prescriptions to the heavily indebted adjusting countries.

As citizens, poor landless and near-landless rural workers are entitled by international conventions to participation – through their own representatives – in the processes of policy-making and negotiating actions that directly influence their well-being. Examples are International Labour

Organization (ILO) Conventions 87, 95 and 141. Yet the influence of rural workers and poor peasants is usually minimal or non-existent. They are scattered in the countryside, unemployed for a substantial period of time during the year, and highly dependent for survival on their many employers and the moneylenders who exercise monopoly power in their localities. In rural localities, large landowners perform multiple functions: influential politician and probably member of parliament, mayor of the village, trader, owner of water pumps for irrigation where water is scarce and, perhaps, moneylender.

These forms of political and economic control are practised – in most cases – within the legal system. Conventional economists view these monopoly powers as a normal feature of a market economy. According to this school of thought, it is inappropriate to describe resulting distributional relations as exploitative, exclusionary or unfair: the market decides what poor peasants and landless workers deserve, as they lack the entrepreneurial abilities and working skills demanded by the market. It is paradoxical that the words 'fair' and 'unfair', 'fairness' and 'unjust inequality', frequently used to describe transactions and market behaviour, are ignored in the analysis of land market outcomes and the construction of its textbook models.

EMPIRICAL EVIDENCE

In this brief review of historical experience, the sequence of presentation of the two main policy approaches, RLR and LMR, neither implies causality nor means the singularity of each approach's occurrence in a given period of time. In many cases they overlap and in some, the adoption of one approach is justified as a reform of the defects of the other, such as the performance or failure of government intervention or the market. Historical experience suggests a sequencing: the promulgation of a radical redistributive reform combined with tenancy regulation was found necessary to amend the cumulative failings of the market (such as land concentration in a few hands, exorbitant rental values, eviction of tenants without compensation and heavy indebtedness of peasants).

Redistributive land reform (RLR)

Prior to the promotion of LMR policy in the 1980s within the context of macro-economic policy reforms, nearly 30 developing countries (in addition to the former Soviet Union and the Eastern European countries) had already implemented different types of RLR, with a wide range in the scope of their land redistribution. Data on the experience of 22 countries appear in Table 5.1. The scope is measured in terms of the ratio of beneficiaries (land-recipient households) to total agricultural households, and the area of redistributed private land to total area of agricultural landholdings, calculated for each country at the time of completion of redistribution (1996 in the case of the Philippines). My measurements of the scope vary widely according to (i) the land ownership ceiling (the maximum private ownership) fixed by each country's legislation; and (ii) the average size of farm unit allotted to beneficiaries (family or subfamily size). Both ratios suggest that the lower the ceiling and the smaller the unit allotted, the higher the proportion of new land recipients. Although these data and their ratios are rough estimates and not perfectly comparable, we should keep in mind that no ceiling was fixed in China and Morocco, and the Mexican RLR possesses the unique feature of being a continual process since 1915 (the first law on agrarian reform, issued in 1915, was confirmed by the 1917 Constitution). No date was fixed for completion of redistribution, as long as there is a demand for land by the large indigenous population.

A comparison of South Korea and Egypt illustrates the importance of the variation in the maximum level of private land ownership for determining the proportion of beneficiaries. In South Korea between 1945 and 1953, a series of land reforms fixed the ceiling at the low level of 2.9 ha, which made it possible for the government to redistribute nearly 65 per cent of total agricultural land area in plots of 0.9 ha on average. This low ceiling enabled nearly 76 per cent of total agricultural households (tenants and hired workers) to own land for the first time. Accordingly, inequality in landholding in terms of the Gini index was substantially reduced from 0.729 in 1945 to 0.303 in 1980.[3]

In contrast, Egypt's RLR, which was intended to correct the wrongdoings of the pre-1952 *laissez-faire* functioning of the land market (see El-Ghonemy, 1953, pp.40–59; 1993a, pp.83–86), fixed a ceiling at the high level of 84 ha (lowered in 1961 to 42 ha). The average area of redistributed family farm units was nearly 1 ha, allotted to small tenants and a few landless workers. This Egyptian ratio of nearly 40:1 made it possible to redistribute only 10 per cent of total agricultural land among 14 per cent of the total agricultural households. The Gini index of inequality of landholding distribution was reduced from 0.740 in 1951 to 0.384 in 1965 when the programme was completed.

Redistributive land reform in both countries was accompanied by two main welfare measures. One consisted of outright transfer of income in real terms from landlords to tenants through a substantial reduction of rent, accompanied by the provision of a high degree of tenure security to tenants. The other comprised government programmes providing highly subsidized complementary production inputs and a rapid expansion of free public health and education, together with the provision of non-land income sources (non-farm jobs in rural areas and increase in livestock assets). Consequently, productivity increased and rural poverty declined substantially. Reliable estimates of absolute poverty reduction show that poverty incidence in rural areas diminished rapidly in South Korea – a

Table 5.1   Estimated ratios of redistributed area and land-recipient households in 22 developing countries (excluding settlement schemes), 1915–90

Countries in descending order of beneficiaries' scale and years of reform acts	Beneficiary households as % of total agricultural households	Redistributed land as % of total agricultural land	Size ratio of ceiling to beneficiaries' units
China (1949–56)	≈90	80[a]	No ceiling
South Korea (1945, 1950)	75–77	65	3/1–2 ha (3:1)
Cuba (1959–65)	60	60	67/30 ha (2.2:1)
Ethiopia (1975, 1979)	57	76[b]	10/3 ha (3.3:1)
Iraq (1958, 1971)	56	60	Varies according to land quality
Mexico (1915, 1934, 1940, 1971)	≈55	42	100 ha irrigated, 300 ha rainfed ceiling/2–5 ha irrigated units (28:1)
Tunisia (1956, 1957, 1958, 1964)	49	57[c]	Mostly recovered French-owned farms
Iran (1962, 1967, 1989)	45	34[d]	
Peru (1969, 1970)	40	38	Ceiling, irrigated 150 ha in coast, 55 ha in Sierra
Algeria (1962, 1971)	37	50[e]	≈40/15 ha (3:1)
Yemen, South (1969, 1970)	25	47	8/2 ha irrigated (4:1)
Nicaragua (1979, 1984, 1986)	23	28	Ceiling 350 ha in Pacific zone and 4 ha. (87:1)
Sri Lanka (1972, 1973)	23	12	25/3 ha irrigated (8:1)
El Salvador (1980)	23	22	120/5 ha (24:1)
Syria (1958, 1963, 1980)	16	10[f]	Rainfed (7:1), irrigated (4:1)
Egypt (1952, 1961)	14	10	40:1 irrigated
Libya (1970–75)	12	13	Recovered former Italian farms
Chile (1967–73)	12	13[g]	80 standardized ha, around 5 ha irrigated (16:1)
Philippines (1972, 1988, 1994)	8	10[h]	5/1 ha corn and rice (3:1)

India (all, 1953–79)	4	3	Differs by states
Pakistan (1959, 1972)	3	4	65/4 ha (16:1)
Morocco (1956, 1963, 1973)	2	4	No ceiling, only recovered French-owned lands

[a]After deducting areas of state farms and non-crop lands.

[b]Area of peasant associations, including producers' cooperatives.

[c] Includes the individualized *habous* on private *Waqf* land.

[d] Includes the area reallocated by the Council of Determination in March 1989, which was occupied by peasants after the owners fled the country.

[e] Includes 2.6 million ha recovered French-owned farms (*auto-gestion* socialist sector).

[f] Does not include 911 201 ha expropriated but not redistributed up to 1990.

[g] These estimated percentages of beneficiaries and land rise to 18 and 36%, respectively, when all *asentados* (potential beneficiaries) were included (Barraclough and Affonso, 1972, p.16).

[h] After the deferment of the distribution of 0.3 million ha to the year 2005, the restitution of nearly 80 000 ha to original owners and the exemptions made in President Ramos's Decree RA7881 of 1994.

Sources: China, South Korea, Cuba, Iraq, Mexico, Egypt, Sri Lanka, India and Pakistan: El-Ghonemy (1990a, ch. 6 and 7, Table 7.1). Ethiopia: Abate and Kiros (1983, pp.160–176). Chile: Castillo and Lehman (1983, pp.249–268). Nicaragua: Baumeister (1994, p.223). Peru: Kay (1983, p.206–217). Ethiopia, Chile and Peru are in Ghose (1983). El Salvador: El-Ghonemy (1984, p.20–21). Algeria, Tunisia and Libya: El-Ghonemy (1993a). Iran: El-Ghonemy (1998, p.157–159). Yemen, South: calculated from FAO (1984). Syria: estimated from FAO (1984, 1991). Philippines: El-Ghonemy (1990b, p.269–272), DAR (1990, p.18) and SENTRA (1997, p.15–31).

private property market economy – from 60 per cent before RLR to 9.8 per cent after the reform (poverty estimates of Keidel, 1981; Dong Wan and Yang Boo, 1984). In Egypt, it fell from my estimated level of 56.1 per cent of total agricultural households in 1951 (one year before the introduction of RLR, when *laissez-faire* market forces and landlords political power were dominant) to 23.8 per cent in 1965 when redistribution was completed. Redistributive land reform was of strategic importance in the early stages of economic development and social transformation in both countries.

From my reading of the history of agrarian systems and the emancipation of the poor classes working on the land, I would argue that two critical development issues spring from land reforms. One is the speedy reduction in land concentration and the incidence of rural poverty; the other is the effect on agricultural growth in general and food production in particular. While we are now able to judge these relationships by employing high-tech statistical analysis, the results do not fundamentally differ from the conclusion reached over 200 years ago by Adam Smith, the fountainhead of economic thought.[4] At present, we are fortunate to have abundant theoretical and empirical information on these issues, though we may disagree about the methodology used in measurements. Contributors to the debate include Dorner and Kanel (1971); Barraclough (1973); Berry and Cline (1979); de Janvry (1981); Ghai and Radwan (1983); Parsons (1984); Cornia (1985); Lipton (1985); El-Ghonemy (1990a, 1993a,b); El-Ghonemy et al. (1993) to mention only a few.

My own inter-country analysis of the results of case studies conducted in a sample of 20 developing countries suggests the following: (i) a strong and statistically significant (95 per cent probability) positive correlation between variation in land concentration and rural poverty levels (in most cases, the high incidence of rural poverty is accompanied by a high degree of inequality of land ownership distribution and *vice versa*); (ii) with a reduction in the degree of inequality (Gini index) by one-third (from an average of 0.66 to 0.44) and a sustained annual average growth of 3 per cent, the average poverty level is likely to be reduced by half; and (iii) without interventionist policy (RLR), this reduction in poverty level by half is likely to be attained in approximately 60 years.[5] Prices (including wages) were not included in the analysis because these data were not available on a comparable basis across the sample of countries.

With regard to food production, a country-by-country review shows, with a few short-term exceptions, that RLR has increased food production.[6] Land recipients have produced more food for themselves and, in many cases, were able to produce more for sale in the urban market. This increase was primarily realized through mixing the hitherto under-utilized family labour with legally secured access to productive land, combined with technological advance. Thus RLR programmes have at least provided their beneficiaries with food command in place of the otherwise landless workers' uncertainty in acquiring food through dependence on an unreliable labour market, the power of grain traders and the inefficient distribution of food aid by class-biased bureaucracies.

In many countries, RLR programmes included the conversion of expropriated or nationalized large farms into government-managed state farms whose main objective was the production of food in order to feed armed forces and to meet the growing demand for food caused chiefly by high population growth, combined with rapid urbanization. This idea was borrowed from socialist countries – especially the former Soviet Union, which had initiated state farms in the 1920s and where these accounted for nearly 67 per cent of total agricultural land in 1980. In developing countries, the proportion of land in state farms to total agricultural land ranged in the early 1980s from 85 per cent in Cuba to 12 per cent in Nicaragua (Baumeister, 1994, Table 8.3) and 5–9 per cent in Egypt, Ethiopia and Mozambique (El-Ghonemy, 1990a, pp.123–27).

Land market reform (LMR)

It was these giant state farms that were the first public enterprises to be dismantled in the early stage of post-1980 market liberalization. For this purpose special laws were passed. They include, for example, Syria's Law No. 10 of 1986, which provided for a joint venture of 25 per cent share by the state and 75 per cent by the private sector, as well as Algeria's Law No. 19 of 1987, and the sale of most state farms in Ethiopia and in Egypt in the 1990s. Those who were able to purchase these farms had the financial capability and political influence which are obviously unavailable to poor peasants and landless workers, resulting in the rise in concentration of land ownership. Because of being heavily indebted and starved of foreign private capital, governments have tended to provide multinational enterprises with generous incentives in anticipation of advances in technology and world market links that will enable these countries to realize the economic policy reform's principal aim of private sector-based, export-led growth.

Some country experiences

Together with the privatization of state farms, the market orientation of land tenure arrangements includes the freezing or slowing down of RLR, and the promotion of land property transfer between willing buyers and willing sellers at market prices, with or without direct financial support from governments and foreign donors. Frequently cited LMR took place in Brazil, Colombia, Kenya, the Philippines and South Africa. In these countries, differing terminology is used to refer to LMR: market-friendly or negotiated land reform, market-assisted land reform, and civil society demand-driven land reform. We may be able to understand this diversity in practical terms after briefly considering each country's programme. A summary indication of their main agrarian characteristics is presented in Table 5.2.

Brazil

Since 1985, this country's land policy has been an excellent example of a lack of political will. Its programme was proclaimed to pacify the millions of discontented poor peasants and landless workers and, at the same time, to serve the interests of influential landlords and multinationals. An October 1985 law typifies this strategy. Article II (section 1.5) was intended to provide 1.4 million rural workers with land ownership between 1985 and 1990 through the distribution of 40 million ha of cultivable but unutilized land, in units of 20 ha on average. The affected farms were those which did not serve 'the social function of land'. While the government was busy defining 'social function', conducting cadastral surveys and studying the legal procedures, however, there was no actual redistribution. Supported by NGOs, rural workers occupied the land in anticipation of ownership, as promised by the politicians. Violent confrontation between the occupants, on the one hand, and the police and landlords' paramilitary organizations,

Table 5.2   Selected agrarian indicators of five countries implementing land market reform

	Brazil	Colombia	Kenya	Philippines	South Africa
Agricultural population as percentage of total population (1995)[a]	19	24	78	42	13
Percentage of rural people in poverty	73	45	55	64	60.6[b]
Land concentration Gini index[c]	0.86	0.86	0.77	0.53	na
Landless farmers as percentage of total agricultural households	39	na	13	34	na
Distribution of income:					
share of lowest 20%	2.1	3.6	3.4	6.5	3.3
share of highest 20%	67.5	55.8	62.1	47.8	63.3
Gini index[c]	0.63	0.51	0.57	0.41	0.58

[a] Agricultural population is defined as all persons depending for their livelihood on agriculture.

[b] Black Africans.

[c] See definition in Note 3. The index is calculated from the results of agricultural censuses. Landless and poverty estimates are for years around 1990 and the distribution of income/consumption is between 1990 and 1993. Income distribution is at national level.

Sources: Agricultural population, FAO (1996b). Rural poverty and landless estimates except South Africa (see text), IFAD (1992, Appendix Tables 2 and 6). Rural population and distribution of income, World Bank (1997a, Table 5). Land concentration Gini index, FAO (1988, Table 3).

on the other, resulted in hundreds of deaths. Eventually, only a fraction (less than 6 per cent) of a total of 1.4 million landless workers received land.

More recently, a programme of 'negotiated land reform' has been in progress. It consists of two main schemes. One involves the transfer to rural workers of property titles to land purchased by the government, supported by the Federation of Agricultural Workers (CONTAG). The other, financed by the International Fund for Agricultural Development (IFAD) and the World Bank, provides credit services to beneficiaries. The programme is monitored and evaluated by a national committee comprising representatives of universities and the government agencies concerned. Available information suggests that landlords sell low-quality land, and that the complex administrative and legal procedures are very slow and costly. It remains to be seen how this programme might resolve the four critical problems characterized in Table 5.2: high land concentration (0.86 Gini index); high landlessness (39 per cent of total agricultural households); high incidence of rural poverty (73 per cent of total rural population); and highly skewed income distribution, in which the share of the richest 20 per cent of households is over 30 times that of the poorest 20 per cent.

Colombia

As in Brazil, Colombia's Law No. 160 of 1994 provides a mechanism for market-based land transfers to reduce the very high inequality of land and income distribution and the persistently high poverty level (45 per cent) in rural areas. The mechanism grants potential buyers of land 70 per cent of the sale price, grouped in project-like activities supported by the World Bank. According to a study by the Economic Commission for Latin America and the Caribbean (ECLAC) (Vogelgesang, 1996), the programme has had very limited success owing to high prices imposed by violent coercion from landlords and narcotics dealers, the refusal of willing buyers to purchase land in any locality, and cumbersome bureaucracy. The study also found that most land buyers are urban, that transaction costs are prohibitive for small peasants, and that 'transfers of property rights through the existing market mechanisms have failed to shift land from one [rich] group to another group [of poor peasants]'.

Kenya

The irony of this poor and overwhelmingly rural country's post-1980 land policy is that it has resulted in the very problems it intended to redress: the vast inequality in the distribution of land and income, and persistent poverty in rural areas (Table 5.2). The privatization of customary land tenure, the consolidation of fragmented holdings and the promotion of land-title transfers through the market mechanism, combined with the deterioration of living conditions among low-income groups after the introduction of economic reforms, have exacerbated land concentration (a Gini index of 0.77), rural poverty incidence (55 per cent) and rising land-lessness.[7] With the agricultural population growing 3.2 per cent per annum, the increasing concentration of land in the hands of a few large landowners and multinationals has increased their power in the land market structure, and the number of landless workers has increased.

Empirical studies show that in Nyanza province, for example, only 3 per cent of all land owned in 1990 was purchased in the open market by large farmers and government officials, while the rest was inherited. Collateral (in the form of land) has been the main obstacle facing small farmers, landless workers and poor peasants seeking loans from both commercial banks and agricultural cooperatives for the purchase of land in the open market. Moreover, a recent study indicates that Kenya's individualization of customary tenure on economic efficiency grounds 'has resulted in landlessness and loss of food security, particularly by women' (Adams, 1997, p.6).

The Philippines

Perhaps in no other country have land reform policy issues engaged the interests of both government and rural people for so long as in the Philippines. It is difficult to assess this country's policy, which has been expressed in a myriad of nearly 15 land reform programmes since 1954. The policy choice – of a combination of half-hearted government-implemented and market-based redistribution – has induced lively debate. During a field visit in 1993, it appeared that official statistics were exaggerated: senior officials tended to discredit previous governments' land reform achievements, giving inflated figures that were, and still are, challenged by the many active NGOs. There also appeared to be a gap between the sophistication of land reform laws, which are ridden with loopholes, and the political will of both government and parliament. Yet the end result of the numerous programmes was that, in 1996, nearly 8 per cent of total agricultural households were able to own land under these programmes, and about half of all agricultural workers were landless (see sources on the Philippines in Table 5.1).

In addition to the slowly implemented 1972 laws of President Marcos and those of the Aquino administration (Republican Act 6657 and Comprehensive Agrarian Reform Law, 1988), President Ramos initiated a market-oriented policy in 1996 as part of his Economic Recovery Programme. This policy reinforced the existing legislative provisions for tenants to purchase the land they till. But a combination of the erstwhile clumsy bureaucracy, the overvaluation of land prices and the local monopoly power of landlords has frustrated the efforts of government, NGOs and university academics to accelerate the private land title transfers in favour of poor peasants and landless workers. International donors, such as the World Bank and the Ford Foundation, are supporting this market-based land reform, which is being implemented in small pilot project areas. A field study by the International Network on Land Market Reform (consisting of representatives of IFAD, the FAO, the World Bank and some NGOs) reports 'the view expressed by both the government and NGOs was that the scope of such a network must go beyond the confines of market-assisted land reforms, which is not the case of the Philippines' experience. It should focus on civil society-driven land reforms' (IFAD/World Bank/FAO, 1997, p.32).

South Africa

Unlike the other four countries, the historical experience of South Africa makes it a special case indeed.[8] Both the agrarian structure and the entire social order were striking manifestations of absolute injustice. They were shaped on racial grounds, beginning with the long colonial rule of the Dutch and the British, and formalized by apartheid in 1948. When constitutional reforms were instituted in 1995, the minority white population – representing nearly one-tenth of the total – owned most of the agricultural land (83 per cent). In contrast, native Africans, representing 77 per cent of the country's population of 41 million, accounted for 61 per cent of all the poor, including 31 per cent of rural households who were landless and with no grazing rights (Government of South Africa, 1995, p.81, Tables 1 and 2). Vast inequalities of income and opportunities are evident from the 1993 data on the distribution of family consumption, which show that the share of the lowest one-fifth of all families in terms of income was only 3.3 per cent of total consumption, while that of the top one-tenth in terms of income was almost half the total consumption (World Bank, 1997a, Table 5)

It is in this context that the present land policy has been pursued as part of the 1995 Reconstruction and Development Programme. Its three components reflect the main land tenure defects to be redressed and the course of action adopted. These components are:

- land redistribution by way of market-based property title transfers between willing buyers and willing sellers, with government financial support; the potential beneficiaries are estimated at nearly one million landless workers and 200 000 tenants;
- land restitution for the black Africans who were dispossessed after 1910–13 without compensation, and who were moved out by whites and concentrated in designated 'homelands';
- land tenure security for strengthening tenants' lease rights and the protection of customary land tenure arrangements, with emphasis on the rights of women.

The programme has been implemented with a strong political commitment and partnership between the Ministry of Land Affairs and NGOs. However, implementation has been slow, owing partly to still rigid racial structures, and partly to exorbitant land prices which are negotiated from very unequal bargaining positions in face-to-face encounters between the many poor peasants willing to buy and the few powerful landowners. These and other obstacles are reflected in the fact that merely 7.5 per cent of all potential land buyers had completed transactions in the pilot area by July 1997. The slow progress is also manifested in the fact that only one-fifth of the beneficiaries are provided with basic services, and that support for production following land transfers is still lacking.

Although it seems easy to criticize this comprehensive programme, several factors are assuredly hopeful: government commitment; support from international aid agencies; and transparency in the management and work of the Monitoring and Evaluation Unit of the Ministry of Land Affairs. Yet there are signs of dissatisfaction with the path chosen. For example, 73 South African NGOs declared in their Charter on Land and Food Security that 'if land reform was left entirely to the market, little if any reform would take place', and 'land reform policy must be driven by the principles of social justice and basic needs as opposed to market forces'. And the National Land Committee (consisting of 10 NGOs) has stated that 'the market is not a solution for a fair land redistribution after the apartheid . . . markets are never truly free'. The Committee proposed 'a more interventionist role for the government to achieve a thorough and speedy redistribution of land' (IFAD/World Bank/FAO, 1997, p.43).

Privatization of customary land tenure in Africa: Côte D'Ivoire, Malawi and Uganda

Linked with the structural adjustment policy package for market-induced efficiency in resource use is the privatization of customary land tenure, the traditional form of land rights in most of rural Africa. The reform is by way of individual titling of land that for centuries has been communally owned by indigenous groups. These groups (tribes, families and communities) devised sets of rules for land rights (use and occupancy) and subsisted by grazing and cultivating food crops when rain permitted. As recognized by anthropologists and geographers, this customary land tenure system has been the suitable socio-ecological system for land use and livestock husbandry in a semi-arid climate. It has been the cornerstone of food security for millions of indigenous people and, in turn, their social security. Likewise, its contribution to economic growth cannot be overestimated. This includes employment of the pastoralists' family members within a rational division of labour of women and children, the production of a considerable part of the countries' total meat, milk, wool and hides, and the conservation of natural resources.

It is ridiculous that some foreign professionals still see this system as backward or primitive and in need of being privatized, according to the conventional Anglo-Saxon conception of efficiency in agricultural production by way of individual private ownership of land linked to the capital market.[9] Despite existing strong arguments for maintaining customary land tenure, including those of the World Bank itself (Fedder and Noronha, 1987, pp.153–169; World Bank, 1992, pp.142–143; Adams, 1997, pp.6–7), and in spite of a lack of empirical evidence on the production superiority of individual private land ownership over communal ownership within customary tenure arrangements, privatization policy is pursued with vigour in most African countries. It is also enforced despite empirical evidence that customary tenure is compatible with the production of export crops and with food production. The experience of several privatizing countries suggests (i) the vulnerability of individual owners to the loss of land to urban land speculators, as well as to mortgage and heavy indebtedness; (ii) the weakening of women's customary rights in land and command over food; and (iii) the shift away from food crops toward cash/export crops. Moreover, because of high transaction costs, the land buyers are businessmen, politicians, senior civil servants, members of the armed forces and larger landowners. These non-agriculturist land speculators know the law and registration procedures, and have contacts with credit institutions and land surveyors. Financially, they can afford the costs of surveying, registration and issuing private title deeds.

Because of space limitations, a few aspects of the experiences of Côte d'Ivoire, Malawi and Uganda are presented to illustrate what is happening in Africa. The primary effect of privatization on rural well-being is increasing insecurity, in terms of both the loss of command over food and the loss of customary rights to land. Before the so-called economic boom of Côte d'Ivoire, the land of the Akan tribes in the south was held communally and, for centuries, produced the yams, cassava, millet and sorghum that provide two-thirds of rural people's calorie supply. With the adoption of an export-led growth strategy, resources have been re-allocated in favour of the cultivation of cocoa and coffee, customarily held communal land has been gradually privatized, and labour shifted to the production of cash/export crops, especially coffee, the area of which expanded eight times between 1979–81 and 1989–91. The net result was a sharp fall in both food productivity and average per capita daily calorie intake during the same period (FAO, 1985, 1986a, 1996b)

In Malawi between 1986 and 1990, the area of customary land that was privatized doubled. Land buyers converted the production of food crops into Burley tobacco, and former landholders became wage workers and net buyers of food. With population growing quickly, at 3.7 per cent per year, food production per person fell rapidly. In contrast, tobacco production increased from 70 000 tonnes in 1986 to 110 000 tonnes in 1991 (FAO, 1993b). In Uganda, the economic policy reform toward export-led growth has facilitated shifting land use from grazing and growing food (cassava and millet) to commercial ranching managed by urban land buyers who have kinship relations with influential policy-makers. For example, by 1991 in Masaka and Masindi districts, nearly half the buyers of 108 500 ha of land were members of parliament, government officials and senior police officers (FAO, 1993b; Nsabagasani, 1997, pp.33–36; Table 5.3). The buyers erected fences around their ranches, depriving pastoral households in the surrounding areas of traditional corridors used for their own passage and the grazing of their animals (and necessary due to the area's highly unpredictable rainfall). Similar problems were identified by Abdalla (1993) in his field study of two Sudanese provinces, Darfur and Kardofan.

No matter how good the economic principles of privatization, falling food productivity associated with market orientation should be of serious concern to governments, international organizations and development analysts. FAO data show a post-1980 downward trend in food production per person in sub-Saharan Africa compared to other regions; the index for 1990–95 is below the average for 1979–81, and the rates of growth in average daily calorie intake per person have also declined in most countries. These trends are very worrying indeed with regard to food insecurity of

Table 5.3 Changes in arable land and pressure of agricultural workforce on land in 13 countries 1970–96, and projection for 2010

Countries[a]	Arable land — Percentage annual growth of actually used arable land (1)			Arable land — Area of balance for future crop production as as % of total land with crop production potential (2)	Agricultural workforce — Percentage annual growth of agricultural workforce (3)			Ratio of actually used land area to agricultural workforce (ha/person) (4)		
	1970–80	1981–90	1991–96		1980–90	1990–2000	2000–10	1970	1980	1996
Algeria	1.2	0.3	1.2	25	0.9	1.2	0.5	4.9	5.9	3.9
Brazil	3.7	1.7	3.0	85	−0.3	−0.7	−1.1	2.4	3.5	3.7
Colombia	0.3	0.4	0.3	88	0.6	−0.2	−0.9	2.1	1.9	1.5
Egypt	0.6	0.0	4.0	3	0.9	1.2	0.5	0.6	0.5	0.4
Ethiopia	0.3	0.0	−0.2	57	1.2	1.0	1.2	1.1	1.0	0.7
Kenya	1.1	0.8	0.0	50	2.7	2.8	2.6	0.5	0.4	0.4
Malawi	0.8	0.3	0.2	59	1.6	1.4	1.2	0.6	0.6	0.4
Mauritania	−3.9	0.5	0.2	65	1.8	2.0	2.3	0.8	0.6	0.4
Morocco	2.5	1.6	0.5	50	0.9	0.5	0.1	3.2	3.1	2.2
Philippines	0.9	0.2	0.1	42	1.5	1.4	1.1	0.9	0.8	0.8
South Africa	1.0	0.8	0.7	–	0.8	−0.6	−0.9	4.8	8.1	7.1
Sudan	0.7	0.4	0.1	82	1.3	0.6	0.9	3.2	2.9	1.8
Uganda	1.5	2.1	0.2	58	2.2	2.3	2.2	1.2	1.1	0.8

[a] Countries (in alphabetical order) whose experiences are briefly discussed in the text.

'Arable' or cultivable is land cultivated with temporary and permanent crops, and land under temporary fallow; it does not include forest and permanent pasture lands.

Potential land or 'balance' is land of varying quality with potential for growing crops; it is a rough estimate and comprises land in actual crop production use (rainfed and irrigated) and land that could be cultivated in future.

Sources: (1) calculated from FAO (1996b, 1993b); (2) based on FAO (1993c, Table A.5); (3) from FAO (1993c, Table A.1); (4) from the same sources as column (1). In these sources the agricultural workforce is termed 'the economically active population in agriculture'.

rural households and their increasing dependence on the imperfect market for food acquisition and the increasing incidence of chronic undernutrition, particularly among young children.

PROSPECTS FOR DISADVANTAGED GROUPS

If the present trends in market-based access to land, coupled with rapid growth of agricultural population and budgetary cuts in public expenditure, were to continue into the twenty-first century what would be the prospects for the hundreds of millions of landless and near-landless rural poor? The post-1980 experiences of the countries implementing LMR examined in this chapter are not only unsatisfactory, but alarming, both in terms of worsening food insecurity and inequality, and in the very slow progress in land property transfers to poor farming people. The estimates of the International Conference on Nutrition (FAO/WHO, 1992) of the present and projected increase in numbers of seriously undernourished people by the year 2005, and those of the World Bank (1992, Table 1.1) on poverty incidence in 1985–2000 (especially the substantial rise in sub-Saharan Africa and the Middle East), show a general deterioration. They sound a warning that policy-makers and international agencies should take this very seriously.

Growing demand for, and declining supply of, land

This section examines what happened to the supply of land relative to the growing numbers of people working in agriculture between 1970 and 1996 (with a projection for the year 2010) in the 13 countries whose experiences have been briefly discussed in this chapter. Because comparable data on land prices are lacking, the ratio of land (in ha) per working person is used as an approximation of the supply of and demand for land. In this context it is worth reiterating that land is not merely a commodity or factor of production; it has significant cultural value, and is insurance against poverty and household food insecurity. It is recognized that the aggregation of land conceals wide variations in quality, cropping intensity and capitalized value between and within countries. In addition, the use of averages obscures two aspects in the land market: rapid urbanization, which takes scarce crop land out of agriculture for non-agricultural purposes; and the increasing costs of land reclamation for new irrigated land settlement schemes, which are particularly costly in North Africa and the Middle East because of aridity, soil texture and water scarcity (FAO, 1986b, pp.40–41; Table 5.11 of Carruthers and Clark, 1981).[10]

With this in mind, let us have a closer look at the data in Table 5.3. With the exception of land-abundant Brazil, Colombia and Sudan, and mineral-rich Algeria and South Africa, there is a very low ratio of actually used crop land to agricultural workforce, particularly in Egypt, Kenya and Malawi. There is also a general downward trend in this ratio, notably between 1980 and 1996. One possible explanation for this decline is the slow growth or stagnation in crop land expansion in many countries, while the population/agricultural workforce is growing at fast rates. Moreover, post-1980 fiscal reforms have required heavy cuts in public investment in land-augmenting technologies, especially irrigation, and for the expansion of land settlement schemes. In my examination of FAO data on irrigation expansion, I found that of the total 87 developing countries for which data are available, nearly two-thirds (63 per cent) manifested an alarming decline in irrigation expansion, especially in North Africa and the Middle East. Also, about 53 per cent of the Middle Eastern population lives in areas with less than the acceptable minimum level of 1000 cubic metres of water availability per person per year, and if present rates of use continue the average is expected to decline by half by the year 2025.

What is of great concern is the fact that in poor countries whose financial capacity to invest in land supply expansion is very limited (Ethiopia, Kenya, Malawi, Mauritania, Sudan and Uganda), relatively large, currently uncropped areas are potentially suitable for crop production (Table 5.3, column 2). The large potential area in Colombia and Brazil is a manifestation of the widespread practice of absentee land ownership, with severely underutilized large estates. According to the results of the 1990 Agricultural Census of Colombia, the number of landholdings in the category of over 200 ha accounts for only 5 per cent of the total, but their area represents 54 per cent of the total. The possibility of transferring land property rights of this large potential area to the present generation of poor peasants and landless workers is extremely low, as suggested by the limited results of the land market reform referred to earlier.

The likelihood of wage-dependent workers purchasing land

Can a wage-dependent, landless worker purchase land in his or her lifetime? How long would the worker have to save all or a fraction of his or her accumulated daily wage in order to purchase land?

The results of available poverty studies show that most of the rural poor are undernourished, landless wage-workers. Before they can save to purchase land, their productivity and earnings from agricultural and non-farm jobs must increase and be sustained in order to raise their purchasing power high enough to enable them to cross their countries' established poverty lines. They are unable to borrow in the open credit market to fulfil this aim. Advocates of market supremacy in the rural economy believe that the private sector's increased investment and production of tradables, linked to the world market, will be the new engine of sustained growth of total and per person output (and income). This, in turn, will raise the purchasing power of wage-workers.

My investigation of the experiences of eight countries[11] in North Africa and the Middle East that have implemented World Bank and IMF market-oriented reforms reveals three disappointing results. First, between 1983 and 1993 only one country, Turkey, had both economic (total GDP) growth and export growth. Second, inflation has soared in all countries as a result of the IMF's conditionality of devaluation and fiscal reforms, sharply raising the overall cost of living. And third, employment opportunities for the growing numbers of agricultural labourers have narrowed, primarily owing to rising unemployment in urban areas and the use of labour-displacing technology in agriculture, which has been facilitated by trade liberalization. With continuing rapid growth of the mostly landless agricultural workforce, post-1980 market supremacy does not permit following the prudent Chinese path of mobilizing excess rural labour for labour-intensive manufacturing in rural areas and for rapid expansion of irrigated areas. The unfortunate result is a rapid increase in poverty incidence (the proportion and numbers of the poor) in six countries, and inequality in income distribution in all eight countries except Tunisia. My findings do not differ fundamentally from the accounts of adjusting countries in Latin America and Asia documented by Stewart (1995) and Berry (1998).

Empirical evidence also shows that it is difficult to find other means to increase earnings enough to purchase a piece of land. Intra-family marriage between a poor landless male and a rich bride is a very remote possibility, for reasons of custom and the values inherent in social stratification. These cultural factors usually give preference to the number of acres owned by the groom or his father. Even landowners would probably lower their status if their daughters were to marry the sons of smaller landowners. Likewise, there is low probability of land property transfer through inheritance arrangements within the poor class of landless workers whose families have very limited landed assets, if any at all [my studies in Gabaris, Bohera Province, Egypt, (El-Ghonemy, 1990a, ch. 5 and note 17); Yemen (El-Ghonemy et al., 1986); and ESCWA/FAO (1986)].

Moreover, there has been a downward trend in remittances from rural migrants who could afford to travel to seek unskilled jobs abroad in the oil-rich Arab states. During the oil boom in the 1970s and early 1980s, this was a good way of increasing earnings in order to be able to purchase land for cultivation and house building. This practice has declined as a result of the slump in oil revenues and the Gulf War (1990–91). The tendency of migrant workers to purchase land with their savings has contributed to land price inflation in labour exporting countries. The Egyptian experience illustrates this situation; the data are given in Table 5.4. The unprecedented rise in land prices between 1975 and 1980 was fuelled by urban land speculators bidding up land prices, not to get an economic return on their investment, but rather for non-monetary gains (such as family security in times of high inflation and political advantages). Such practices may incite small landowners to sell parcels of their land at very high prices, leading to loss of

Table 5.4   Average land values and daily wages in Egyptian agriculture, 1930–97

Values in Egyptian pounds and current prices	Market-forces period		Land reform period	Liberalization policy and market-forces period	
	1935–40	1945–51	1952–56	1975–80	1997–98
Market sale price (*P*)	119	415	180	3,000	35,000
Annual rental value (*R*)	7.1	22.7	17.5	29.5	1300
Adult male wage (*W*)	0.029	0.102	0.110	0.365	8.000
Deflator (1966–67 = 100)	25	56	69	270	2,540
R as percentage of *P*	6.0	5.4	9.7	1	3.7
P in year's rent	16.7	18.5	11.1	101.7	26.9
P in year *W*[a]	19.5	19.4	7.8	39.1	21.0

One Egyptian pound equalled US$4.13 up to September 1949 and was devalued to US$2.87 until 1977. Between 1982 and 1986 it equalled US$1.22, in 1997 and 1998 it equalled US$0.34. The sale price and rental value are for one feddan of land (0.42 ha or nearly 1 acre).

[a] Assuming 210 working days per year. The deflator is the cost of living index for rural areas established by the Institute of National Planning, statistically linked with 1966/67 = 100.

Sources: Rental values are from El-Ghonemy (1953, Tables 10 and 37) for 1929–51. The rest are from the Egyptian Ministry of Agriculture's Bulletin of Agricultural Economics, several issues (in Arabic). Adult male wages for 1937–51 are average rates collected by the writer from 98 villages in Lower Egypt and 83 in Upper Egypt during his work in the Fellah Department. The rest are from Radwan (1977, Table 3.2) and the Ministry of Agriculture. 1997–98 data from Department of Agricultural Economics, Ein Shams University, Cairo. The deflator is from the CAPMAS Statistical Yearbook, Cairo.

land by peasants who then join the misfortune of their landless fellows (Radwan and Lee, 1986).

To understand the dynamics of land prices over the period 1935–98, I have calculated these and daily wage rates from several sources, and from my interviews in villages.[12] The data are divided into three periods: (i) the sub-periods in which market forces were dominant, 1935–40 and 1945–51; (ii) the period of intensive government intervention, including the implementation of redistributive land reform (1952–56); and (iii) the *Infitah* or abrupt start of economic liberalization combined with the oil boom period (1975–80). The prices during the implementation of redistributive land reform (1952–56) are the land tax-based official average prices used by the government to establish the sale price to new owners and compensate the affected landlords. (The sale price is 70 times the land tax, and the rental value is seven times the land tax.) Beyond this formal use, land sale price was never enforced, while fixed rent seemed to be enforced only in areas administered by land reform cooperatives and public farming corporations. These arrangements may explain the sharp rise in average land prices by 17 times in 1975–80 relative to that in 1952–56, while rent increased by 1.7 times and wages rose by nearly three times as much. These changes in nominal values should be seen in real terms, that is, relative to the rise in the cost of living index for rural areas, 1966–67 = 100 (the deflator rose from 69 to 270, or a rise of 201).

Assuming 210 working days per annum, the data in Table 5.4 suggest that a landless worker has virtually zero opportunity to buy one feddan (0.42 ha) during his or her lifetime through the land market, since the average sale price of land in market-based transactions periods (1935–51, 1975–80 and 1997–98) was equivalent to between 19 and 39 years' average daily wage of an adult male. The landless worker would need to accumulate *all* his earnings, without spending anything on living costs, for these years in order to purchase one feddan. If the worker spent half his or her total wage earnings, and assuming a constant wage–land price ratio, the period would double, that is, it would extend beyond a worker's life expectancy of 55 years, so that he or she would go to the grave without being able to realize the dream of purchasing one feddan of land. During the period of strong government intervention (1952–56) the waiting period was reduced to between a quarter and one-fifth of that for the period of domination by market forces. The chance of a landless worker becoming a tenant (leasing-in one feddan under fixed cash rent using accumulated wages) is also better during the period of government intervention than that of reliance on the market. Moreover, during the period of dominant market forces mortgages have been unobtainable, as tenants and landless workers had (and still have) no access to institutional credit which required land as collateral (in addition to the Islamic condemnation of mortgages).

Land prices and wage rates in Morocco in 1998 and Kenya in 1986 reveal a situation similar to that in Egypt. For example, in Kenya in 1984–86 a landless farmer's hope for purchasing 1 acre of land at the average price of 10 000–15 000 shillings per acre was an unrealizable dream. The annual income of a poor Kenyan rural household was about 1700 shillings (Collier and Lal, 1986, p.129; Livingstone, 1986, pp.11–15). These figures mean that the entire household has to accumulate earnings, without *any* expenditure, for eight to nine years to purchase 1 acre (0.4 ha) of land in the open market.

Rural women's access to land

Three issues have emerged during the post-1980 market-orientation policy. First, in the process of individualization of communally held land and collective farming, land has been allocated to households. In practice, men are the household heads who pool and manage labour use and income. The second issue concerns the (consequential) adverse effects of the tendency toward cash crop production resulting from the privatization of communally held land, particularly in Africa. Not only have women tended to lose their long-established (under customary tenure arrangements) equal rights in land use and inheritance, but they have also been deprived of customary entitlement for self-produced food crops. In these situations, and depending on the male/female division of labour, the opportunity cost is likely to be high for women in terms of the loss of secure tenure, diminishing family food security and displacement of their labour. Cash/export and food crops as substitutes grown in individualized communal holdings tend to re-allocate labour to the disadvantage of women. When husbands migrate, women assume all the farming responsibilities as household heads, in addition to the year-round domestic workload and livestock husbandry. In short, these institutional changes, combined with commercialization of agriculture, increase the uncertainty of women's individual access to land and often threaten household food security.

Finally, women's share in the total number of landholdings (owned and rented) is proportionally very small compared to their share in the total agricultural labour force. With the exception of the South African 1994 land policy, in which women are guaranteed equal rights with men in landholding, there is injustice and male bias in most of the countries' programmes. This judgement is based on the results of the 1980 and 1990 agriculture censuses and of recent labour surveys and population censuses. Needy female wage workers with no access to land and few or no non-land assets are most likely to be at a high risk of undernutrition, and represent a proportionally high number of their respective countries' rural poor.

CONCLUDING REMARKS

It is my hope that the reader will see in the following remarks an appeal to common sense. I begin by suggesting some ways to improve LMR. But I have serious doubts with regard to a short-term land-policy shift, because market-based reforms of land tenure arrangements are held in bondage by the present economic reforms and foreign debt crisis, and because countries are busy privatizing all economic activities.

First, in view of increasing poverty levels and numbers of landless workers and minute landholdings,[13] any private or public action that would secure access to land for these disadvantaged people is welcome. The recently propagated LMR is an example. Its presentation as a new policy instrument is misleading because market-based land transactions and state-assisted functioning of private enterprises in agriculture existed long before the introduction of government-administered RLR, to which LMR is portrayed as the alternative. What is new is the treatment of the land market just like any other commodity market (e.g. fertilizer), and the prescription of LMR as an internationally standardized land policy reflecting a single ideology. It prescribes to developing countries not a set of policy options, but a unique path intimately linked to World Bank/IMF-induced economic reform packages. Common sense and countries' experiences teach us that (i) the land market is a social institution, not just a mechanism to equilibrate supply and demand; and (ii) we should not jump from broad theoretical concepts constructed under restrictive assumptions to a single path of concrete policy advice that is not culturally determined.

Second, the experience of the countries examined in this chapter suggests that, in many ways, the implementation of LMR, within the context of economic reforms, offers few prospects for disadvantaged rural groups to secure access to land. It curbs public investment in expanding crop land and enhancing human capabilities among the poor, and reduces the funds needed for government purchase of private land for sale to poor peasants. These budget cuts have resulted from the obsession with fiscal reform – that is, to achieve a zero budget deficit at any social cost. Moreover, LMR has made land purchase dependent on the formal credit market and the temporary financial support of foreign donors, without (i) a parallel reform of land-title registration or cadastral surveys; or (ii) the provision of land laws and land market information required to allocate resources efficiently, competitive and efficient agricultural credit institutions, and post-land-purchase production support. To be socially acceptable, LMR should also provide for land tenure security, particularly the protection of tenants from unlawful eviction, and for collective negotiations between sellers and representatives of tenants (e.g. old land reform cooperatives and trade unions of rural workers). Empirical evidence suggests that the survival of LMR depends on what governments do in these areas. Of equal importance is the retreat from privatizing customary land tenure systems, especially in Africa, which has led to the loss of household food security as a safety net against poverty and to greater land concentration among buyers who are mostly urban land speculators.

Third, progressive land taxation as a component of land market reform has, for political motives, been frustrated. Levying higher tax rates as size of land ownership increases might induce large landowners to sell part of their land (to the state) and so increase public revenue, which could be used to activate the land market in favour of land purchase by poor peasants. The apparent success of landlords, in alliance with bureaucracies, in frustrating this policy is likely to make peasants lose faith in governments that evade crucial issues. Research is needed on this hitherto neglected policy issue.

Fourth, the results of countries' experiences and the empirical evidence indicate the fallacy of some assumptions behind post-1980 remedies, including LMR. Among these faulty assumptions are (i) privatization of communal lands and changes in customary tenure arrangements, operating within a competitive market mechanism, are good for the rural economy and indigenous peoples because they facilitate the mobility of resources from non-tradables (e.g. self-produced food and non-cash services) to tradables (cash/export crops). Past experience suggests that customary land tenure arrangements are compatible with the production of both, and are flexible enough to accommodate the modernization of agriculture; (ii) economic growth is accelerated by market-determined land property transfer and large private farms are productively superior to small family farms (the higher the land concentration, the higher the rates of agricultural growth); (iii) RLR programmes inhibit the adjustment of national economies to crises and external shocks; and (iv) liberalization of the agrarian system, in particular formal credit and the market-determined distribution of land ownership, is a basic policy instrument for improving the access of landless peasants to land and for poverty alleviation in rural areas.

Fifth, the responses of NGOs to market-based land policies pursued by national governments and international agencies are critical to poverty alleviation, and should be taken seriously. Depending on the nature of the political system, historical experience shows us that people gain more benefits as groups than as individuals, and that government tends to respond more to group demands than to those of individuals. We have noted from countries' responses to LMR that the voice of reason and prudence has come from coalitions of NGOs and university academics in Brazil, the Philippines and South Africa. The FAO, IFAD and the World Bank are governmental organizations, and the FAO has abdicated its leading role in RLR (entrusted to it in 1979). The work of the United Nations Research Institute for Social Development on equity issues could be strengthened by closer links with the ILO, whose tripartite structure gives rural workers, including agricultural trade unions, equal status to that of governments. In addition, the ILO monitors government ratification and enforcement of international conventions on minimum wage-fixing, rural workers' freedom of association and rights to organize.

Finally, some of the biggest problems in assessing the two contrasting land distribution policies, RLR and LMR, arise from the avoidance of issues of fairness and moral perception (in which equal weight is given to the sufferings of the losers and the benefits to those who gain), and the neglect of the policies' social impact on the sum of well-being. It is true that RLR focuses on rapid poverty reduction, but it permits affected landlords to retain the best land while that of lower quality is allocated to new owners. It also tends to disregard the fair compensation payments to the losers and the impact on trade. Land market reform, on the other hand, concentrates on economic efficiency of resource-use relationships and export-led economic growth, because it is intimately bound up with the structural adjustment programmes of the World Bank and the IMF. With this narrow economic focus, and the post-1980 muddle over means and ends in development strategy, LMR disregards the distributional consequences of market transactions and the social importance of enhancing human capabilities. It justifies such socially undesirable outcomes as increasing inequality and unemployment, destitution of the landless poor, and the loss to the indigenous peoples of Africa of their traditional command over the food they produce. This tolerance or justification of the policy's undesirable social impact is grounded in a belief in the narrow economic principle that one's well-being or otherwise is decided by the market. This fetishism makes LMR neither culture-dependent nor concerned with total well-being.

Throughout this chapter, I have tried to suggest what the main features of a socially acceptable LMR might be. They are tentative but may help us to see that a land market with morality is possible.

Peasants' Pursuit of Outside Alliances and Legal Support in the Process of Land Reform

Krishna B. Ghimire

INTRODUCTION[1]

Peasants' need for external support

Experience has shown that poor, weak rural social groups such as small farmers, tenants and agricultural workers require external support if their attempts to access productive land, secure formal titles and improve productivity through subsidized credits, use of appropriate technologies, markets and other facilities are to have any hopes of success. Examples of such alliances and actions by rural groups and stronger outsiders are not lacking, but many are spontaneous and rather short-lived.

On the whole, as Scott writes:

> In the Third World it is rare for peasants to risk an outright confrontation with the authorities over taxes, cropping patterns, development policies, or onerous new laws; instead they are likely to nibble away at such policies by non-compliance, foot dragging, deception. In place of a land invasion, they prefer piecemeal squatting; in place of open mutiny, they prefer desertion; in place of attacks on public or private grain stores, they prefer pilfering. When such stratagems are abandoned in favor of more quixotic action, it is usually a sign of great desperation (Scott, 1985, p.xvi).

Well coordinated, assertive and long-term direct action is seldom likely by those who are entirely occupied with the daily struggle for survival. In fact, peasants and other poorer rural groups may intentionally wish to avoid open confrontation with authorities and domineering landowners for fear of further repression. On the other hand, trustworthy external allies and assistance, combined with growing consciousness and organization, have strengthened peasant mobilization and action (Huizer, 1980, pp.1–5).

Reliable external allies and support are crucial if the livelihood interests of marginalized rural populations are to receive the attention of authorities and powerful landowners. Progressive administrators, technicians and politicians can help peasants mobilize around land issues. Genuine international solidarity and financial and technical assistance programmes are important as well. National and local farmers' associations, cooperatives and some development non-governmental organizations (NGOs), academic centres, political parties, trade unions, and religious and professional organizations that interact with peasants and other rural groups on a sustained basis can assist peasants and the land-aspiring rural poor in various crucial areas.

First, these types of organization can play an important role in mobilizing peasants and the rural poor. In many cases, marginalized groups may not be aware of land reform issues, including their rights, what they might gain from land reform, and the actions that would be necessary to achieve their goals. Outsiders may assist by organizing self-help groups, literacy campaigns, leadership and training programmes, internal political mobilization, coordination of actions, networking and dissemination of useful information. They may also be able to influence the way land reform issues are portrayed by the mass media, lobby political parties, local governments and the bureaucracy, and organize the rural poor for direct electoral participation aimed at wider land reform and tenurial security. They may assist with organization of direct action campaigns such as squatting on private or public land, removal of crops by tenants/sharecroppers from landowners' fields, pressuring officials and landowners for lower land rents or crop sharing, etc. Finally, these organizations may encourage debate and imaginative project planning concerning wider resource-use options, comprehensive redistribution/restitution of cultivated land, flexible access to and use of common property resources, and security of tenure for indigenous peoples, women, pastoralists and fisherfolk.

Second, organizations and individuals concerned with social causes may work to acquire tenurial security and improved working conditions for marginalized rural groups. They can help identify available land and acquire formal title. They may be able to mobilize peasants and other sympathetic groups to oppose evictions of tenants and landless labourers by landowners. In some cases, they may mediate between landlords and tenants in disputes (e.g. written/customarily binding and longer lease contracts, lower rents or crop sharing, more equitable sharing of input costs). They may also make arrangements with authorities to take official steps to improve access to common property resources, and lease or rent terms.

Third, rural societies undergoing profound transformation are marked by a great deal of tension. Sympathetic outsiders may mediate internal conflicts of interest within the peasantry, as well as between peasants and other rural social groups and outside forces. Settlement of contentions between different rural groups – such as squatters and earlier tenants, small farmers and pastoralists, residents and migrants, small farmers and agricultural labourers, households selected and rejected for land redistribution – is complex but crucial. So is the prevention of conflicts across tenurial classes. Grassroots organizations and influential progressive individuals could help to resolve conflicts involving access to common property resources and expropriation of indigenous peoples' customary land rights. They could also provide assistance to peasants and other weaker rural social groups by assisting them in the development of skills for long-term crisis management.

The fourth key area where outsiders can be of assistance is in the identification of cases where the human rights of peasants have been violated. Such violations may include arbitrary evictions, injuries, or destruction of their crops, animals and houses. In addition to monitoring cases where peasants' basic human rights have been infringed, human rights activists, lawyers and legal aid services can defend individuals or groups in legal circles, or refer cases to a competent authority or independent human rights organization.

Fifth, providing marginalized rural groups with extension services – credit and loan guarantees, appropriate inputs and other services, as well as markets for outputs – in conjunction with land reform is extremely crucial. External forces can play an important role in organizing land reform beneficiaries into cooperatives, user groups, informal production bodies, etc. Their assistance is also likely to be vital in establishing land committees or other organizations for land improvement, erosion control, watershed protection schemes and sustainable agricultural practices. Monitoring of the living and working conditions of the beneficiaries is equally important, especially to verify that they hold on to their land, their production potential is fully exploited, and they do not become indebted.

Peasants' legal needs

The land question is essentially political. In most developing countries, those who possess most of the cultivated, fertile land also hold most of the political power. Moreover, government policies concerning the use and management of uncultivated land and access to other common property resources frequently reflect the interests of dominant social groups. Powerful landowners can thus avoid, delay or make land redistribution measures ineffective through the use of legal loopholes or outright manipulation of legal and political systems. They tend to have influential allies in high places, and at times even outside the country. They may skilfully employ reasoning that conforms to the approaches, methods and interests of multinational companies, banks and most bilateral and multilateral agencies. Their arguments may include the higher potential productivity of larger farms and their capacity to generate foreign exchange through cultivation of cash crops, or the need to retain large, consolidated land areas for the development of agro-processing zones, for example. Indeed, such explanations also provide the national landed classes and agro-industries with a convenient alibi for their continued hold over large tracts of land or, in some cases, for new claims over subsidized public lands, even after land reform measures have been introduced. Land reform legislation alone can do little to change the existing power structure and wider political, economic processes. It can help, however – especially when there is strong popular mobilization at the local level combined with a supportive national and international environment.

In recent years, some attempts have been made to portray agrarian reform and access to land as fundamental human rights (Anon., 1988). But land rights have been marginalized in the human rights discourse, where they are eclipsed by cases of torture and lack of general civil and political rights.[2] In many cases, however, human rights violations are linked to the absence of land rights in rural areas (Plant, 1993). Peasants are victims of human rights violations especially when they try to reclaim or validate their land rights through actions such as squatting, claiming property or crops, or bringing to public attention cases of administrative mismanagement and corruption, exploitation by landowners, displacement by cash crop plantations and so forth. These actions make them targets of physical and legal harassment, and sometimes imprisonment. Human rights activists, lawyers and other concerned actors can help increase peasants' awareness of their rights and defend them when their rights are violated. Peasants' legal needs are vast, but due to their other pressing needs they may not consider their legal requirements priorities at all times. Nevertheless, if legal assistance is available to peasants during times of land conflict, potential hardship may be avoided.

Land and legal issues are intimately related. For example, activities linked to access to land; its use, possession and ownership; the sharing of its produce/rents; and land transactions and sales must adhere to legal principles if they are to be fair and take place smoothly. These legal principles may be customary or modern, and in reality they have tended to be a mixture of both.

Wide differences exist among countries in legal codes, traditions and social structures. Peasants' legal needs seem to be substantial in most contexts. In the context of land reform, the type of legal assistance sought and expertise available, as well as legal education and training, and the financial and technical inputs required for action, may differ significantly from country to country.

Legal aid is important at all stages of land reform – from identification of land that might be made available, to negotiation, to acquisition. Direct actions by peasants such as land invasion often provoke retaliation from landowners for which marginalized groups need legal support. Legal protection is especially crucial in actions against eviction of tenants or exploitation of agricultural labourers by their employers. Disagreements between the landowners and tenants on rents, taxes and other obligations may result in the landowner taking the case to the police, local administration or court. Tenants and labourers need legal advice and support if their interests are to be effectively defended. Conflicts between landowners and tenants could be prevented or better handled if conscientious lawyers set up locally agreed mechanisms of arbitration or dispute resolution. This might make it unnecessary for poorer peasants to go to higher courts, and result in saving money and time.

One major problem in this context is that peasants are generally unaware of many legal aspects of land issues – in part because land laws tend to be complicated and may change frequently. When peasants are ill-informed about land laws, reform measures, their rights and what they stand to gain from reform, misunderstandings are likely and disputes may occur. Raising peasants' legal awareness is crucial during the land redistribution process and during the post-land-reform period. For example, they must be made aware of their legal obligation to repay loans obtained to purchase land or agricultural inputs. Indebted peasants, who may have used their land as collateral for a loan, must also be made aware of their own legitimate rights and of the possible legal manoeuvres of their adversaries. They must know how to protect their land from unscrupulous land speculators, moneylenders and merchants if they are to preserve any gains obtained through land reform.

In addition to human rights and legal organizations, development NGOs, peasant organizations and other progressive civic associations, the state may also provide legal support to peasants. The state promulgates new land laws and seeks to implement them effectively and judge conflicts, and in doing so it may aim to reflect the interests of marginalized groups. In order to provide legal assistance to the land-aspiring rural poor, the state can mobilize the resources necessary to create new legal institutions, recruit lawyers and paralegals, organize training programmes, disseminate information and promote community-level legal education. In Bangladesh and the Philippines, for example, as discussed below, the effectiveness of legal support services and systems at the local level has depended upon a solid, country-wide legal framework, whether or not the state attached importance to initiating assistance measures and programmes.

Are lawyers reliable allies?

Various social groups and individuals may support peasants' actions if they are perceived to be victims of social injustice. For example, local students may participate in peasants' protest rallies or land-invasion activities. There may be some solidarity from urban and rural trade unions, although the former tend to be distant, and the latter tend to be active where there is favourable political space and agricultural modernization has resulted in a class of agricultural labourers. Farmers' associations and cooperatives may also support peasants' movements when their own interests are directly affected, but many may be controlled by rich farmers and local elites. Political parties may also support peasants' movements on a long-term basis, but in some cases peasants may simply be considered as 'vote banks', or local authorities and landowners may repress peasant movements when the latter seek alliances with underground political parties. Rich or middle-class farmers may form alliances with peasants when they perceive a common interest, such as reduced land taxes or higher crop prices. Their interests are likely to diverge, however, over peasants' demands for greater access to land or tenurial security. Professional groups or individuals, such as development NGOs, teachers, human rights activists, lawyers and extension specialists, may have few interests in common with peasants' groups, although some may be truly concerned about social inequality and improving peasants' welfare.

Lawyers, as an occupational or economic category, are not usually a socially oriented voluntary group (as community development workers, priests or teachers, might be, for example). Most lawyers have few contacts with ordinary peasants and agricultural labourers, who are unlikely to be considered promising clients. It is usually peasants who need lawyers; lawyers seldom need peasants.

Most lawyers provide their advice and assistance on the basis of a negotiated fee, seeking maximum remuneration that peasants would frequently be unable to provide. Peasants may avoid seeking legal advice for this reason. Peasants may also be victims of deceitful lawyers who claim money, labour or produce from peasants but provide little in return. Some lawyers, allies of rich and powerful groups opposed to peasant issues, can be among the worst enemies of peasants when they defend the interests of landlords, moneylenders, merchants and agribusiness. The majority of lawyers in developing countries provide their services and assistance to those groups which are able to compensate them generously. This may not be surprising, as the majority of lawyers tend to come from the elite classes.

But lawyers can be fine allies when they are supportive of peasants' interests and aspirations, or when their own interests coincide with those of peasants. Certain lawyers and legal associations may build rural constituencies to acquire national or foreign recognition of their work or to attract outside funding. Recent graduates from law colleges and universities may find it difficult to find jobs in urban areas and may therefore begin their careers in rural areas. For lawyers who have political ambitions, peasants may be reliable supporters. And lawyers harassed by repressive regimes because of their origins or beliefs may find that alliances with peasants and rural workers aid their own self-protection. Of course, under repressive regimes, lawyers may distance themselves from rebellious peasants and workers for fear of persecution. Unfortunately, this means that legal assistance may not be available for peasants and rural workers when they need it most.

Whether or not peasants and rural workers can count lawyers among their allies depends upon specific socio-economic and political contexts. It is difficult to establish a typology of situations or outcomes. Rural conflicts and the mechanisms for their resolution vary depending on place and time; and the type and quantity of legal aid required also varies. Generalizations about legal needs across countries and poor rural social groups is scarcely helpful if specific policy measures are to be formulated.

Lawyers' ability to assist peasants

Lawyers can play a crucial role in ensuring that peasants receive legal information and that laws granting them specific rights and resources are enforced in their favour. Due to high rates of rural illiteracy and difficulty in accessing information, legal expertise is generally absent in rural areas – especially when it comes to the interpretation and application of modern land laws. Indeed, some specialists have argued that legal activities should not be the exclusive prerogative of lawyers and judges as many public policies, legislation and legal cases directly affect ordinary people and groups. Furthermore, they emphasize that laws should not aim only to defend the interests of the poor or the disadvantaged, but rather to eliminate the structural causes that underlie their condition (Soliman, 1987, pp.46–47).

During the late 1980s, the International Commission of Jurists (ICJ), an international association of independent lawyers, held a series of seminars in South Asia, South-East Asia and Latin America, focusing on the role of lawyers and legal services for the poor in rural areas. These seminars assessed rural legal services and encouraged debate and reflection on the role of lawyers in rural development. The term 'legal services' was preferred to legal aid, as it 'encompasses training of paralegals, the production of simplified legal materials and information dissemination, counselling, mediation and negotiation' (ICJ, 1997, p.15).

All seminars pointed to the poor provision of legal services in rural areas. In Peru and Colombia, for example, government legal services are concentrated in urban areas, making it difficult for the rural poor to access them. A second problem, confronted by indigenous peoples (often a significant proportion of rural populations) who have lost customary lands, was a feeling of alienation as a result of linguistic and cultural differences. This often leads to their marginalization in the few legal aid programmes that do exist (García-Sayan, 1987). The South and South-East Asian seminars brought out the social and geographical distance separating most lawyers from peasant issues, which may lead them to be viewed with suspicion rather than as potential allies in defending local interests. In all regions, however, the importance of having peasant organizations, NGOs, church groups and other local organizations incorporate legal services into their agendas was highlighted.

Many popularly oriented NGOs and local voluntary organizations are getting involved in 'legal literacy' and awareness-raising campaigns, which use simple techniques such as translating laws into local languages, publishing information pamphlets and using theatre and rural radio programmes to disseminate information on land rights and legal assistance to the rural population. For example, the Association of Female Jurists in

Cameroon discusses women's land rights on both radio and television. The Youth Association of the Ziquinchor Region in Senegal translates laws and relevant documents from French into local languages and disseminates this information via seminars and workshops. The Society for Participatory Research in Asia (based in India) transcribes relevant land laws into accessible languages for rural legal activists and leaders. Casa Campesina in Peru holds radio and television discussions on legal aspects of agrarian questions.[3]

Given the high cost of professional legal services, the training and use of paralegals has grown in recent years. For many NGOs this has been a way to avoid costly outside professional help, yet still provide marginalized rural groups with some legal assistance. Paralegals are generally local actors (community leaders, social workers, teachers, law students, development workers, etc.) who receive training and education on legal questions, and act as assistants to lawyers in locating evidence and other information that might be necessary to defend their case. They may also conduct research on certain cases and provide referrals to lawyers where necessary. Furthermore, they often play a wider social role, mediating situations of conflict, mobilizing communities and assisting in the establishment of people's organizations (Ravindran, 1988, p.7). Their role in society can potentially encompass far more than a lawyer's, and because they come from local areas they are often deemed more credible than outsiders. Because they may be more aware of customary law and can thus use it where applicable, their approach may be more flexible.

Lawyers may play a central role in training paralegals, however, as may social workers, academics (sociologists, psychologists, etc.) and others (ICJ, 1997). Paralegals are often hired by local organizations or are requested to assist on a voluntary basis, although the latter appears to be rare.

The fact that pay is less, and rewards in terms of other material and social gains fewer, may dissuade lawyers from providing legal services to the rural poor. Dias, in his discussion of obstacles facing 'law as a resource for the poor' in South-East Asia, points to the desire of lawyers to monopolize information and knowledge on legal matters (Dias, 1987, p.27–42). In other words, they may fear losing their professional hegemony of knowledge about land legislation. According to this specialist, rural communities and individuals require lawyers to impart a degree of information and skills.

However, lawyers do sometimes get involved in local legal service programmes. A noteworthy case is the Legal Resource Foundation (LRF) in Zimbabwe, a non-profit organization whose board of trustees includes a former Chief Justice, a Supreme Court Judge, as well as other prominent lawyers (Coltart, 1993). The foundation's lawyers actively train paralegals, provide legal advice, carry out research, and litigate in public interest cases through Legal Project Centres set up in rural areas. In order to overcome resistance by lawyers who might perceive the group's activities as potential competition, the LRF formulates and implements its programmes in close collaboration with the Law Society of Zimbabwe (Coltart, 1993).

Similarly, the Legal Resources Centre (LRC) is one of eight legal institutions in South Africa helping the urban and rural poor in land restitution cases. It represents poor black communities in land conflicts, contending land claims in protected areas and the provision of formal titles. It also provides legal education and training on subjects including acquisition of land, subsidies for land purchase and loan repayment (LRC, 1995). But demands for legal services are much greater than LRC and other organizations are able to offer (personal communication with a lawyer working for LRC, October 1997); significant conflicts over land-related issues and land reform persist in the country.

In the Philippines, Structural Alternative Legal Assistance for Grassroots (SALAG) was formed as a 'socio-legal action group' aimed at providing an expanded legal assistance programme to the marginalized sectors of Philippine society (Valera et al., 1987, pp.54–56). SALAG works to empower local rural populations to be active participants in the legal process, rather than simple clients dependent on lawyers. The group provides legal assistance and non-formal legal education; networks with other NGOs, people's organizations and government organizations; and organizes an apprenticeship programme to sensitize law students to rural issues (Valera et al., 1987).

Although there are examples of lawyers and legal institutions working to protect peasant rights, to enforce laws that support the claims of the rural poor to land, agricultural extension services or other resources, and prevent the 'appropriation' of law by those with more political, social and economic clout, many such attempts are not wholly effective. The individuals and institutions so inclined usually lack human and financial resources and are thus able to cover only a small number of cases. Some may have promising beginnings but fail as a result of diminishing capacity – although most of the time this is due to factors beyond their control (lack of funding, for example) rather than absence of will. Also, their energies may be diluted through pressures to include activities more solicited by donor agencies. Some of these issues are considered in the following discussion.

COMPARATIVE PERSPECTIVES FROM BANGLADESH AND THE PHILIPPINES

The first part of this section provides a general picture of land reform experiences in the two countries. The importance of legal aid in the context of land reform will be examined, as will the roles of lawyers and legal institutions in promoting the interests of peasants and rural workers. The second part assesses some ongoing land reform processes, and looks in particular at peasants' aspirations for land and the extent to which legal aid has been made available at the local level. This review is based in large part on information collected by the author during field observations, unstructured interviews with peasants and NGO workers, and a review of 'grey' literature.

General overview of agrarian reforms and the importance of legal aid

Bangladesh

The high level of landlessness or near-landlessness and rural social deprivation are quite closely related in Bangladesh. Nearly half of all rural households are considered landless, and out of a total of 14 million agricultural households, 11 million possess no more than 0.05 acres (0.02 ha) (Uddin and Akhter, 1997, p.72). Since the 1950s, the state has formulated land reform laws with a view to providing 'land to the tillers' and improving the living conditions of the rural poor. At the same time, however, national elites have lacked the political commitment required to implement legislation and promote land reform. This is primarily because both state institutions and local power structures have tended to be strongholds of landlords (Mannan, 1990, pp.398–399). Until the beginning of the 1980s, land reform measures were limited to the fixing of a land ceiling at around 33 acres (13.4 ha) per household, and attempts to acquire the excess land for eventual distribution to the landless (Saha, 1997). In a country where landlessness is so widespread and the average land holdings are unusually small, the land ceiling for the landlord has remained remarkably high. Moreover, attempts to appropriate land beyond the ceiling from landlords have been slow and largely ineffective.

Over the years, although some land was redistributed to small peasants (mainly *khas* land – i.e. land under government jurisdiction), rural agricultural cooperatives established, and more advanced technology provided (mostly high-yielding varieties of seed), the wider structural issues of inequalities in landholdings, the large number of landless, and questions of who was actually accessing, controlling and benefiting from new technologies remained unaddressed (IFAD, 1992; Sobhan, 1993; Jannuzi and Peach, 1994).

In 1984, in a populist move by the Ershad regime, a new Land Reforms Ordinance was promulgated. The ordinance set a new land ceiling at 20 acres (8.1 ha) per family, and stipulated that the *baragadar* (sharecropper) had the right to cultivate 5 acres of land. This was to be explicit in a legally binding contract between the landowner and the *baragadar*, thus doing away with the tradition of oral contracts, which proved to be increasingly precarious. The contract set up the terms and conditions of cultivation and was valid for five years, and could be renewed if the conditions were satisfactorily met by the sharecropper (Jannuzi and Peach, 1994; Saha, 1997). Furthermore, the ordinance included a clause giving the sharecropper the option of purchasing the land. It obliged the landowner to give notice of intent to sell, and the sharecropper had a period of 15 days to make an offer. With the provision of rural credit facilities, it was hoped that tenants would be able to secure loans and gain title to land in this way.

This ordinance has remained virtually unimplemented. Clauses guaranteeing security of tenure have been timid in their formulation. On the question of the legally binding contract aimed to guarantee security of tenure for the sharecropper, a significant number of escape clauses can be used by landowners to their own advantage. Those pointing most eloquently to tenurial insecurity state that land can be repossessed if the landowner believes that 'it is not being "personally cultivated" by the *bargadar*'. Furthermore, the owner can 'simply decide to take back the land "for personal cultivation"' (Jannuzi and Peach, 1994, pp.43–44). The vagueness of the terms could lead not only to land repossession, but potentially to eviction of sharecroppers. Land purchase by a sharecropper may also be circumvented by landowners who sell or give land to their relatives (Jannuzi and Peach, 1994).

Unlike rural elites who have easy access to credit (and are also the biggest defaulters on loans, as their social clout often saves them from repaying), the rural poor have extremely limited access to institutional credit facilities (Jannuzi and Peach, 1994; Saha, 1997). They must borrow money from landowners and moneylenders who charge high rates of interest. A cycle of indebtedness and loss of land may ensue, in which the end result may be rising rural unemployment and poverty.

The local power structure is thus stacked against the rural poor in Bangladesh. Landowners pull not only political, social and economic weight, but also legal weight. They know, or are able to hire specialists who know, all possible loopholes in the existing legislation in order to prevent tenants, sharecroppers and poorer farmers from accessing land. And they may not hesitate to use phoney charges, produce false land ownership documents claiming title to land, or exert their influence over the local land administration, lawyers and police.

NGOs and grassroots organizations working to fight rural poverty commonly encounter the power of landlords, and in some cases they help peasants and other marginalized rural groups to file suits against landlords. But due to the lack of effective, low-cost rural legal services, the costs of taking landowners to court are enormous for NGOs, even if the ruling were in favour of the rural poor (ALRD, 1993). The legal system may also be prone to corruption. Even though the law states that tenants and sharecroppers can appeal in writing in cases where wrongdoing has occurred, this is an extremely weak form of legal recourse given the high rates of rural illiteracy, limited financial resources, and the probability of waiting months before any action is taken. Even where recourse is possible, most peasants refrain from using it, given the traditional social authority of landowners and fear of reprisal.

Despite land-related disputes and rural violence arising mainly from the appropriation of *khas* land by local landowners, the government of Bangladesh has done little to set up rural legal services (Jansen, 1990; ALRD, 1993; Westergaard, 1994). In recent years, NGOs and people's organizations have attempted to fill part of this gap. A number of rural organizations include legal issues in their overall activities. The case of Nijera Kori will be discussed in greater detail in the following section, but Bangladesh Legal Aid and Services Trust (BLAST), Gonoshahajjo Sangstha (GSS) and the Association for Land Reform and Development (ALRD) also provide valuable legal assistance to rural populations.

BLAST, one of Bangladesh's largest voluntary legal aid organizations, provides legal assistance for the marginalized population. In 1996, it covered some 11 districts and had two law clinics in Dhaka. It employed 390 lawyers and handled 1037 cases. It also held training courses for lawyers and worked quite closely with other NGOs by providing legal aid and assistance to their beneficiaries and customers (BLAST, 1996, 1997).

The GSS provides legal assistance in disputes arising from violence against women, false charges to intimidate the poor, and the rights of peasants to *khas* land (Westergaard, 1994, p.16). It covers 25 per cent of legal costs, administrative and financial services for members and non-members. GSS also provides legal education involving marriage, divorce and inheritance laws; land disputes concerning hereditary rights are especially numerous in Bangladesh.

The ALRD, an organization concerned with the coordination of NGO activities on land reform, also includes a legal aid programme as part of its activities. The organization recognizes the importance of legal awareness-raising and services in a context where over 80 per cent of rural litigation has to do with land disputes, especially false titles (Rahman, 1995, p.32). But its capacity to handle the legal cases by itself is limited: in October 1997 ALRD had only one legal facilitator (personal observation). Nevertheless, through its contacts with other NGOs and government agencies, it has the ability to mobilize legal assistance when it is critically needed.

Most of the legal aid available in rural Bangladesh has gone to defend cases of repression of women, maltreatment of children, gross violation of human rights, and support to tribal and ethnic minorities. For organizations such as BLAST, GSS and others – including the Bangladesh Human Rights Enforcement Committee, Bangladesh Human Rights Commission, Ain O Shalish Kendra, Coordinating Council of Human Rights of Bangladesh, and Commission for Justice and Peace – land disputes represent a small part of their overall activities and involve 'exceptional cases'. For example, out of the 1037 cases handled by BLAST in 1996, only 25 were land cases (BLAST, 1997, p.18). Furthermore, as most of these organizations are based in Dhaka or in the principal provincial towns, much of the legal aid tends to be limited to urban areas.

In sum, therefore, only meagre legal aid is available to peasants and other marginalized rural groups seeking access to land or better livelihood possibilities. Even when the government of Bangladesh has attempted to impose land ceilings and fairer rent policies, landlords have found legal loopholes that enable them to maintain their holdings, or have done so through patron–client relationships, including alliances with officials, political elites, and even some parts of the peasantry (Khan, 1989, pp.91–128). In this situation, legal assistance is crucial to ensure that *khas* land is distributed to the rural poor, inform local populations of their legal rights and defend peasants in land disputes. Lawyers and paralegals can also help by obtaining land surveys and documents from relevant land administration bodies and mobilizing village support for particular cases (Jansen, 1990, p.233).

The Philippines

Land distribution has been a thorny issue in the Philippines ever since independence in 1946. By the mid-1990s, the country had witnessed 11 agrarian reform programmes, each promising to be more progressive and true to the 'land to the tiller' ideal (SENTRA, 1997). What has been lacking is successful implementation.

In recent years issues of access to land, combined with improvement in livelihood conditions, have gained in importance due to several factors. First, 56 per cent of the population is rural, with half living below the poverty line, and accounting for two-thirds of the country's poor. Second, extremely biased landholding patterns persist – 3.4 per cent of farms are larger than 10 ha each, but control one-third of prime agricultural land, while almost two-thirds of all farms, which cover 30 per cent of total area, are less than 3 ha each (ANGOC, 1997). Traditional landowning families have managed to retain power in the countryside through a network of patron–client relations and political alliances. Third, more than half the total agricultural population in the late 1980s consisted of landless labourers (Riedinger, 1990). Fourth, several large foreign and national corporations occupy the most fertile land, and their position is protected by the liberal free-market policies of the government.

Presidential Decree 27, the land reform programme promulgated under the martial law regime of Ferdinand Marcos in 1973, was limited to land growing rice and maize. However, as this left untouched the export-oriented sector of cash crops, it did nothing to transform power structures in the countryside. The whole issue of landless labourers was also ignored. Other programmes, involving the conversion of sharecropping tenancies to leaseholds, and government acquisition and redistribution of private estate land to peasant beneficiaries, also yielded dismal results. Approximately 5 per cent of the country's cultivable land was redistributed to less than 8 per cent of the total landless population (Riedinger, 1990). Nevertheless, this period witnessed remarkable peasant mobilization, the formation of local rural organizations and widespread protests. Thus when Corazon Aquino came to power in 1986 under a democratic banner, the situation was one of severe agrarian unrest with large discrepancies in landholdings, despite land reform policies. Her administration placed agrarian reform at the centre of the political agenda by launching the Comprehensive Agrarian Reform Programme (CARP).

CARP started out with the goal of redistributing 8.1 million ha of private and public lands among 4–5 million rural households (ANGOC, 1998). It was considered a progressive agrarian reform because it covered all agricultural lands, including large estates and corporate land (via voluntary or compulsory acquisition), and because of its 10–year deadline (which has now been extended to the year 2004 due to financial and administrative setbacks). The Comprehensive Agrarian Law placed ceilings on land holdings, limited holdings to one farm per person, and placed a 5 ha limit on landowners (although each heir is allowed an additional 3 ha) (ANGOC, 1998). Furthermore, policies were put in place to safeguard indigenous lands, provide rural credit and extension services, and organize potential beneficiaries into Agrarian Reform Committees. Also, for the first time, the Department of Agrarian Reform (DAR) was endowed with extra-judicial powers to ensure efficient implementation of the programme and provide secure legal land titles to beneficiaries (Anon., 1997c; SENTRA, 1997; ANGOC, 1998).

CARP's extensive coverage and use of a variety of tenurial arrangements (renting, leaseholdings, communal holdings) seemed, in theory, to be the necessary ingredient for success. But it has been criticized by NGOs and peasant groups for a number of reasons. One main critique is that agrarian reform was used as a campaign tool to gain power, but once elections had been won, dedication to actually implementing the programme waned (Riedinger, 1990). Peasant organizations are also critical of the fact that despite provisions for distribution of private lands, the bulk of lands were taken from government-owned public properties, leaving the holdings of large landowners virtually intact. Out of the 2.6 million ha distributed between 1987 and 1996, only 15 per cent (a mere 640 000 ha) were private agricultural lands (Anon., 1997c, p.2). The fact that 5.7 million ha of agricultural land that could have been included for distribution in CARP were excluded from the very start, and by September 1996, out of the total 2 221 254 ha of private land included in CARP, only 583 413 ha had actually been distributed, speaks for itself and points to the continuing influence of landowners on agrarian policy making (SENTRA, 1997, p.16). The government has side-stepped the fact that it is precisely on these private lands where levels of conflict are most intense, and the stakes are higher for both landowners and tenant farmers.

Complications and setbacks have also been pointed out in the poor provision of extension services and rural credit facilities to the beneficiaries (actual, as well as potential). It appears that, as in other developing countries, the bulk of government funding has gone into paying compensation to landowners (who often claim that what is offered is not sufficient, and use this as grounds to repossess the land). In its plan for the 1999–2004 phase, DAR estimates that most of its funding for Land Acquisition and Distribution will go to paying compensation to landowners (45 754 out of 52 853 million pesos), whereas the total budget for Program Beneficiaries Development is 35 984 million pesos (DAR, 1997a). The government has pointed to the lack of donor support in supplementing its budget (Riedinger, 1990; ANGOC, 1997). It asserts that although international aid agencies pushed for non-conflictual, voluntary-based transfers, they refused to fund any government land acquisition activity due to its 'political' nature (ANGOC, 1997).

Peasants, NGOs and legal aid groups have denounced the continuous harassment of beneficiaries by landowners, who have used legal loopholes and resorted to outright violence, often with the aid of paramilitary forces, to evict tenants. Other miscarriages of justice have involved the issuing of false claims, slowing down or cancelling the issuance of legal land titles, multiple titling of the same plot, and the rapid and sometimes illegal conversions of agricultural lands to industrial or commercial plots (ANGOC, 1997, 1998; Anon., 1997c; DAR, 1997b; SENTRA, 1997). Certificate of Land Ownership Awards (CLOAs) are frequently not handed over to beneficiaries as promised (Anon., 1997c). Land titles may be awarded to people who are not qualified beneficiaries. For example, there have been cases where land titles were apparently given to people who were not residents of the area, as well as to those who were not peasant farmers (Anon., 1997c, p.5).

In other cases, land certificates given to farmers have been annulled by DAR on the grounds that legal errors were made. It is estimated that 67 442 ha affecting some 25 062 farmer beneficiaries have been confiscated in this way (SENTRA, 1997, p.24). Other excuses for land repossession include neglect, or the exemption of land from CARP due to loopholes under Presidential Decree 27. Such misuse of the legal system seems fairly widespread and clearly undermines the steps taken by CARP.

In a country with a tradition of feudal relations, where the power of rich landowners and multinational corporations is entrenched, various means are used to hold on to land. They are fiercely opposed to their land being distributed, give the least productive land to beneficiaries when it is unavoidable, or purchase and 'stockpile' prime land, to push up land prices (SENTRA, 1997). The use of productive agricultural land for speculative urban or industrial recreational projects, with the backing of local governments, is also a problem. Furthermore, the government has been eager to promote export-oriented crops and indeed for the latest phase of CARP (1999–2004) has invited international agribusinesses to invest in peasants' Agrarian Reform Committees, without considering the long-term impacts on local food security, the environment or social relations (DAR, 1997b).

Despite CARP's many problems, however, it has (for the first time) created a space for collaboration between NGOs, people's organizations and government organizations. Civil society groups have used this tripartite relationship to involve themselves actively in agrarian policy dialogues at all levels. A concrete manifestation is the Tripartite Partnership for Agrarian Reform and Rural Development (TriPARRD) launched by the Philippine Partnership for the Development of Human Resources in Rural Areas (PhilDHRRA). TriPARRD began in three provinces in 1989 extending nationwide by the mid-1990s. It comprises 57 people's organizations and 15 NGOs, as well as government agencies involved in agrarian reform – the DAR, the Department of Environment and Natural Resources and the Land Bank of the Philippines (LBP). TriPARRD is mainly concerned with three main areas of CARP: improving land tenure; building and strengthening social infrastructure; and developing productivity systems (PhilDHRRA, 1997). Although a paralegal component is part of TriPARRD's agenda, few concrete measure have yet been implemented.

One major government action in support of peasants' and rural workers' interests has been the creation of courts at the provincial and central levels to adjudicate agrarian reform matters. Decisions of these agrarian courts cannot be challenged in other courts. As such, landlords' ability to bring cases to higher courts (which would be too costly and time-consuming for peasants) is limited. Agrarian courts are also charged with determining 'just compensation to landowners' (DAR, undated, p.40). An official estimate suggests that since 1989, agrarian courts have handled over 500 000 cases (DAR, 1997b, p.6). However, landowners may seek to take peasants to trial in regular courts as opposed to the agrarian judicial bodies, under allegations that they are 'squatters', resisted eviction orders, or did not pay share rent (SENTRA, 1997, p.28–29), because the regular courts are more prone to the influence of landowners and their allies.

All legal needs of peasants associated with land issues cannot be met by the agrarian courts, however. They take a small number of cases involving landowner–tenant disputes related to land distribution; for other land controversies, peasants must seek legal advice from independent lawyers (or other NGO-provided legal services) and follow standard legal procedures in other courts.

Besides the government's agrarian courts, NGOs and peasants' groups also continue to lobby for more active and central roles, providing policy alternatives and suggestions to reduce loopholes. Given the ambitious agenda CARP has set for itself, such groups argue that more measures, including greater involvement of civil society groups, are required to stem the use of illegal land conversions, the cancellation of land certificates, and the appropriation of various laws by landowners to suit their own purposes (Anon., 1997c).

Over the years, a number of NGOs, farmers' groups and legal organizations have provided legal assistance to peasants and rural workers during various conflicts with landowners and employers. SALAG has provided not only legal assistance, but also initiated long-term awareness-building and training programmes on land questions. Similar work is undertaken by the Kaisahan Tungo sa Kaunlaran ng Kanayunan at Repormang Pansakahan (KAISAHAN) and the Legal Resources Centre. Local and provincial groups also provide legal assistance to peasants; one such group is the Malay Mindanao Foundation and Center for Alternative Rural Technology (CART) in Mindanao. Several rural development NGO groups such as SENTRA, the Philippines Peasant Institute, ANGOC and others also provide legal counselling, advice and support.

But organizations with an exclusive mandate to provide legal assistance to the rural landless and poor in relation to land reform are few. Most of the NGOs and other organizations providing legal aid are unable to meet existing demand. As in Bangladesh, they often take the simplest cases requiring limited personnel and financial resources. They are thus eager to take cases involving family disputes, inheritance issues and property claims, which can be handled in local courts. Moreover, these cases do not create direct conflicts with powerful local landowners and elites – which is especially important if local groups and NGOs are to be able to function. National and more determined groups may be able to provide legal assistance in a more defiant manner, although many of them tend to be based in Manila. Some of these aspects will be elaborated below in discussing two local cases in Mindanao.

Case studies

Nijera Kori's work with the Char Bajja and Char Majid communities: cases from Bangladesh

Nijera Kori is one of many non-governmental development organizations in Bangladesh, but its strong participatory approach and activism have given it increasing prominence in recent years. The organization was founded in 1977 to assist famine-affected destitute urban women. Although women remain the focus of Nijera Kori's programme activities, since the 1980s the organization has been working in rural areas to help men and women, landless and marginal farmers, fisherfolk, artisans and small traders. Over the years, it has emphasized the need to change the unequal nature of the rural power structure and resource distribution, arguing that 'the cause of poverty in Bangladesh is not paucity of resources or overpopulation, rather unequal distribution of wealth' (Nijera Kori, 1997a, p.1). It further argues that the unequal distribution of resources has led to 'divisions amongst the people and has exacerbated the problems related to social injustice, dowry, discrimination, oppression of women, exploitation, unjust possession of public resources by power cliques and corruption' (Nijera Kori, 1997b, p.1). It views popular mobilization and consciousness-raising as essential to changing the situation in favour of the rural poor and deprived social groups, including women.

In Bengali, 'Nijera Kori' means 'we do it ourselves'. As such, the organization encourages self-help, autonomy and awareness-building activities, and motivates the rural poor to form collective groups to resist social injustice, as well as seek to improve their livelihoods

The projects of Nijera Kori are spread across the country, with the exception of the north and north-east. In June 1997 they covered 1016 villages (Nijera Kori, 1997b, p.3). By June 1997, 6561 self-help groups were created, bringing together 146 394 core members of whom just over 50 per cent were women (Nijera Kori, 1997b, p.3). Group meetings, training and workshops permit people to exchange views, discuss specific events, devise plans and develop professional and leadership skills. In order to make group members financially self-reliant, or at least make them avoid going to fraudulent moneylenders, it urges people to develop the habit of saving and to contribute to various savings schemes that can make money available during emergencies. Group members are also encouraged to invest in pisciculture, agriculture, livestock-rearing, small cottage industries and small trading. A great number of Nijera Kori's activities, however, concern political mobilization and collective action against social exploitation, repression of women, and access to local resources, especially *khas* land.

Nijera Kori considers title to *khas* land by the landless an integral part of poverty alleviation in rural areas. In theory, *khas* land should be more accessible to the poor than privately held land, especially in view of the government's policy of distributing these areas to the landless. In practice, however, powerful individuals tend to grab any land that becomes available, which provokes conflict. Part of the problem is that it is often difficult to establish whether land is *khas* land or not; also, powerful individuals can enlist the help of officials to produce false ownership documents. Indeed, even in cases where possession is recognized, powerful people can evict the landless with the help of local police and thugs. To discourage the landless, land grabbers have been known to bring false charges (such as theft) against the landless (Kabir, 1994, p.72). This makes it difficult for the landless to have access to *khas* land, especially when they are not sufficiently organized and lack wider support.

Nijera Kori has thus sought to organize the landless and to influence public opinion and government departments, as well as providing legal support to its group members. In 1996–97 it provided legal support to approximately 100 cases, a number of which involved defending its own employees, who were often considered the main foe by landlords and elites. Cases involved access to and formal titling of *khas* land, land dispossession for shrimp cultivation, oppression of women, and sometimes even deaths related to these issues.

Nijera Kori considers its legal aid highly successful. In most cases suits brought against peasants and the rural poor have been unfounded, with encouraging verdicts in favour of the landless. By registering legal suits, the poor are becoming aware of the weak points in the administration and local power structure, and group members are acquiring competence in rural arbitration (Nijera Kori, 1997b, p.16).

Most of the NGOs providing legal assistance in Bangladesh have not been able to cope with the demand, and Nijera Kori is no exception. It does not have a legal division of its own and hiring lawyers is costly, particularly when a case must be tried in higher courts. Landlords and corrupt elites usually try to exploit this situation. Nijera Kori generally approaches broad-minded lawyers to handle the cases, where possible at a moderate rate. This is not always feasible, however, as lawyers are in great demand. The organization also seeks legal help from organizations with greater capacity, but others may be reluctant to accept additional cases as they are usually unable to meet even their own needs for legal aid.

Char Bajja and Char Majid are two 'villages' situated a few kilometres apart at Sundaram Thana in Noakhali district in the Bay of Bengal (Map 6.1). A considerable amount of 'new land' has surfaced in the area in recent decades as a result of a gradual deposition of soil washed down from the Himalayan region. In Bengali, *char* means 'land rising from water'. In theory, all *char* lands are government (*khas*) land. In practice, however, these lands are subject to individual claims. Conflicts over the possession and use of land may therefore arise between poorer households – for example, between those with land titles and those claiming to have possessed earlier titles; old and new settlers; households selected for entitlement and those rejected; households already settled and those buying the land from the proclaimed owner(s). Many such conflicts are resolved locally (at times with the help of NGOs and locally respected individuals) unless powerful landlords or elites incite one group against the other. Conflicts between poorer households and those with economic, political or judicial power tend to be especially complicated. Given that the price of land is attractive and because of its suitability for shrimp farming (because salt and fresh water are available), powerful landlords, local political elites, land speculators and shrimp cultivators have sought control of land in the area. Increased government and foreign funding for shrimp cultivation and its potential as a foreign exchange earner have also swayed local politicians and administrators in favour of powerful groups (Nijera Kori, 1996). Indeed, they may already belong to the same circle of people.

The land question in these two villages (or more appropriately, settlements) depicts this process well. Char Bajja was established in the early 1980s when new land appeared on the banks of Mejna river due to soil deposits and the construction of a dike for flood protection. By 1997 some 200 households, mainly flood victims from the area, had settled there, each with 1 acre (0.4 ha) of land to cultivate. As a result of the growth in shrimp cultivation and related earnings prospects in the late 1980s and early 1990s, powerful landlords, local elites and businessmen also sought possession of

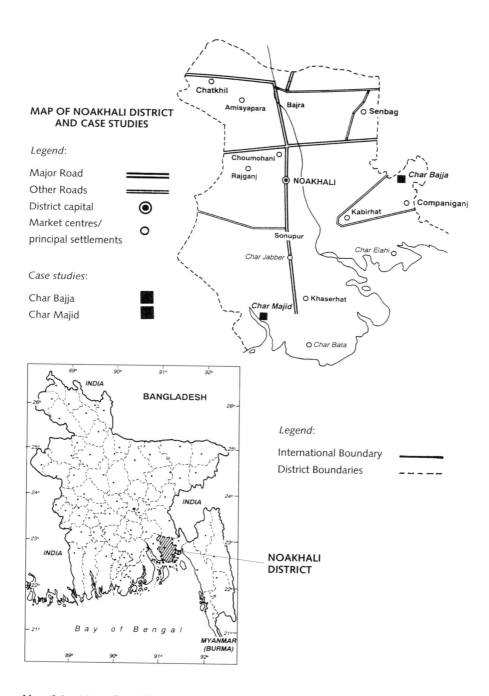

Map 6.1 Map of Noakhali District and case studies

this land, first by producing false land 'ownership' certificates, and subsequently by using legal and then more coercive means. They also attempted to influence government departments in their favour by suggesting that the land in question was not suited for peasant agriculture because of poor quality soil and its high saline content.

In October 1997, when this author visited Char Bajja, all available land was under the cultivation of paddy, sweet potatoes and several types of vegetables. People acknowledged that the land was not very fertile, but with their care, construction of bunds and use of manure, it had become more productive. In 1996, an average of 50 munds (2000 kg) of paddy per acre were produced. Crop production was combined with limited livestock-rearing, fishing and some outside wage employment, especially by young boys. In the settlement, peasants had their own dwelling and thus did not need shelter on their employer's land.

But over the past four years there have been intense conflicts in the area. In the beginning, landlords and their associates threatened the settlers and sought to divide them. Money was offered to potential collaborators. When it became clear that those manoeuvres were not working, harsher means were used. Local administrators were called upon to undertake police assaults, peasants' huts were burned, and crops were destroyed. At the same time, lawsuits were brought against the peasants in the local and high courts. In 1997, three peasants were in jail serving life sentences, convicted in a bogus rape case. Landlords and other elites in Bangladesh have such influence over the judiciary and administrative system (especially at the local level) that abuse of the system is not difficult. Here, they had combined the land dispute case with another (fictional) criminal lawsuit as a way of discouraging peasants.

Without timely legal aid from Nijera Kori, the peasants would probably have been evicted from their land. When the case of rape was brought to local and then high court, and the peasants could not pay for legal assistance, Nijera Kori hired three defence lawyers. Nijera Kori was also able to publicize this case and attract the attention of independent NGOs that provide legal support. One of these, the Dhaka-based Bangladesh counterpart of Amnesty International, dispatched two of its local lawyers to investigate the case. Ironically, and to the great dismay of Nijera Kori and the peasants, these two lawyers recommended that the case be decided in favour of the landlords and local elites, apparently after being offered bribes (personal communication with a Nijera Kori activist). This indicates that many of the lawyers can be bought easily by peasants' adversaries, especially when they lack compassion for the peasants' cause.

Many comparable processes were discernible in the case of the second settlement as well. Char Majid was established in 1982, with 235 households and a total cultivated surface of 560 acres (233 ha). A slightly larger plot per household and higher land productivity explains relatively improved living conditions in this village (larger and more solid houses, higher school attendance, etc.).

The main problem in this settlement was that, despite having settled and cultivated the land for over 15 years, peasants had not received legal title. Instead, the government (for political reasons) distributed land titles to people who had fought for independence from Pakistan in the late 1960s and early 1970s. Some 196 'freedom fighters' were thus given title to the entire area in 1991–92, apparently without the settlers' knowledge. According to the peasants, not all of the people who obtained title were freedom fighters. Moreover, some title-holders were in commerce, or had other professions and had no interest in or previous knowledge of cultivating land. Their main interest was the resale value of the land. And, because of the high demand for land for shrimp cultivation, prices had surged in the area, especially for registered land. This created a strong alliance between the freedom fighters and shrimp cultivators in the area. Moreover, shrimp cultivators were not in favour of peasants' ownership of land, as they were likely to continue to use land for crop production. If it were controlled by the freedom fighters and could be subcontracted or bought, the land use could be changed to shrimp cultivation.

In this settlement there have been repeated conflicts during the harvest season, as freedom fighters use hired men to intimidate the peasants and collect harvested produce. However, due to strong peasant solidarity and generally supportive public opinion in the surrounding villages, people continue to reside in the area and manage to keep the bulk of their crops. The help of NGOs such as Nijera Kori has proved especially important.

Nijera Kori has brought peasants together in self-help groups and co-operatives to resist the control over their land by freedom fighters and improve economic conditions. More importantly, it has maintained contacts with the local administrators involved in the case, as well as with influential freedom fighters, and probably helped avoid direct confrontations between peasants and freedom fighters. During the field visit negotiations were taking place, with Nijera Kori as mediator. One possible compromise was the allotment of 50 per cent of the land to peasant households and 50 per cent to the freedom fighters, but the peasants were totally opposed to handing over their land to people who they deemed 'undeserving'. They also feared that acceptance of this formula would lead to the conversion of additional land to shrimp cultivation. This would make adjacent plots unsuitable for crop production because of potential infiltration of saline polluted water and diseases from shrimp farming. Solutions were far from clear and the tension was high, especially with the paddy-harvest season near.

Carruf and MAPALAD: cases from the Philippines

The Carpio-Rufino Agricultural Corporation (Carruf) and MAPALAD, a multipurpose peasant cooperative for coordination of land acquisition and livelihood improvement, are two of the best-known cases of land conflicts in the Philippines. Both concern the provision of land and land titles to resident tenants and agricultural labourers where this has been fiercely opposed by previous landowners. The latter have repeatedly used professional 'security guards' to intimidate peasants and agricultural labourers. They have sought to exploit all possible legal loopholes and have brought peasant groups to courts on a variety of criminal charges. The Carruf and MAPALAD cases have come to the attention of the regional and national media, government departments and political parties. A number of NGOs working on rural poverty alleviation and land questions have mobilized peasants and provided legal assistance and advice, which have been of crucial importance in MAPALAD in particular.

The Carruf and MAPALAD cases are located in the province of Bukidnon on the island of Mindanao (Map 6.2), near one of the island's principal roads. Although they are quite integrated with nearby market centres and an urban way of living, agricultural activities remain the main source of employment and income in the area. Fertile soil, high rainfall and irrigation possibilities, on the one hand, and abundant rural labour, on the other, have attracted transnationals and agribusiness to the area. Cash crops – sugarcane, pineapple and banana – are produced for export, although rice (the main crop), maize (increasingly used as animal feed) and various legumes are also produced for the market (Municipality of Valencia, 1997). Both tenants and wage labourers work on the large estates, and land conflicts in both Carruf and MAPALAD have grown out of contentions between estate owners and these groups.

Carruf, previously a private cash-crop estate belonging to an affiliate of former President Marcos, is located in Barobo, Valencia. The area is planted mainly with sugarcane and some maize, and part of the estate was also used for cattle ranching. The owner lived in Manila and the estate was operated through farm administrators and resident hired labourers, who maintained dwellings and home gardens on the estate.

In the late 1970s and early 1980s, Valencia was marked by political agitations and actions against plantation owners, rich farmers and local elites cooperating with the regime. The owner of the Carruf abandoned his estate during the unrest, and the estate's labourers immediately took over the land. They agreed upon division of the land, but maintained earlier landuse patterns.

In 1986 DAR placed the estate under compulsory acquisition. Some 148 ha of the property were to be made available for acquisition by 111 landless households, but screening of beneficiaries and preparation of the CLOAs took 10 years (until February 1997). On behalf of the households, DAR negotiated a loan with the Land Bank of the Philippines (LBP) to purchase the land from the owner for 8 million pesos. It also sought to organize the beneficiaries into three production cooperatives, and the implementation of this task was given to a local NGO, Malay Mindanao Foundation and

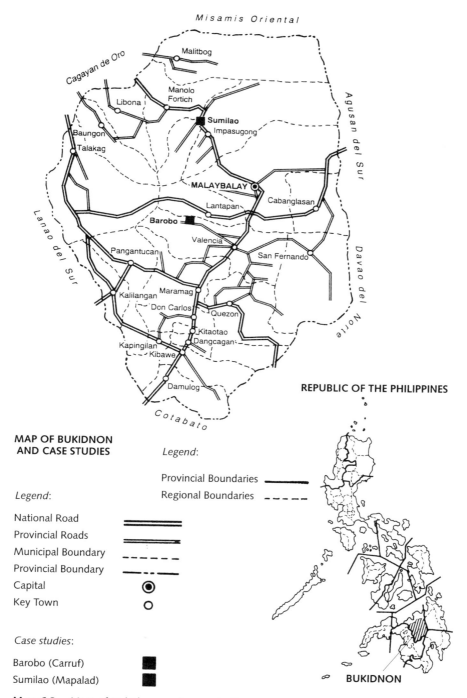

Map 6.2   Map of Bukidnon and case studies

Center for Alternative Rural Technology (CART). The beneficiaries would gain full ownership title in 2007 (after 10 years of provisory entitlement). At the end of 1997, each household paid about 2000 pesos to the LBP towards the mortgage, which extended over 30 years. This represented about 10–15 per cent of their annual produce (personal communication with peasants).

Delays in obtaining ownership documents and constant harassment from a 'security agency' hired by the estate owner to protect his property created an environment of uncertainty for the beneficiaries. There were few incentives to improve the quality of land or crops, and many households sought employment in the local market centres (such as Valencia), or as daily agricultural labourers in the surrounding areas. Such wage employment has been scarce, however.

In recent years land prices have risen sharply in the area, and cattle ranching has become an increasingly profitable use of land. The powerful absentee owner thus attempted to recover possession of land by a variety of means. In the early 1990s two cases were filed before the Department of Agrarian Reform Adjudication Board (DARAB) in Manila and Malaybalay (the provincial capital), claiming that the CARP beneficiaries were 'squatters' and had entered the property unlawfully, and thus that the land certificate given to them should be cancelled (DARAB, 1997). There were also attempts by the landowner to use the local power structure (the mayor of Valencia) in his favour (Anon., 1997a, 18 April 1997). The DARAB decided that the peasants were the rightful owners of the land.

When the legal cases were ruled in favour of the peasants – who were subsequently provided with the ownership certificate – the previous estate owner took a more confrontational attitude. He hired the Tagabagani security agency, comprising 20 armed men to intimidate the peasants. They fired guns at night to frighten the peasants, and enclosed the cultivated fields with barbed wire to prevent the peasants from harvesting their crops. A truck used by peasants for transporting sugarcane and maize was also seized by the security agents (personal communication).

In another act of coercion, a 30 ha plot of sugarcane was burned one night in April 1997. This meant the loss of a year's work for the affected households. Peasants protested this act both in Manila and in the province, with the support of DAR and NGOs such as CART, Kaunlaranng Kanayuan, Balay Mindanao Foundation and Partnership for Agrarian Reform and Rural Development Services. These protests received significant national media coverage. The government was urged to uphold its promise for land reform and provide police protection for the beneficiaries of land reform. The local mayor (who had permitted the private security agents to operate in the area in the first place) was pressed to initiate a dialogue between the two opposing groups (Anon., 1997a, 23 April 1997; Anon., 1997b).

Ultimately, the peasants were again able to cultivate their land. But when this author visited the area in November 1997, the Tagabagani security guards were still intimidating the farmers. In May 1997 President Ramos ordered the investigation of a case of harassment by the agency, but no report was issued until the end of November 1997. Peasants still lived in uncertainty. Fear of eviction from their plots had receded due to widespread publicity and outside support for their cause. But economic hardship was forcing some households to borrow money, and others were making arrangements to sell their plots to moneylenders as soon as title was granted to them (personal communication with a local development worker).

The MAPALAD peasants have endured a similar situation, although the landowner in this case has been even more hostile and has exerted influence over local landholders and elites, as well as government officials in Manila. Tribal origin (and thus unfavourable socio-political standing) and their overwhelming reliance on daily wage employment for survival have made the position of the MAPALAD peasants extremely precarious, but they have been well organized, received extensive public sympathy, and attracted a great deal of support from NGOs, professional organizations, the media and DAR.

MAPALAD was established by peasants after they were offered the possibility of acquiring 144 ha of land in Sumilao, Bukidnon. The land, generally well suited for agriculture and endowed with irrigation facilities, had been leased to Del Monte Philippines by its owner. Before the expiration of the 10–year lease in 1990, DAR included the area in its compulsory acquisition scheme and sought to distribute it to 137 landless agricultural labourers in the area. Most of these workers were employed by the Del Monte estate.

The decision by DAR to expropriate the estate, and subsequent moves by the beneficiaries to begin cultivating their parcels in July 1997, were opposed by the landowner in a variety of ways. The landowner applied to DAR to convert the farm into an agro-industrial zone, suggesting that the scheme would create more employment and improve the municipal economy.

At the same time, the landowner hired 50 armed men from the Tagabagani security agency to protect the property. Agents evicted the peasants, burned peasants' huts, seized farm implements and other belongings, and told peasants that land mines had been placed in the area and that fences around plots were electrified. Other local landowners and former employers of the peasants were urged by the estate owner not to hire workers belonging to the MAPALAD group (Anon., undated, p.2). The landowner also filed a case before the Regional Trial Court in Malaybalay seeking to annul title and to obtain 10 million pesos in damages from the peasants.

The Malaybalay court decided in favour of the landowner, and the peasants were ordered off the land. Moreover, although DAR rejected the estate owner's application to convert the land into an agro-industrial zone, the governor of Bukidnon, the local mayor and large landowners supported the landowner and encouraged him to appeal to President Ramos. The president reversed DAR's decision and approved the landowner's proposal to convert the farm into an agro-industrial zone (Anon., 1998c). The peasants were thus totally helpless.

The regional office of DAR, a few paralegal workers and local NGOs had been assisting the peasants in various ways. A MAPALAD Task Force was formed by the MAPALAD cooperative and several NGOs [Panaghiusa sa Lalawigang Maguuma sa Bukidnon (PALAMBU)–Pambansang Kilusan ng mga Samahang Magsasaka (PAKISAMA); Balay Mindanao Foundation; PhilDHRRA–Mindanao], and youth and religious groups. Some larger agrarian NGOs, such as PAKISAMA, AR Now! and PhilDHRRA, gave the MAPALAD case national exposure. And several newspapers began reporting on the case, especially the violent eviction carried out by the estate owner. Farmers' groups and academic institutions, such as the Philippine Peasant Institute, called on the president to reverse his earlier decision on the MAPALAD and several other similar cases in the country (Anon., 1997a, 8 November 1997; Anon., 1997d; Anon., 1998c; Anon., undated).

The MAPALAD peasants received legal aid and advice from Balay Mindanao Foundation, Sentro para sa Alternatibong Lingap Panlegal and KAISAHAN, who investigated the cooperative's legal standing and possible legal steps to be taken. These lawyers were supported by the Ateneo Law School and the Integrated Bar of the Philippines. The task force created by the NGOs to review the legal arguments of both sides found overwhelming evidence in favour of the MAPALAD peasants, and submitted these findings to the office of the president. No concrete reaction was forthcoming (Anon., undated, p.11).

Peasants sought to convince President Ramos and the Regional Trial Court in Malaybalay to revise their decision by initiating a hunger strike in October 1997. Twelve peasants camped out in front of the DAR central office in Manila, and seven peasants staged a hunger strike in Cagayan de Oro city in Mindanao. This was the first occasion in the country's history that a hunger strike was used to draw attention to the plight of peasants' struggle for land, and it attracted a great deal of radio and television coverage. NGOs and other supporters had helped the peasants prepare psychologically for their hunger strike, and advised them on the selection of the location, visibility of the camp, and consultations with the media and concerned government departments (Anon., 1998c). During the 28–day strike the peasants also received medical check-ups. The hunger strike ended with Ramos's announcement of a compromise solution: 137 peasant households would have the option of purchasing 100 ha, with the remaining 44 ha going to the landowner.

The striking peasants returned to Sumilao to a hero's welcome; their action was expected to encourage other groups to organize and mobilize in the face of similar problems elsewhere in the country (Anon., 1997a, 7 November 1997). Although the president's decision appeared to have been accepted by both parties, the peasants were not able to take possession of their property until the beginning of 1998.[4] The proposed compensation of

6 million pesos, rejected by the landowner, was still the object of negotiations, however (Anon., 1998c). Furthermore, the preparation of land parcels, issuance of new land certificates, and guarantee of loans from the LBP still had to be completed before peasants could settle on and begin cultivating their plots. Most of the peasants had used their limited savings during the mobilization and protest; preparing the land and ensuring family subsistence before the first harvest was realized (personal communication with peasants). The DAR regional office and NGOs that had supported the peasants during the land entitlement process did not have the resources to provide further assistance to peasants during the post-entitlement period.

CONCLUSION

Outside alliances and support are crucial to peasants and other marginalized rural groups during the land reform process. Political mobilization, leadership development, organization of land acquisition actions and protests, networking, and influencing the media, political parties and government land policies are important, but are often beyond the means of peasants without the assistance of more informed, resourceful outsiders. External assistance is frequently handy in the identification of land for redistribution, selection of beneficiaries, acquisition of titles, prevention of eviction of tenants by landowners, improvement in wages for agricultural labourers, and negotiation with landowners or government departments. External support is similarly critical in resolving land conflicts among the rural poor themselves, as well as across tenurial classes, and in ensuring that the beneficiaries of land reform have access to essential agricultural inputs and support services. In short, the benefits of external alliance and support are enormous.

In practice, however, landless peasants and other marginalized rural groups can seldom count on the support of external forces. The landless rely mainly on traditional authorities, religious leaders and elders. A supportive teacher, extension worker or village counsellor can often provide tremendous backing for the peasants' cause, as they tend to have a better knowledge of the functioning of the government bureaucracy and, perhaps, land legislation.

The cases from Bangladesh and the Philippines show that legal aid has been critical to the struggle of landless peasants for land. In these two countries, even though legal assistance did not enable the peasants to break the power of landowners, it did help to restrain the latter in some cases. Despite the fact that landowning classes were sometimes able to manipulate the legal system to their advantage and were able to pay top price for legal advice, they could not completely ignore the interests of their tenants, the local landless peasants, or public opinion. Legal proceedings often went together with complex negotiations with the landless, their representatives or opposing lawyers.

Copious land reform legislation exists in both countries; the problem lies in its effective implementation. Lawyers have an important role to play in this regard as well, especially in advocating the interests of the near-landless, tenants, agricultural labourers and other marginalized land-seeking rural groups. With their knowledge of national and international legislation and legal covenants, lawyers can work to advocate and sustain an independent judiciary, monitor government policies, signal human rights violations, and ensure that land reform legislation is implemented. But it is rare that marginalized groups can retain the services of lawyers, as they are costly and are based mainly in urban areas. Furthermore, even among lawyers willing to work for peasants, very few would be fully sensitive to the peasants' cause.

Despite recognition of the usefulness of legal services, provision at the official level has been insufficient in both countries. In the Philippines, the DARAB has protected the interests of a significant number of tenants and landless peasants seeking access to land. This experience is unique, and could provide useful lessons for other developing countries promoting land reform. This also demonstrates that state capacity to defend the interests of the landless through regulatory institutions and processes is necessary – despite calls by international funding institutions to curtail state involvement in agricultural and economic planning. Demands on agrarian courts are overwhelming even though they deal exclusively with disputes over land acquisition. Of course, the case studies also revealed the tactics of some landlords, who may concoct 'diversionary' cases (such as damage to property, acts of violence or theft) so that cases will be tried in criminal courts over which peasants have little influence. Because of a prolonged history of land disputes in the Philippines, a number of Filipino NGOs have given considerable attention to the agrarian question, especially since the fall of the Marcos regime. However, the legal component has tended to remain weak in their overall activities, and demands for legal assistance can scarcely be covered. In Mindanao, for example, NGOs have been able to accept approximately one case out of every 10 (personal communication with a CART paralegal activist).

In Bangladesh, the government's recent land reform measures have been limited mainly to the distribution of *khas* land to the landless. The government has thus avoided the political risks involved in radical land reform (reduction in the land ceiling, progressive land taxation, greater provision of credit and other institutional production support services to the poorer farmers). The government has also managed to evade direct conflicts with the powerful landed classes, and the influence of the latter over the local administrative and judiciary machinery remains staggering. As a result, even redistribution of *khas* land has been far from smooth. The government of Bangladesh has made no specific provision for agrarian courts that would protect the interests of the landless. Furthermore, few NGOs working in rural areas focus on land reform, and even fewer provide legal services relating to tenurial disputes. Indeed, there is not a single rural development organization in the country with a specific mandate to provide legal assistance to the peasant and landless populations. Nevertheless, the activities of those which have integrated legal assistance into their programme, such as Nijera Kori, have been highly effective.

Ideally, for land reform measures to be more successful, landless groups and peasant organizations should have their own lawyers. Alternatively, a cadre of motivated lawyers should be available to pursue the peasants' cause. Clearly, more lawyers would not automatically mean that more legal aid would be available to the land-aspiring rural poor, but a legal curriculum more sensitive to agrarian problems, land laws and rural poverty could help increase future lawyers' awareness of land disputes and perhaps increase their support of land reform measures. Raising the awareness of school teachers, agricultural extension workers, NGO activists and so forth about land laws and reform initiatives could produce a valuable local pool of paralegals, as these actors constantly interact with the landless and marginalized rural population. Efforts to raise rural people's consciousness through literacy classes, community training programmes and legal education could also yield results.

Cases in both countries indicated that social mobilization by NGOs, peasants' organizations and professional organizations has been more decisive than the supply of legal aid *per se*. Naturally, this would not have happened if the local populations were not active as well. But it does reveal that social actions surrounding land questions are more effective when the process of mobilizing and empowering the rural poor, as well as the wider public, is combined with the provision of concrete legal tools and support.

CHAPTER SEVEN

Peasant Mobilization for Land Reform: Historical Case Studies and Theoretical Considerations[1]

Gerrit Huizer

Peasant protest against land alienation has a long tradition. As various authors (Huizer, 1967; Landsberger, 1969; Wolf, 1969) have shown, movements of peasants to defend, conserve or recover their ancestral land and livelihood have proliferated during this century as a reaction to aggressively advancing large-scale modes of production. However, during the past few decades not much progress has been made by such movements due to the resilience of commercial landed interests and the state in their support. Rural development literature has not paid much attention of late to the difficulties peasants face in this context.

Having studied and worked with peasants and their small or large-scale organizations for many years (Huizer, 1967, 1972, 1980, 1991), I have the impression that a considerable misunderstanding about peasants' human, political or even revolutionary potential prevails. Despite empirical evidence to the contrary, many policy-makers and scholars (mainstream as well as Marxist) consider materially poor peasants to be passive, apathetic and fatalistic or, on the other hand, spontaneously or almost irrationally rebellious when their life becomes unbearable. Rarely is attention or appreciation shown toward the rational and pragmatic approaches of relatively powerless and submitting (apparently submissive) peasants and women to the often irrationally brutal ways that those with power (landlords, merchants, moneylenders, party cadres, development bureaucrats) try to control and maintain peasant behaviour – generally strongly supported by army and police – in an exploited state. This is well documented by the late Ernest Feder (1971). Despite this disadvantage – or perhaps because of it – peasants and their movements have been able to bring about drastic or even massive revolutionary social and political changes in a number of cases in the past.

As regards the present, Korten (1995, pp.293–294) sees a hopeful trend towards 'an awakened civil society' in the Zapatista rebellion in Chiapas, Mexico as 'the first revolution of the twenty-first century'. This Zapatista Army of National Liberation came dramatically to the foreground on 1 January 1994, the day that the North American Free Trade Agreement (NAFTA) officially came into effect. A number of small towns in Chiapas were occupied by indigenous peasant rebel forces to demonstrate that they would no longer tolerate brutality and land usurpation by local landlords and politicians, made possible in part by the recent changes in agrarian legislation and Article 27 of the Mexican Constitution which formerly protected communal land possession but now, as part of the NAFTA agreement, favoured large-scale privatization. Many cases had been reported of violent dislodging of peasants and assassination of their leaders, but the situation only worsened. Armed resistance – more symbolic than real, but well propagandized on the Internet – appeared the only way to get some kind of attention and justice. The rebel action had been prepared carefully and had a cultural component, strongly rooted in the Maya indigenous spirituality with an ecological and earth conservationist component. Will it inspire other, similar social movements?

There is a need for a careful assessment of the effectiveness of past peasants' movements for land reform. The relationship between social mobilization and land reform has been an issue for discussion (and some experimentation) in UN circles, including some specialized agencies, since the 1950s. This culminated in the organization of the World Land Reform Conference in 1966. The conference recognized that mobilization of peasant communities was an important element in national development. A main question related to the increasing interest of the UN in popular participation in agrarian reforms during the 1960s was: why do social movements emerge and become large scale and effective in some places and not in others? An even more pragmatic and important question was: how exactly do they emerge, and what can be done to stimulate or support them?

In order to answer these questions, the most spectacular and effective movements that took place in different parts of the world will be described and analysed in a more-or-less chronological order, from the early experiences of Mexico, Russia, China, Japan (and Taiwan), Bolivia, Cuba and Indonesia, to the recent one in Zimbabwe. Cases where effective reforms did not come about, such as the Philippines, Brazil and India, will also be dealt with. After presenting the relevant case studies on these movements, generalizing strategic and theoretical considerations will be given on the kind of dynamic processes involved in their emergence and growth, and in their success or failure.

MOBILIZATION IN MEXICO

One of the first and most important peasants' movements for land reform was the rebellion headed by Emiliano Zapata between 1910 and 1919 in the Mexican state of Morelos. During the last decades of the nineteenth and the early twentieth century, the aggressive expansion of sugar plantations (haciendas) disowned many traditional peasant communities from their life-support system (the communal *ejido* lands). This process provoked a reaction which, after several years of collectively organized struggle, achieved a recovery of lands by the *ejidos*. The struggle began as a collaboration between village committees (from Zapata's village and others) for the legal recovery of lands that had been usurped. Legal action for recovery had been tried in vain (most judges were landlords themselves), and land was recovered when peasants from those villages took down the fences that had been put up illegally by the haciendas. Landlords and (para)military reacted violently to this land 'invasion', causing the struggle to escalate and spread more widely. Weapons were taken from the nearby hacienda, Chinameca. After one month the group had grown to about 1000 men. The leaders of the movement, supported by a local schoolteacher and priest, drafted a land reform plan, which was signed in Villa de Ayala in 1911.

This *Plan de Ayala* proclaimed that the people should take immediate possession of the lands they had illegally been deprived of, and for which they still could show title. Those with difficulty in proving their title could receive lands from the expropriation, after previous indemnification of the landlords, of one-third of the hacienda lands. Small properties were respected by the Zapatistas. In addition to the distribution of land, a credit programme was initiated for the peasants in 1915 and 1916. To appease the peasant armies that had sprung up in various parts of Mexico, certain elements of the *Plan de Ayala* regarding the restitution of communal lands (*ejidos*) to peasants were included in Article 27 of the 1917 Mexican Constitution in a Constituent Assembly at Aguascalientes.

The movement began to suffer setbacks after 1917 because of the severe measures taken by government troops. Whole villages were eliminated in order to cut off support for the movement. Zapata was treacherously assassinated by an infiltrator, an army officer, on 10 April 1919. His prestige among the peasants was so strong that some continued to believe that he was still alive. He has been called the 'apostle of the peasants' or the 'Christ of the Americas'.

During the following two decades the legal provisions for land reform were implemented only in those areas where peasants created militant organizations on their own behalf – mostly despite considerable oppression – in the states of Vera Cruz, Michoacan and Yucatan. By the mid-1930s the government of the reformist general Lazaro Cardenas was relying heavily on peasants' organizations for defence against military coups staged by conservative forces opposed to his moderate, but firmly reform-oriented, policies. During his government (1934–40), almost 18 million ha of land (many irrigated) were distributed among 770 000 peasants. Because of often violent opposition to the distribution, peasant organizations were strengthened by the government, which provided them with weapons for self-defence.

It should be noted that during the Cardenas years there was not only a mobilization of popular support, but new forms of popular participation were institutionalized. Peasants' organizations and labour unions were brought together in the Confederacíon Nacional Campesina (the National

Peasant Federation) and the Confederacíon de Trabajadores de Mexico (the Mexican Workers' Federation), respectively, both of which were integrated into the official national political party and which, under different names, remain in power until today.

The period of intense land reform ended in 1940, and the spirit of mobilization gradually disappeared thereafter. Political power soon came under the influence of those sectors of the middle class that were not interested in pursuing the vigorous programme of social change and reform. The official peasants' organization put up only verbal opposition to this trend. Various observers have noted that discontent and unrest among the peasantry increased, and that many peasants turned to unofficial channels and organizations. In 1958 an independent peasants' organization led by the socialist leader Jacinto Lopez, the Unión General de Obreros y Campesinos de México (UGOCM), gained sufficient strength to stage massive demonstrations and symbolic land occupations, particularly those possessed by large landholders in circumvention of the law. This occurred mainly in the Pacific-northern states of Mexico, where the government had encouraged the cultivation of cash crops on relatively large commercial farms on newly irrigated lands. These were the same lands claimed by the landless peasants under the land reform legislation. But the reform process has stagnated and general unrest, at times leading to acute turmoil, has continued in Mexico to this day, as illustrated by the Zapatista movement in Chiapas.

MOBILIZATION IN RUSSIA

In the transformation of Tsarist Russia into the Union of Socialist Soviet Republics, peasant mobilization played a decisive role. At the time of the 1917 revolution the peasantry formed about 80 per cent of the population, and although the most spectacular aspects of the revolution occurred in the cities and were brought about by intellectuals, workers and soldiers, the revolution was only consolidated into a new regime after the peasantry had joined in a massive way.

Peasants in Russia lived under appalling (semi-)feudal conditions until their 'emancipation' in 1861 under a system in which they had to pay, over the course of a number of years, for their liberation and a plot of land. After 'emancipation' the peasants became subject to the demands of the village commune, the *mir*. Though viewed as a 'kind of collective superego' with 'a truly religious aura' (Wolf, 1969, p.62), the *mir* showed considerable internal tension, a minority of better-off peasants often dominating the rest, as well as most of the land. Thus during the last decades of the nineteenth century a group of wealthy farmers was able to grow considerably at the cost of the old nobility and the poor peasantry. This trend created new rural contrasts and conflicts, as most peasants continued to cherish egalitarian communal ownership.

One consequence of the dissatisfaction among the mass of poor peasants was the emergence in 1905 of the Peasants' Union. Because peasants believed they had a natural right to the land, a radical agrarian reform programme based on land expropriation was proposed. Peasants' assemblies in the villages spread, and this idea was increasingly discussed. Many peasants from backward areas had worked at times as migrant workers in more developed areas, or in the mines, and they brought new and sometimes revolutionary ideas back to their villages. The unpopular war between Russia and Japan in the Far East added to the dissatisfaction. A general peasant rising embracing 300 districts of 47 provinces took place at the end of 1905. Over 1000 manorial houses were ravaged, and in many places tax payments were withheld (Owen, 1937, p.20). The movement was crushed early in 1906 after concessions had deprived it of some of its impetus. One major concession was participation in the legislative process by representatives of the people, including the peasants. It was hoped that the peasants' views on property rights would be changed by means of the individualization of property through the dissolution of the communal villages via Land Settlement Commissions. Minister Stolypin's legislation of 1906–11 formed the framework for this approach.

The various stages of legislation enacted by Stolypin represented an effort to strengthen the government by supporting the wealthier farmers, or 'betting on the strong' as the expression went (Owen, 1937, p.49). The peasants who cultivated small plots on communal lands could become proprietors of these plots through the new laws. Farmers who cultivated larger plots could become owners of theirs. As a result of this process, a certain amount of protection of the weak that had resulted from communal cultivation and from common grazing lands was lost. Four million people left their villages to look elsewhere for work. Better-off farmers were able to survive this change and benefit from it, but for the majority of small peasants, securing a livelihood became more difficult. This increasing insecurity and dissatisfaction found expression in the acute unrest of March–October 1917. Furthermore, in many areas there was not enough land outside the estates to supply plots sufficiently large to sustain individual peasant families. This is a main reason why most peasants, particularly the peasant-soldiers who returned from the war, supported the 1917 Revolution.

After the fall of the Tsar in February 1917, local (village and cantonal) committees took over local power and staged or tolerated seizures of estate land, often by violent means. In some areas actions were undertaken against farmers who had separated from the communal villages according to the Stolypin laws. Peasants' assemblies, also called 'agrarian soviets', and their executive committees began taking control over most of rural Russia. In March 1917, in some areas, the cantonal committees were mainly composed of local intellectuals, but within a month they were exclusively of peasant membership. In many areas seizures of estates and, at times, of smaller private plots, continued, sometimes led by the cantonal land committees. Elsewhere, small landowners and efficiently cultivated estates were not touched. In general, the initiatives of local peasant committees could not be limited by any authority except the villagers themselves, who became increasingly radical and violent. Soon cantonal committees were in control of virtually all of rural Russia. Assemblies and conferences were held frequently to decide on local policies and to consider candidates for the Constituent Assembly or the Second All-Russian Congress of Soviets of Workers', Soldiers' and Peasants' Delegates. At this congress in November 1917, Lenin proposed the Land Decree and obtained the massive support of the peasantry for his government (Reed, 1977). This was a decisive occurrence in the Russian Revolution. The Land Decree confirmed what was already effective in many areas of the country: private property of the estates was abolished. Land could no longer be sold, bought, leased or otherwise alienated; it would be distributed according to local needs among those who desired to work it with their own hands. This would be done by local committees, the soviets of peasants' delegates, who would effectively control land use. This legislation rallied the peasantry behind the communist government during the crucial years of the Civil War (1917–21) and foreign intervention. Although it was adapted to the needs of national economic policy several times, the Land Decree of November 1917 formed the base of the agrarian policy of the USSR in the first years after the Revolution.

After a decade, collectivization of agriculture became problematic because agricultural production by rich (*kulak*) and middle peasants did not keep pace with the exigencies of the rapid industrial growth that took place. Relatively low prices paid by the state for grain were an important reason, and agricultural exports (to pay for imports of machinery) declined precisely when the new Five-Year Plan required an increase. The Communist Party Congress thus decided that small-scale agriculture had to be replaced by large-scale, mechanized agriculture (Ladejinsky, 1977, p.27).

All agriculture was collectivized in support of extremely rapid industrialization. And under Stalin, popular participation was not only abolished but effectively destroyed, at the cost of many lives. Although there was considerable resistance, highly oppressive measures prevented any kind of social mobilization of the peasants.

MOBILIZATION IN CHINA

During the 1920s, about half of the Chinese peasantry were landless or semi-landless. Peasant exploitation had become blatant because of corruption and regional power struggles between the so-called warlords. Peasants' movements emerged that would result in outright revolution. This resistance started in the south near Canton (now Guandong) in the areas where the anti-imperialist Taiping Rebellion (1850–65) had originated.

Nationalist sentiment played a role in these efforts from the outset, and the movement spread to other provinces of China.

Thus considerable rural unrest and local social movements were encountered by Mao Ze Dong when he returned to his province of origin, Hunan, after his efforts to rally the Shanghai working class for a communist revolutionary movement had been ruthlessly crushed by the Kuomintang Government in 1926. Mao's 'Report on an investigation of the peasant movements in Hunan' (Mao, 1971) shows the strength of the movements, and also the surprise of its author in finding peasants organizing on their own behalf when, according to his theoretical Marxist conception, the urban proletariat should be the class to take such an initiative. Learning by trial and error from and with local people, Mao Ze Dong followed the age-old folk tradition of (mostly Taoist-inspired) people's rebellions in Hunan when he helped the peasants and their secret societies to become better organized. Thus the Red Army was gradually created. One of the great feats of more than 20 years of struggle by the Chinese peasant guerrilla armies was the Long March in 1934–35, in which the communist army escaped total annihilation by the overwhelmingly superior armies of Chiang Kai-Chek by withdrawing to isolated areas of Yenan (now Yunan) province. Here the numerically weakened but spiritually and morally strengthened communist army could establish a base and distribute land to the tillers, which served as a base for the conquest of all China in the late 1940s.

The peasants' mobilization, in order to be successful, had to use a sophisticated strategy of alliances between different classes of peasants and other parties. In order for mobilization to be effective, it was necessary to study, in each local grassroots situation, the composition of the prevailing (class) contradictions and to distinguish between those which were fundamental and those of secondary importance. Mobilization could often be achieved along the lines of the most fundamental contradiction, for example, against the 'enemy' provoking the most widespread or acute opposition. This could be the local gentry (rich farmers), or the middle farmers or foreign interests. But the poorest members of society and their interests were always the basic point of reference in a stratification. Mao was also aware that if the rebellion was to become a true revolution, he had to ensure the participation of women (Stacey, 1979).

The social movements of the Chinese peasants increasingly became a militant political organization, not merely struggling for concrete benefits and abandonment of unjust practices, but with the objective of gaining state power to achieve those goals for the country as a whole. Thus a social movement that had resisted state power for over two decades took up state power itself, and became able to bring about the reforms that the peasants and women had been agitating for. The most important effects were the land redistribution policies giving all tillers access to land, and later, in the mobilization initiated from above, movement toward the gradual formation of cooperatives and collectives in rural areas to support rapid industrialization.

However, as industrialization became the main target of the communist government, after 1958 the people were victims of disastrous experiments, such as the Great Leap Forward, and famine. Because of the increasingly absolutist rule of the Communist Party and internal policy struggles, the Chinese population suffered intensely and many lives were lost, as described by Stiefel and Wolfe (1994, pp.117–118). But despite these ups and downs, industrial growth averaged a spectacular 10 per cent yearly in China between 1950 and 1980 (World Bank, 1983), and living standards of the population also gradually improved.

MOBILIZATION IN JAPAN

The Chinese revolution also indirectly influenced rural and industrial development in a few neighbouring countries. Wolf Ladejinsky, key adviser to the US occupation forces in Japan, stated in 1951 how General MacArthur 'stole communist thunder in Japan with democratic land reforms, our most potent weapon for peace' (Ladejinsky, 1977, p.151). In Japan, the First World War had also brought about changes in the rural areas that were mainly favourable to the landlords. Land prices rose and landowners had new opportunities for profitable speculation, while many small farmers lost their lands through indebtedness. Absentee landlordism increased and tenant farmers were forced to pay higher rents in kind. Because of this trend, some tenants had insufficient rice for survival. The result was the last and largest spontaneous peasant revolt, the Rice Riots of 1918, which spread to more than 30 prefectures and lasted 42 days.

After the First World War, industrial crisis led to the dismissal of many workers. When they returned to their already overcrowded villages, rural unrest grew. Tension increased rapidly as the backward conditions in which tenants generally lived were more acutely felt by those who returned. The organizing experience they had gained in industry was soon applied to bargaining for better conditions. The first formally organized tenant unions grew up in the areas around the new industrial centres, particularly Nagoya.

The need for an organization at the national and prefectural levels was increasingly felt but did not materialize until 1922. A group of intellectuals, journalists, a missionary and a labour leader took the initiative in creating the Japanese Peasant Union (*Nihon Nomin Kumiai*, abbreviated *Nichinō*). By 1926 the *Nichinō* claimed a dues-paying membership of about 68 000 peasants. Its main aim was to reduce rents, but it also had political aims such as legislation to protect the tenants, as well as the rather vague objective of 'socialization of the land'. After universal suffrage was introduced in

Japan in 1925, and the number of voters rose from 3 million to 14 million, *Nichinō* became politically more influential.

In the campaign to spread the movement, those tenant unions (*burakus*) were chosen where the most severe and acute problems existed. Very large landowners were helped by police repression of tenant organizations; smaller landowners used their traditional paternalistic control to pressure tenants against joining a union. Kin relationships, favours and threats to force people to pay their debts were used to pressure the tenants.

As peasant unions spread throughout the country and became better organized, their demands changed. Initially, demands were mostly for postponement or reduction of rent payments when harvests were bad, or other emergencies. Later, demands for a permanent rent reduction of 30 per cent were increasingly heard. Landlords often tried to evict peasants when they started to organize unions. The fact that more and more disputes, rather than being solved through negotiation, were brought to the courts generally ruled in favour of the landlords and made the peasants' organizations more aware of the need for political action at the national level. The (leftist) Workers' and Peasants' Party, on the whole supported by the *Nichinō* (both undergoing parallel splits and mergers), won considerable influence during the 1928 elections to the Diet.

In September 1931 an explosion engineered by the Armed Forces near Mukden in China was used as a pretext for the occupation of Manchuria. This action considerably increased the authoritarian tendency of the Japanese government and the influence of the armed forces, and marked the beginning of a period of serious repression. It is striking that despite all the repressive measures, the number of disputes continued to increase.

After the defeat of the Japanese army in 1945, the peasants' movement was still alive, although many of its leaders had spent years in jail, and it was quickly reactivated and pressed for land tenure reforms similar to those tried out in some areas in China. The Supreme Commander for the Allied Powers pressured the post-war Japanese government to abolish feudal-type relations in the countryside and avoid the risk of peasant rebellion. Between 1946 and 1949, almost all land property in excess of 1 ha of irrigated paddy was redistributed among the tillers, mainly through purchase and resale. Organized peasants played a crucial role in this process, together with the rich farmers and landlords, whose tight grip on rural social life, however, was broken.

MOBILIZATION IN THE PHILIPPINES

At the beginning of the twentieth century, commercial agriculture, introduced under US colonial rule, caused a serious deterioration of the conditions for peasants in the Philippines. An increasing amount of land was dedicated to commercial crops, particularly sugar and tobacco, which could be exported to the USA with considerable tax facilities. Land owner-ship became increasingly concentrated as a result. In addition, a more business-oriented approach was introduced on the new plantations, modi-fying the patronal relations that had existed on the traditional estates. Absentee landlords became increasingly common. The paternalism that had helped to maintain some appearance of benevolence in the old system disappeared, and landlords became hated strangers (Jacoby, 1961, pp.199–201). Average tenancy rates rose from 38 to 60 per cent between 1903 and 1946.

An additional source of frustration for the peasantry was 'land-grabbing', by which large owners claimed adjacent smallholdings, and won their case in the courts because of their influence and ability to pay lawyers. Thus thousands of once independent and self-sufficient farmers were reduced to the status of tenants and landless farm labourers (Jacoby, 1961, p.201). Several local and more-or-less spontaneous peasant uprisings took place in protest.

Already in 1919, a sharecroppers' union had been created by a commun-ist leader, Jacinto Manahan, which became known in 1924 as the National Union of Peasants in the Philippines (Katipunan Pambansa ng mga Mag-bubukid sa Pilipinas, KPMP). Although this organization was later forbid-den, it maintained strong roots among the peasants.

In 1930, a socialist party leader, lawyer and wealthy landlord in Pampanga, Pedro Abad Santos, created the League of the Poor Labourers (Aguman Ding Maldong Talapagobra, AMT), which became strong in the Pampanga area by organizing strikes and protest demonstrations. One of the important collaborators helping Abad Santos to spread his movement was Luis Taruc, the son of a peasant, who had acquired some education. Such (often voluntary) collaborators went to live in the villages, where they organized meetings and explained the purpose of the organization.

The peasant organizations generally used non-violent methods, such as demonstrations and sit-down strikes. If there were any arrests they went together as a group into jail. Dramatic stage presentations and similar cul-tural activities were used to teach the peasants about the labour struggle, and to turn the strikes into public manifestations. By 1938, 70 000 members participated in the AMT. This socialist peasant organization had good chances to develop during the 1930s while the communist KPMP was offi-cially prohibited. Landlords organized armed groups, such as the 'soldiers for peace', to oppose and clash with the socialists, which led to consider-able violence in the rural areas of Central Luzon. When the socialists were also prohibited from holding meetings, the organizers used any kind of gathering, such as Protestant religious meetings, to make propaganda for the peasant cause.

In 1939, shortly before the Communist and Socialist parties merged, the AMT joined with the stronger and better organized KPMP. As a re-action to the Japanese occupation, on 29 March 1942 the united peasants' organizations created the People's Army against the Japanese, or Hukbalahap (Hubko ng Bayan Laban sa Hapon). The aims of the Huk movement were expressed in a manifesto emphasizing opposition against and expulsion of the Japanese, cooperation with the Allied armies, apprehension and punishment of traitors and collaborators with the Japanese, complete independence for the Philippines, and the establishment of a democratic government with land reform, national industrialization and guarantees for a minimum standard of living (Salmon, 1968, p.12).

Beginning in 1942, the peasant organization accepted the use of military means, with many peasants carrying arms for the first time and forming squadrons of approximately 100 men each. Thus the armed struggle against the Japanese was initiated. The armed units operated in the areas around the homes of their members. Support for the units was organized in the villages through the Barrio United Defense Corps (BUDC), in order to guarantee a supply of food and other necessities. BUDC councils created in the villages where the resistance movement spread brought forms of democratic decision-making to the villages which had traditionally been dominated by the *caciques*. The BUDC councils formed the local government in the areas controlled by the guerrilla forces. This system functioned particularly well in the areas where the peasant organizations had gained strength before the war.

The Huk movement rallied many people and became so strong that it controlled whole areas of Central Luzon, which the Japanese could not enter. In those areas, *de facto* political control and local government were in the hands of the resistance forces, which had their base in the peasantry. The lands of many landlords who collaborated with the Japanese and lived in the towns were taken over by the Huks in the areas they controlled, and harvests were no longer handed over. Landlords who supported the Huk movement were allowed to remain on their land, but had to accept a fixed rent. Although the efforts of the Huks considerably facilitated the American army's liberation of the Philippines from the Japanese, relations between the Huks and the Americans were never good. It was feared that the Huks would radically change the social order in the Philippines if they had the opportunity to do so.

A few months before he died in 1948, the American-supported president, Roxas, outlawed the Huk organization. His successor, Quirino, attempted to negotiate an amnesty inasmuch as Roxas's policy of armed repression had failed. Reconciliation was attempted with the minimum demands presented by the Huks mainly peasants' demands. They were: (i) division of estates and resale to tenants with government assistance; (ii) migration from overcrowded to less crowded areas; (iii) laws establishing fair sharing of the crop by landlords and tenants; (iv) curbs on usury; and (v) a minimum wage scale. A 70–30 Rice Share Tenancy Act in favour of the peasants was soon promulgated, but implementation was very defective, and no truce between the government and the Huks actually resulted.

Magsaysay's 1953 presidential campaign and the reforms that were promised, particularly land distribution, also helped to appease the peasants. The possibility of a peaceful solution to agrarian and other problems appeared to emerge. Divisions of opinion between Taruc and the more doctrinal leaders over this and other issues came into the open. Taruc surrendered in 1954, under a pledge of amnesty by President Magsaysay, although the pledge was not kept. Taruc was jailed for many years. The peasants took up a wait-and-see attitude, and the Huks had to withdraw due to decreasing support among the peasants and increasing effectiveness of the army. Between 1952 and 1954, several institutions and programmes were created to deal with the peasant problem in various ways, as an alternative to the violent struggle in which the peasants had become involved.

One programme was the Philippine Rural Reconstruction Movement, a private community development agency, sponsored by Dr Y.C. James Yen of the Joint Sino-American Commission on Rural Reconstruction, which had been active in Mainland China before 1949 and later carried out rural development activities in Taiwan. Another effort to neutralize radical peasant mobilization was the creation of the Federation of Free Farmers (FFF) in 1953 by a group of Catholic laymen, headed by Jeremias Montemayor, a lawyer and lecturer at the Institute of Social Order in Manila. Montemayor became member of the committee created by President Macapagal to draft the 1963 Agricultural Land Reform Code, but he later recognized that this law was too elastic and left much to be desired.

Because of the resistance in influential circles to even moderate land reform, the FFF gradually became more openly radical. At times it organized public demonstrations in which a great number of individual cases were brought together and given wide publicity. At such events, student sympathizers played an important role. A whole series of individual cases was resolved after a spectacular demonstration was staged in Manila in September–November 1969. The demonstration consisted of a marathon picket of almost two months in a park (the Agripina Circle) in front of the Bureau of Lands, and sometimes extended into the lobby of the building itself.

The assassination of several local FFF leaders also had a radicalizing influence. However, this did not stop other, more radical peasants' organizations from emerging, until President Marcos declared martial law in 1972. Many organizations were banned and went underground to join the outlawed Communist Party of the Philippines and its armed wing, the New People's Army (NPA). This organization, led by José Maria Sison, waged an armed guerrilla struggle along Maoist lines. During the 1980s, NPA had about 3000 fighters and a considerable base in the wider population. However, internal divisions due to policy changes in China have weakened the NPA's influence (Karunan, 1992).

Land reforms promulgated under Marcos in the 1980s were directed mainly toward 'betting on the strong', including multinational agribusiness corporations. The World Bank-supported agrarian reform programme of the Aquino government, which came to power on a wave of protest in 1986, was also disappointing. But peasants continued to organize, in the Kilusang Magnubukid ng Philipinas (KMP, National Peasant Movement in the Philippines), and under the leadership of Jaime Tadeo became increasingly vocal in favour of more radical land reform (Karunan, 1992, pp.88ff).

MOBILIZATION IN BOLIVIA

Up to 1952, the agrarian structure of Bolivia was similar to Mexico's before the Mexican Revolution, but the exploitation of the Quechua- or Aymara-speaking peasants (a majority of the country's population) by the small, white, Spanish-speaking land-owning aristocracy, allied with the 'tin barons', was perhaps even more intense. Indian serfs (*colonos*) who lived on haciendas had the right to farm small subsistence plots (*sayañas*) for their own use, in return for which they had the obligation to provide free labour to the hacienda owner three or four days a week, either on the hacienda itself or at the owner's town residence.

Scattered peasants' revolts have occurred in Bolivia for centuries as a reaction to the abuses of the prevailing system of servitude. The Chaco War between Bolivia and Paraguay (1933–35), related to a conflict over oil concessions between Standard Oil and Royal Dutch Shell, fuelled such rebellion because it exacerbated the disintegration of the traditional system as thousands of Indian soldiers left the haciendas for the first time and entered into contact with the outside world. Bolivia's defeat left many frustrations and much political bitterness.

In the aftermath of the war, peasant unrest increased in many areas of Bolivia. In 1936 a rural syndicate was formed in Ucureña, in the temperate, fertile Cochabamba valley, one of the country's most prosperous agricultural regions. In this area, the Santa Clara monastery was leasing some of its land to local large landholders, and the lease included the right to the services of the resident peasants. The latter organized a union in order to rent the land from the monastery themselves, and thus avoid the onerous labour obligations that were imposed on them. Their efforts encountered strong opposition from various local landowners, who saw in the peasants' initiative a direct threat to their customary rule. These landowners thus bought the land from the monastery and evicted the peasant families who had been living and working there for years, destroying their homes and forcing them to leave the area or to revert to serfdom. A young, radical peasants' leader, José Rojas, whose father had been dispossessed in this fashion, had to escape to Argentina where he worked as a labourer and acquired a political education. He returned secretly to Bolivia a few years later and revived the peasant movement in Ucureña, becoming its undisputed leader.

In the meantime, the urban middle class became increasingly dissatisfied with the traditional oligarchical control based on landed and mining interests. They initiated a number of political movements which culminated in a revolution under the leadership of Paz Estenssoro's MNR (National Revolutionary Movement) with the widespread support of the urban and mining proletariat and the organized peasants. On 9 April 1952 the army and other defenders of the conservative government who had tried to prevent the electoral victory of the MNR were defeated by a short, bloody revolutionary movement, directed by the MNR in La Paz and other towns.

In the power vacuum created in rural areas by the disappearance of forces that traditionally supported the landowners, new power relations took shape. Peasants' syndicates were organized all over Bolivia, virtually taking over local government functions. New leaders were elected in massive peasant concentrations or community meetings. The newly formed Ministry of Peasant Affairs and leaders of the MNR directed this drive. One of the strongest centres of organization of this movement was Ucureña, in Cochabamba, where the movement grew rapidly when rumours circulated that conservative forces were trying to regain control. Many haciendas were invaded and buildings burned down. The movement pressured the government to take radical land reform measures. On 2 August 1953, the Bolivian agrarian reform was officially launched by presidential decree in a public ceremony in Ucureña, attended by thousands of peasants. One of the main functions of the peasants' syndicates, belonging to newly formed federations in all departments and united at the national level in the National Confederation of Peasant Workers of Bolivia, was to petition for land for their members under the new land reform programme. An armed peasant militia was created to support the government and the peasants against counter-revolutionary violence. Many landlords fled their estates, and the *de facto* distribution of hacienda lands by the organized peasants often took place well in advance of the slower legal proceedings.

After the mid-1950s, the rate of implementation of land reforms declined. Benefits for the peasantry were largely neutralized because land property was mostly privatized, and the market remained under control of rural elites. The reforms, however, were effective enough to prevent the peasantry from joining a 'focus' of revolutionary guerrillas created by Ernesto Guevara in Bolivia in the mid-1960s. The official national peasants' federation institutionalized by the government in 1952 continued to have a certain political impact, partly through the Ministry of Peasant Affairs (see Stiefel and Wolfe, 1994).

MOBILIZATION IN CUBA

In Cuba the peasants' struggle against large estates and corporations goes back to the colonial epoch. Peasants began mobilizing after the introduction of railways around 1830. This had made the cultivation of sugarcane profitable, and as a result the owners of sugar estates began to extend their lands aggressively at the cost of the small tobacco producing farms, and through eviction of peasants and usurpation of the plots they cultivated.

Peasant resistance was initially sporadic and isolated, but when armed struggle for independence flared up in 1868, the peasants joined the movement. This rebellion was repressed, but many peasants in the Mambi army participated in the revolution of 1895 against the Spanish regime, in which 400 000 Cubans and 80 000 Spaniards lost their lives (Wolf, 1969, p.254). Peasants were 'concentrated' in closed villages by the colonial regime in order to counter their guerrilla tactics, and as a reaction to this form of eviction the peasants joined the liberation struggle in ever greater numbers. When the fighting ended, due to American intervention, the Americans took more and more power in Cuba, replacing the colonial forces. Instead of institutionalizing the armed forces of the liberation as a national army, as proposed by the Cubans, the Americans created the *Guardia Rural* (rural guards), members of which were not identified with the peasantry. With the support of the *Guardia Rural*, peasants were evicted from communal lands and small private plots in order to create plantations for American companies or individuals. Thus sugar production and cattle rearing became the dominant activity in Cuba (Wolf, 1969, p.255).

Between 1910 and 1920 the peasant struggle in Cuba was influenced by the growing urban labour movement and by socialist and communist ideas. But it was not until large estates began expanding rapidly between 1915 and 1925, mainly in Oriente province and Camagüey, that the peasant struggle became more effective and increasingly radical. Thousands of peasants were evicted and pushed into the mountains, or forced to work as labourers on estates or in sugar factories often owned by foreign companies.

In 1928 the peasants mobilized to retrieve lands or prevent usurpation by the United Fruit Company, which received help from the *Guardia Rural* in several places along the north coast of Oriente province. By 1933–34 the peasants became more formally organized. One outstanding leader, a veteran of the 1895 revolution, was Lino Alvarez. Particularly at the beginning, his strategy was to try all legal means possible to defend the peasants' lands. More radical leaders denounced his 'excessive legalism', but his approach provided time to organize the peasants effectively and mobilize them into big demonstrations when it became clear that the legalistic approach was failing dismally.

In 1939, the Peasant Federation of Oriente was created at a peasant congress. The struggle everywhere for concrete and moderate goals encountered rigid negative reaction from landowners and companies, leading the peasants to realize that those forces were practically their class enemies. As a result of this awareness, the small local groupings saw the need to become more strongly and rationally organized and to give a more radical content to their demands. Thus a more-or-less organized struggle gradually emerged. At the Second National Peasants' Congress in Havana in 1941, in which over 800 peasant delegates participated, the Asociación Nacional Campesina (National Peasant Association) was created.

The need for fundamental changes in rural social structures such as broad agrarian reform, rather than small gains, was increasingly felt by the peasants' associations. During the 1940s government promises about land reform were made, and some weak steps in that direction were taken. Efforts to neutralize the increasingly radical peasant movement and the increasing demands for structural change were also made through the creation of an alternative organization, the Confederación Campesina de Cuba (Peasant Confederation of Cuba), led by persons related to the government.

After the military coup d'état that brought Batista to power in 1952, the peasant struggle became more outspoken again as a reaction to the increasing demands of large landowners and companies. The Asociación Nacional Campesina organized many meetings, and pro-land reform committees were created in most sugar producing areas. An attack on the Moncada barracks by young revolutionaries headed by Fidel Castro on 26 July 1953 had a considerable impact on the militancy of the peasants and workers. The sugar strike of 1955, which paralysed over 100 sugar mills, was an expression of the trend towards radicalization. The confrontation between peasants' associations and the King Ranch (from Texas) when it usurped lands for livestock rearing in Adelaide, Camagüey province in 1954; and the Francisco Sugar Company, which seized land in 1958, provide other examples. After peasants were imprisoned when they tried to prevent these companies from taking their lands, women took over the efforts to halt the bulldozers destroying their houses and crops. Similar activities were taking place in Oriente province. When the small group of revolutionaries headed by Fidel Castro started a guerrilla struggle in Oriente province after landing with the *Granma* to stage an aborted uprising in December 1956, they found the peasantry ready for insurrectionary action. Traditional resistance against the violence of large landowners and companies had radicalized the peasants to such an extent that they were prepared to support or even join the guerrilla forces. The trade unions of sugar workers and the Communist Party were initially hesitant to support the rebellion in the *Sierra* (Wolf, 1969, pp.268–273), but once successful, joined or even supported them, together with anti-American elements of the middle classes.

Repressive actions of the Batista regime, as it tried to concentrate the rebellious peasants in areas where they could give no support to the guerrillas, further radicalized peasant resistance. The careful way in which the guerrilla forces approached peasants in the areas they dominated, along with the reform measures they encouraged, received immediate support from the local peasants' associations. Particularly Law No. 3 of the Rebel Forces, promulgated on 10 October 1958, and giving up to 26 ha of land to its cultivators free of charge, helped to mobilize the peasantry behind the revolutionary forces and ensure their victory on 1 January 1959.

Soon after the revolutionary regime came to power, a land reform law was promulgated (17 May 1959) which prohibited the possession of land beyond 30 *caballerias* (about 390 ha). More than 100 000 tenants, sharecroppers and other precarious cultivators thus became proprietors of their plots without any obligation to pay for the land. The large estates (many of which were foreign-owned) were expropriated and transformed into co-operatives or state farms.

MOBILIZATION IN BRAZIL

As in Cuba, after the few indigenous communities had been extinguished, the best lands in the coastal belt of the Brazilian north-east were occupied in the colonial period by rapidly expanding sugar plantations (*engenhos*) producing for the world market. The dryer inland areas were occupied by large cattle ranches. When the traditional sugar estates could no longer compete effectively on the world market, many workers were dismissed. Modern sugar factories (*usinas*), often built with foreign capital, were introduced and the government took measures to protect the sugar industry.

Many peasants' movements emerged in the heavily populated areas in Brazil's north-east. Ligas Camponesas (Peasant Leagues), organized in 1955 by peasants on the Galileia sugar estate, formed an association to raise money to purchase from the landlord the estate on which they worked. A socialist lawyer and charismatic leader, Francisco Juliao, sympathized with the peasants and defended them in the courts. Soon the idea emerged to extend this local initiative to the state of Pernambuco, then all of north-east Brazil. As the movement gained strength and became more radical in reaction to the landlords' opposition, competing unions were established by the Catholic Church to counterbalance the influence of the leagues. Soon also these other groups became increasingly convinced of the need for radical reform. A programme of *concientizaçao*, which aimed through literacy to assist the peasants to express their needs, introduced by Paolo Freire, supported this. During the early 1960s, the left-of-centre Goulart government began promulgating agrarian reform legislation that could have largely satisfied peasant demands. Probably as a reaction to the growing strength of the overall reform movement, in which the peasant leagues and some church-sponsored unions participated, the army staged a coup d'état in April 1964. Under the military government, the peasants' leagues and other groups were ruthlessly oppressed. The grassroots movement, originally sponsored by the Catholic Church to compete with the leagues, soon allied with them after it also faced the intransigence of the landlords. This later became known as the 'theology of liberation'.

In the hope that some redistribution of land would take away the motive for peasant mobilization, the military did legislate land reform in 1964: the *Estatuto de Terra*. This land reform did not affect the underused land of large estates; it was designed to encourage resettlement on virgin land in Rondônia, in Amazonia. At the same time, in the south, commercial agriculture (*soja*) was stimulated on large estates.

In 1979, as a reaction to this modernization and commercialization in the southern states, many small-scale peasants who had been dislodged or had lost their tenancy began the 'landless movement' through which they sought to defend their land or occupy what they were entitled to. This took place in isolated cases all over Brazil (Mançano, 1996, p.66). The peasants were often supported by the Comisao Pastoral de Terra, created by the Catholic Church to deal with the increasing injustice. The movement continued to gain strength and created, in 1984, the Movimiento dos Trabalhadores Sem Terra (MST), which had its first National Congress, with 500 participants, in 1985 (Fatheuer, 1997, p.73). The movement intensified its increasingly militant and, at times, confrontational policy of occupying lands, thus achieving *de facto* land reform in many different local situations. Wide publicity regarding invasions of mostly underused land gained considerable support among the peasantry. By the early 1990s about 2000 peasants had been killed in massacres during land occupations, but 140 000 peasant families obtained land through these activities since the 1980s (Grzybowski, 1994).

The intensified use of violence by the landlords was related to the rapidly increasing concentration of land in a few hands, which occurred not only in the south, but particularly in Amazonia where several *latifundia* of over one million ha were created (Mançano, 1996, p.39). As a reaction to the aggressive occupation of huge tracts of land in the latter by foreign companies (such as Volkswagen) and commercial farmer settlers, the local population, seeing its life-support system threatened, gradually began to mobilize. Encroachments were resisted with some measure of success by rubber-tappers (*seringueros*), who had traditionally lived and worked sustainably in Amazonia. The rubber-tappers' movement gained worldwide recognition after the assassination of its leader, Chico Mendes, in 1988. By that time the movement had created a national organization and was receiving considerable support from environmental and other NGOs to defend peasants' rights and set up sustainable projects going beyond land reform as such.

MOBILIZATION IN INDONESIA

One of the most spectacular peasants' mobilizations in Asia was the Indonesian Peasant Front (Barisan Tani Indonesia, BTI), created and directed by the Indonesian Communist Party (PKI) after Aidit became its

Secretary-General in 1953. The need to organize peasants was emphasized, taking as a point of departure their most strongly felt demands and grievances. It was suggested that local organizations be created around such demands. Party cadres were instructed to identify the most acute problems in each particular area or community. Activists had to 'live together, eat together and work together' with the peasants. They also helped solve all kinds of practical day-to-day problems, such as rent payment, legalization of titles, etc. Such 'small but successful' actions were seen by the PKI and BTI cadres as the best way to be accepted by and to mobilize the peasantry (Hindley, 1964, p.16).

Strong, new, local leadership was needed to rally the people against traditional elites, in order to mobilize them to oppose the deteriorating land tenure situation. Identification with the fate of poor peasants was the initial step in gaining their adherence and admiration. Loyalty to charismatic and particularly able or courageous leaders brought together the Javanese peasants in their struggle for improvement and change. Such leaders also took on the 'fatherly' role traditionally played by landlords and wealthy farmers among the peasants in their village. Once traditional patronage was undermined and new leaders enjoyed enough prestige, it was possible to compete successfully with old leaders in elections for *lurahs* (village heads) and even higher positions in local government. In several areas, particularly in Central Java, BTI and PKI leaders were gradually taking over official positions from the established local elite.

At the end of 1953 BTI counted several hundred thousand members, and claimed 8.5 million members in September 1964. The growing strength of the communist and communist-oriented mass organizations provoked a strong response from the armed forces. A PKI Party Congress planned for 1959 was initially forbidden by the army but was later allowed, thanks to support from President Sukarno. However, the scheduled elections of 1959, which could have given the Communist Party a majority in parliament or made it the most influential party, were not held. Instead, presidential rule or 'guided democracy' was initiated, and President Sukarno tried to keep a balance between the army, the Communist Party and other forces, checking one force with the other.

The bargaining position of the BTI as a mass organization was, however, strong enough to take up the land reform issue successfully at the national level, and to obtain the promulgation of a land reform law in 1960. According to this law, landowners who had more than the official ceiling of 5 ha of irrigated paddy land had to make the surplus available for redistribution to the landless. Implementation of the law was, however, very slow.

In order to speed up the reform programme, in 1963 Aidit endorsed a 'unilateral action movement' (*Gerakan Aksi Sefihak*) of the peasants. The tactic most frequently used was occupation of the lands to which landless peasants were entitled under the law. In August 1964 President Sukarno more-or-less endorsed the movement, and during the second half of 1964 drastic steps were taken to accelerate the stagnant land reform programme.

A ferociously violent reaction came, however, in October 1965. After an abortive coup, allegedly by leftist officers, a military regime came to power. Sectors of the army, together with the youth of the mainly Islamic rural elites, assassinated more than half a million peasants and peasant leaders, as well as other communists or alleged communists. After this massacre the BTI was virtually non-existent, and land reform stagnated.

MOBILIZATION IN ZIMBABWE

In 1890, the 'Pioneer Column' headed by L.S. Jameson (of Cecil Rhodes's British South Africa Company, BSAC) occupied Mashonaland. The Pioneer Column did not encounter resistance. The Shona people may have expected the whites to offer protection from possible Ndebele raids – it did not occur to them that the whites would steal their land, which was considered sacred, protected by the spirits of their ancestors, and held in trust by elders and allotted to those needing it. Once the Shona realized that the whites had come to stay, taking more land, 'an uprising was inevitable, and in this the spirit-mediums, the link between the dead and the living, were to play a vital role' (Martin and Johnson, 1981, p.45). The spirit mediums of Chaminuka, Nehanda and other supra-tribal founding ancestors had a particularly strong influence on the rebellion.

Various efforts have been made to explain the relatively strong impact of the Shona uprising as compared with rebellions elsewhere in Africa. Ranger (1967, pp.352–354) ascribes it to charismatic leadership and religious enthusiasm, combined with a utilitarian and disciplined approach. Thus European goods were not looted, but were promptly delivered to the spiritual leaders. There is also evidence of millenarian elements in the movement, based on prophetic warnings against the seductions of the white man's way of life and goods. Although the millenarian and supra-tribal impact of the movement are debatable, its strength was obvious, as it took the BSAC's two armed columns, entering from Beira and Bulawayo, more than a year (to December 1897) to gain control – and this happened only after the two most important spirit mediums had been captured. In the rebellion, 400 whites were killed, about 10 per cent of the settler population at that time (Martin and Johnson, 1981, p.49). After the 1896–97 rebellion was put down, relative peace seems to have prevailed between the white minority and the great majority of black people, though more and more land was occupied by the whites.

After the Second World War, the white population doubled to about 150 000, and more Africans were expelled from their lands. There was rising discontent among the Africans, as many had served in the war yet on their return were again treated as second-class citizens. Trade union activity, which had been almost impossible previously, emerged in 1945 and in 1948 resulted in a general strike. In 1951 the Native Land Husbandry Act forced rural families to reduce their cattle herds and change land tenure practices. This contributed to radicalization, which was further enhanced by the fact that in the early 1960s many African countries gained independence. But whites in Rhodesia resisted pressures from Great Britain to give the Africans a greater share in the government and, under the leadership of Ian Smith, declared themselves unilaterally independent from Britain.

Following the example of FRELIMO, the Mozambican liberation movement, the Zimbabwe African Nationalist Liberation Army (ZANLA) began a guerrilla war in Zimbabwe in 1972. The important role of the traditional spirit mediums was soon acknowledged by both the nationalist organizations and the Rhodesian government. Some of the ZANLA leaders, most of whom were Marxists, were initially circumspect about the powers of the Nehanda and other spirit mediums. Tungamirai, one of ZANLA's top leaders, was among them. His scepticism arose from his Catholic background and his political education, but he later changed his mind when he became closely acquainted with the spirit mediums.

The Zimbabwe African National Union (ZANU) forces used the Maoist model of a liberation war, in which combatants sought the support of the local population through political education, as well as mobilizing and defending them, extending the 'liberated zones' (Lan, 1983, p.11), but avoiding possible confrontation with the technically superior military forces of the state. In order to gain real acceptance among the peasants, the guerrillas could not rely on – and in fact had to replace – the traditional chiefs. The latter had lost much of their authority because they had been integrated into the colonialist system of indirect rule. Here the spirit mediums were to play an important role, their influence being so important that it was officially recognized and honoured by the newly elected Prime Minister, Robert Mugabe, at the independence celebrations in 1980.

Recovery of much of the ancestral land by the peasantry, however was postponed by the Lancaster House Agreement, which was signed by the liberation forces and the colonial government before independence became official. Although land reform was recognized as a key reason for social mobilization, the agreement stipulated (under international pressure) that a radical redistribution would not take place during the decade following 1980. Recently within the ruling party, Zimbabwe African National Union/Popular Front (ZANUPF), pressure has been building up to finally return much of the land to its original African inhabitants. After years of waiting, a first spectacular return of peasants to 'the land of their grandparents', organized by ex-guerrillas on white farms in the fertile Marondera area, was reported in *The Economist* (Anon., 1998d) as a sign of growing 'peasants' revolt'.

MOBILIZATION IN INDIA

In India, social mobilization of peasants for agrarian reform was also an integral part of the nationalist liberation movement from the beginning. As Sen (1982, p.28) described, Congress-leader Gandhi was crucial in mobilizing tenants against *zamindari* land tenure and tax systems imposed by the colonial government. Working from his Bihta ashram, Swami Sahajanand Saraswati – a Brahmin and disciple of Gandhi – took a leading role in the creation of a central organization, the All-India Kisan Sabha (AIKS) in 1936. One of its demands was the abolition of the *zamindari* system of feudal landownership. The Congress Party's national leadership was not in favour of this trend because the party championed landlords and rich farmers. Socialists and communists had an increasingly strong influence in the AIKS (Sen, 1982, p.73) while few Congress leaders were part of it. Intellectuals, including Swami Sahajanand Saraswati and N.G. Ranga (many with a Marxist orientation), held leadership positions in the AIKS. The AIKS formed peasant cadres who, in turn, mobilized at the local level. In 1938 AIKS had 500 000 members. A ban on the Communist Party and jailing many of its leaders brought a setback, but after the ban was lifted in 1942 the organization quickly recovered (Sen, 1982, p.77).

As a reaction to the 1943 famine in Bengal in which many peasants died, the *tebhaga* movement emerged against landlords. The movement demanded that two-thirds of the crop be remitted to the cultivator, as recommended but not implemented by the 1940 Land Revenue Commission. The *tebhaga* struggle was supported by the Bengal Kisan Sabha which organized massive demonstrations in 1946. Because of the strong influence of communist leaders in the movement, the Congress Party leadership responded with severe police repression. This caused the collapse of the movement but radicalized the peasantry even more, indirectly strengthening the Communist Party in Bengal. This laid the base in West Bengal for the coming to power through regular elections in 1967 of a United Front government, dominated by the Communists, which later carried out moderate but more or less effective land reform in that state. A similar transition had already occurred in 1957, through an elected United Front government in the state of Kerala.

The AIKS also had a considerable impact in the Telengana region in Andhra Pradesh. In the colonial period this state was ruled by Nizam and Muslim elites. The feudal conditions prevailing in the rural areas came under pressure in the 1940s when a class of rich peasants emerged and supported the nationalist cause. When the Nizam declared independence for Hyderabad in 1947, the Congress joined the radical agrarian struggle against the Muslim feudal elite. In the areas where the communist-oriented AIKS had gained peasant support, the Muslim elites mobilized a paramilitary force that killed or jailed thousands of peasant militants (Sundarayya, 1979, pp.545ff).

The peasants' mobilization achieved a short-lived land redistribution (of over a million acres), and local village committees abolished feudal servitude. In 1948, however, the Indian army moved in to 'pacify' the Telengana area and integrate the state into the Indian union. This action, as well as internal divisions over the strategy to follow – insurrectionary armed struggle, as in China, or parliamentary politics – brought an end to this movement in 1951 (Karunan, 1992, pp.42–44).

During the 1960s Maoist-oriented Communists came to the foreground in India. The growing contradictions between rich and poor in the rural areas led them to initiate rebellions among peasants and tribal communities under the guidance of their ideologue, Charu Mazumdar, in Naxalbari (Darjeeling district) and Srikakulam. These 'Naxalite' rebellions remained rather isolated, and when they became increasingly violent they were isolated by army and police intervention (Sen, 1982, pp.212ff; Karunan, 1992, pp.47ff). One effect of years of agitation in different parts of India was some measure of tenancy reform, mainly in the areas where peasants' organizations had been active in the late 1940s. However, these reform efforts remained relatively localized or were not systematically implemented. With ups and downs, rural unrest remained endemic in most of India despite, or partly as an unforeseen result of, top-down rural development efforts.

To appease the peasantry other, less radical rural development strategies were designed in India in the early 1950s. A community development programme was initiated in 1952 with support from the Ford Foundation and the Indo-American Technical Cooperation Fund. This approach was soon adopted on a large scale, and in a few years became a nationwide programme widely propagated to meet the communist challenge (Bowles, 1954, p.2). As part of this strategy, community development and agricultural extension workers generally accepted that 'communicating' new ideas via established leaders in the villages would automatically benefit the whole community. Information about improved technology, such as better seeds or fertilizers, was given to the more advanced farmers, the 'opinion leaders', who were prepared to adopt new practices. The expectation was that the other farmers would eventually follow their example. This approach completely ignored the uneven distribution of land and other resources in rural areas. It strengthened the economic position of those who were already better off, widening the contrast between poor and rich at the village level. This community development strategy in fact sharpened the contradictions and the potential for social conflict in the villages. This rich–poor polarization was accelerated by the green revolution. Although food production increased considerably, growing contradictions between rich and poor led to social discrepancies, tenant displacement and increasing landlessness, enhancing unrest in many rural areas. The Ministry of Home Affairs (1969) reported that considerable and alarmingly violent 'agrarian unrest' had emerged precisely in those areas where the green revolution had been successful.

Jannuzi (1994, p.140) pointed out that the shattering of Congress Party dominance in the 1967 elections showed that formerly submissive peasants were beginning to act on their own behalf, contrary to the expectations of the landholding elite. He further observed that land reform for India as a whole has been a lost opportunity, but that for electoral reasons and because of growing tensions and contradictions the future governments of India will have to deal with it: 'Early in the twenty-first century, if not sooner, any remaining proponents of agrarian reform and land reform may finally have their day, and meaningful steps may be taken to resolve India's persistent dilemma in its agrarian sector' (Jannuzi, 1994, p.215).

CONDITIONS FOR THE ORGANIZATION OF PEASANTS

Generalizing from the case studies above, one could say that extreme frustration has caused peasants to take the risk of mobilizing or joining a peasants' organization. The areas where important regional or nationwide movements began were not necessarily the poorest and most marginalized agricultural areas, but those where 'modernization' or 'development' had created growing discrepancies. This was true of the sugar plantation area in Morelos where the Zapata movement began, and of the Department of Cochabamba, one of the richest agricultural areas of Bolivia. Hunan province in China and the areas relatively close to cities in Central Luzon, Japan and Java in Indonesia had similar problems. Another shared characteristic of these areas is that they were not isolated – most had easy access to urban centres – and that, with increasing absentee landownership, rigid traditional, feudal relations were modified. The case-study areas were also more densely populated. More recently, while rapid urbanization, entailing migration of the rural poor to city slums where their chances of survival are supposedly better, may have relieved some acute landlessness, movements often emerged in areas with relatively good communications with urban centres, such as mines and industrial centres (e.g. the Zapata, the Bolivian, and the Chinese and Japanese movements).

In most areas the erosion of the status quo, generally through economic development, caused the peasants to organize. A change for the worse in living conditions often incited them to defend what little they did have. This occurred, for instance, in the area where the Ligas Camponesas began in Pernambuco, Brazil. The desire of the landowners to introduce sugar-cane production on lands that, for years, had been cultivated on a tenancy basis for subsistence and commercial crops, and efforts to effect this change through violent means, provoked the peasants to organize and defend their interests.

In Java, commodification and increasing absentee landownership implied slowly worsening conditions for the rural population. In Japan, the economic crisis affecting industry and agriculture at the end of the First

World War caused rural tension. Also, in Morelos, Mexico at the beginning of this century, it was not the question of balance between *latifundios* and indigenous communities, but the usurpation of the land of those communities by the land-hungry sugar estate owners and the despoliation of indigenous peasants, which set off what may have been one of the bloodiest revolutions in modern history. And in Cuba, the aggressive extension of plantations and eviction of peasants set in motion an increasingly effective peasant organization effort that ended in a revolution.

An important side effect of the trend toward 'modernization' and concentration of land in the hands of mainly absentee landowners was that the traditional bond between landlords and peasants underwent a change. Exploitative aspects of the traditional system became clearer. One result of increasing absentee landownership was a decline in the paternalistic type of control (or patronage) that the landlords traditionally had over the peasantry.

Furthermore, the increasing exigency of economic power-holders or their resistance to improvement initiatives, or rising expectations among peasants, sometimes created the conditions for the rise of militant movements. For instance, the wish to turn back the clock in land tenure conditions in Ucureña, Bolivia transformed a small peasants' organization into a radical, large-scale movement. In China, the exploitation caused by increasing commercialism and warlord influence incited peasants to rebel.

Although there is great differentiation within the peasantry, from landless rural proletariat to indigenous *comuneros,* the case studies suggest that effective organization was possible among most types once the condition of frustration existed. The only group that appeared difficult to organize was the most destitute peasants – those who lived below subsistence level, were highly dependent on their 'patron', or lived in isolated conditions or as migrant workers. Such peasants only joined in a movement when their fate became unbearable, at which point a violent explosion often resulted without much organization.

Yet considerable differences in the potential to organize do emerge among various categories of peasants. For example, tenants or sharecroppers, who had a certain degree of independence and managed their own plots, were relatively more apt to feel frustrated and to take the initiative to organize than other types of landless peasants. Despoliation of tenants without reimbursement for the improvements to the land they brought about, insecurity of tenure related to arbitrariness of the landowners, and excessive rents or their frequent increase were often major causes of frustration. Absentee landowners, and the knowledge that a large share of the produce or cash surrendered to the landowner was in most cases conspicuously wasted in the cities in a luxurious lifestyle, often contributed to the feeling of frustration.

Often some precipitating event, a concrete case of strongly felt injustice, suddenly bolstered the unity of the peasants who had been attempting to organize a common action of protest for some time. Zapata was a clear case. In other cases protest actions came about more gradually: for example, the desire for recovery of ancestral land is a basic motivational force in many peasant movements. This came into the open, however, only after the peasants had gained some strength through united action around smaller issues, thus gaining confidence that their deeply felt aspirations could be realized.

LEADERSHIP

Charismatic, or at least solidarity-inspiring, leadership among the peasants has been highly important to the organization of peasants sufficiently to confront elites. A characteristic of such leaders is that they have been able to express clearly the sometimes vague frustration felt by the peasantry. On one hand, this capacity of the leader helped the peasants in their process of consciousness-raising. On the other hand, it facilitated a strong identification with the leader.

When the leader of a peasants' organization took on a paternal role because of his personal qualities, the danger existed that the organization could become dependent on that specific leader. In such cases, when the strong and dynamic leader disappeared or was eliminated, the organization collapsed because no one person or group of persons could replace the leader. This happened to Zapata's movement after his assassination in 1919, and to the Huk movement after Luis Taruc gave up under pressure. The continuation of an organization in the face of 'decapitation', imprisonment, or elimination of its main leader(s) can be ensured only when a core of replacement leaders is available. In the process of creating a peasants' organization it was therefore essential for the initial leader(s) to stimulate leadership qualities in potential successors.

Thus the common idea that all peasants' movements and organizations are created by agitators who come from outside, particularly from urban areas, is a misconception. Most of the movements referred to in this study were started by leaders from the peasant class who had certain special experiences that qualified them for leadership of an organized movement. Emiliano Zapata had army experience and had worked in the city. José Rojas of Ucureña had trade union experience in Argentina; and Luis Taruc in the Philippines had received more education than the majority of the peasants.

But the studies also suggest that once a rudimentary organization existed, sympathetic urban political leaders, such as Mao in Hunan province, Lino Alvarez in Cuba and Franciso Juliao in the north-east of Brazil, could help the organization gain regional or even national impact by assuming the overall leadership. On other occasions in Ucureña and Morelos, authentic peasant leaders (Rojas and Zapata) received important assistance from more urbanized personalities such as university teachers, lawyers and politicians, but they retained control of the organization. In Japan, Indonesia and Zimbabwe, outsiders with some kind of political agenda (electoral support or national liberation) were, from the outset, the crucial mobilizers. In Zimbabwe and, to some extent in Indonesia, they had to rely on close collaboration or support from local spiritual leaders.

It may be argued that the emergence of a certain type of leader was problematic for some organizations. For example, in many cases the influence of a leader over his followers was personal and more-or-less charismatic, while the organization may have benefited from a more rational and institutional type of leadership. It was thus not infrequent for a union to transform itself into the 'following' (or clientele) of one specific leader. As a result of this phenomenon, struggles between potential leaders arose, each having his own internal 'following', and each worked for domination of the organization as a whole. This obviously led to divisions within, and sometimes to the break-up of the organization. It was not always easy to find a proper balance between strong leadership and solid institutional structure, so that a change in leadership would be possible without threatening the organization's existence.

In many countries the lack of democratic traditions made disciplined, orderly organizational effort a hazardous undertaking. Autocratic remnants of a feudal or colonial society may be detrimental to active participation in organized groups. But the cases illustrate that unions can function effectively at the local level, with a high degree of participation.

SOCIAL MOBILIZATION STRATEGIES

The examples in this chapter suggest that peasants' movements generally develop only when there is a concrete event or acute conflict about which people become acutely concerned. It seems that even if conditions are bad and growing worse, peasants will be mobilized only when there is clear-cut conflict. Moderate demands, however, can sometimes lead to such a conflict because of the intransigence of the elite. Peasant organizers often sought sensitive issues at the local level if a clear, rallying issue was not too immediately obvious. In Java, for example, this strategy was utilized consistently and successfully, introducing clearer awareness of existing, but often hidden, local contradictions and conflicts (between rich and poor, for example) in a society in which *rukun* (harmony) was highly appreciated. This also happened in Japan and the Philippines.

In introducing such conflict awareness it was important to determine the kind of peasants on which the organization would base its strength. In countries where there was a clear polarization between rich landlords and poor tenants, organizations represented the tenants' interests. They rallied the peasants in the villages or on the haciendas around such issues as security of tenancy, better tenancy legislation, sharecropping arrangements more favourable to tenants (e.g. 40–60 sharing instead of 50–50 or more), or even land reform, as a final or principal demand. Land reform *per se* came up particularly when landlords insistently rejected other, more moderate demands, or took illegal measures such as eviction.

Where the land tenure pattern was more complicated, it was more difficult to determine the most appropriate kind of organization. There were often sharecroppers who tilled land belonging not to large landholders but to slightly better-off neighbours and relatives, who themselves had only a small plot and let part of that to the sharecropper, more to help him than to exploit him. To organize such sharecroppers in their own exclusive interest would have been extremely difficult; many peasants who leased a part of their plot would have opposed this approach. Whenever the differences between tenants and the lesser landlords were minor, both could be united into one organization that benefited the small owners in such a way as to enable them to give more favourable sharecropping or tenancy conditions to the tenants.

The degree to which certain tenure patterns, or changes in such patterns, occur in a particular area or village (even more than in a clear-cut landlord–tenant division) also merits careful investigation. It appears that the approach of the BTI in Indonesia was successful, preceding organization and action by such research into the various class contradictions in the villages. Such action–research has been non-existent in most other cases, but in countries with complicated land tenure structures it seems crucial to any organizing effort that possible contradictions be evaluated.

Once a peasant organization had come into existence, a process of consolidation generally followed. Cases of abuse argued successfully in the courts, and mass demonstrations and public meetings held to support petitions for justice or land, often served to increase support for an organization. Initially, only steps to obtain justice were undertaken, as intended by the existing laws. Meetings were held and a petition, with or without the direct support of a sympathetic or paid lawyer, was presented to the competent authorities. Often, however, the authorities stood aloof, or openly chose the side of the large landholders. Continuous frustration encountered when following the slow course of legal procedure prepared the ground for more radical peasant action even beyond the limit of legal possibilities, such as civil disobedience.

The way in which peasants' organizations presented their demands, and demonstrated the bargaining power to back them up, were also important to bringing about change. Generally some form of direct action from the peasants made it clear to the authorities, as well as to landholding groups and other vested interests, that the demands were serious. Among these forms of direct action, the peaceful occupation or invasion of land considered to be expropriable was probably the most effective, as well as the most generally practised.

Land reforms tended to occur only after such direct, usually non-violent, action by peasants' organizations. 'Unilateral actions' in Java, the occupation of estates by Bolivian peasants in 1952, and the activities of MST in Brazil are examples. Some such actions were symbolic, designed to draw public attention or exercise pressure. In other cases they did lead to immediate changes in the system of cultivation or property relations.

While the peaceful occupation of unused or underused lands has been used frequently by peasant organizations as a means of pressure, such acts cannot always be considered a form of civil disobedience. Several countries have laws allowing squatters on unused lands to claim property rights after they have worked these lands for a number of years. This generally involves lands in areas of scarce population where property rights are poorly defined. The situation becomes more complicated when such lands are registered in the name of large landholders, who either leave them unused or use them extensively or partially, in areas where many landless peasants live under marginal conditions. In such areas, landless peasants are often allowed to cultivate these lands in small plots for their own subsistence in exchange for a fee or for work on the landlord's holding. The trouble arises when the owner wants to extend operations and starts dislodging the peasants who have been in possession of these lands for some time. The peasants then become perceived as invaders, and the police, army or hired gunmen are called in to remove them. Such actions often provoke resistance from the peasants, who come back in numbers to re-occupy the lands they have been cultivating. The Cuban situation before 1959, and presently that in Brazil, are cases in point.

Until today, indigenous communities and 'tribal' groups in many countries have effectively recovered lands (through occupation), to which they have age-old titles, after many years of unsuccessful litigation in the courts. Occupation may consist of building symbolic living quarters on the 'recovered' lands, ploughing the land or grazing their cattle on it. Branding such acts 'violence' and trying to restore the *status quo* with the aid of the police or the armed forces has cost the lives of many indigenous peasants and does not solve the basic problem. Human rights activists and NGOs have sometimes stepped in to denounce such actions and pressure authorities to implement the law. Yet severe repression of peasant actions may create the belief among the peasantry that self-defence, weapons in hand, is the only means left to defend their fundamental human rights. Thus a strong revolutionary consciousness may emerge, with peasants demanding radical changes in the rural, or even overall national, power structure. The present Zapatista movement is a clear example.

There were thus considerable variations in the dynamics of mobilizations. Some organizations began at a certain moment in one place and then spread into surrounding areas where essentially the same conditions prevailed, as in the state of Morelos and around Ucureña. It also happened that attempts to organize occurred spontaneously in scattered communities or areas in a country. Such attempts could, at times, be included in a nation-wide movement being created by political leaders to gain mass support for a reform programme. Mobilization began this way in Cuba and, to some extent, in the MST dominated areas in Brazil. The first type of process is predominantly horizontal, while the latter is largely vertical. Most mobilizations combine the two approaches, with the vertical approach often following the horizontal one after it has been successful in a given area.

A creative use of existing or growing contradictions between classes or categories has been another main force in organizing strong peasant movements. This is often a complicated affair – in most countries there exist not only powerful landlords and poor peasants, but a great variety of (sub)categories of peasants that can be played against each other or form alliances against a common enemy. Mao Ze Dong, and to some extent the BTI in Indonesia, searched among locally existing differences and contradictions for the most fundamental and antagonistic ones. This proved to be effective, but was also risky.

OBSTACLES

Characteristics of power structures that impede organizational processes also deserve special attention. There is considerable evidence that certain strategies used by large landowners are often supported by the state to prevent peasants from organizing when the conditions are ripe. Irrespective of legislation regarding human rights, such as freedom of association, large landholders may use their authority and economic power to hinder popular mobilization. This was often accomplished by firing agricultural workers or evicting tenants who were potential or actual leaders, and who took the initiative to organize the peasantry. When such measures did not have the desired effect, or were impossible, potential leaders might be offered money or privileges in exchange for moderating or halting the organizing efforts. And if this did not work, threats of arrest or persecution for 'subversion' or similar acts might be employed. It should be stressed again that such approaches were used regardless of the existing legislation, since the application of the law in rural areas was often influenced or controlled by the large landholders. If such actions did not prevent an organization from emerging, the assassination of the most important leader(s) has, in the worst cases, been used to block the organization process. Despite such severe, often systematically applied countermeasures and human rights violations by landowners and their supporters, peasants' movements have been able to survive and grow, and even be successful. The moral courage of leaders who have consciously risked their life for the cause of social justice in the rural areas is well worth special attention.

All case studies indicated that the human rights situation, particularly regarding freedom of association and the formation of representative organizations of peasants, left much to be desired in most countries. This remained true even following ratification by most countries of at least one of the International Labour Conventions, designed to deal with various aspects of such basic freedoms such as the rights of association and combination of agricultural workers; freedom of association; and protection of the right to organize and bargain collectively. Peasants and workers in the countries that have ratified one or more of the conventions related to freedom of association have not necessarily enjoyed better conditions, because too often these conventions remained a dead letter.

Another strategy sometimes used by landowners and their local elite allies or by the state to prevent peasants' organizations from consolidating and bargaining for essential structural changes is the creation of parallel unions that restrict their range of activities to petitioning for limited improvements, such as higher wages, better housing conditions and more appropriate tenancy rates, etc. On several occasions, unions that work towards such limited goals have been purposely stimulated in order to undermine those pressuring for more fundamental structural changes. For example, the Free Farmers Federation in the Philippines and the church-sponsored unions in Brazil in the early 1960s competed in this way with the Huk movement and the Ligas Camponesas, respectively. Ironically, these parallel movements sometimes became considerably radical because of the landlords' opposition to even their moderate demands.

It often occurred that the 'obstacles' placed in the way of peasant organization became counter-productive in the long run, sometimes forcing initially moderate movements into greater cohesiveness out of self-defence. There is considerable evidence that where the landholding elite most violently and harshly opposed orderly peasants' organization and bargaining for legitimate demands, the peasants, with or without urban political support, have sought to strike back more drastically. Thus Zapata's movement, the occupation of haciendas in the Cochabamba valley in 1952–53, and the cases described in Russia, China and Cuba illustrate how elite intransigence caused revolutionary movements to grow.

At the same time, a radical politicization of movements sometimes became an obstacle to the effectiveness of peasant organizations, although the pros and cons of being strongly linked with a certain political party or ideology are difficult to weigh. In China and Indonesia, a strong, sustained link with the Communist Party was essential to consolidation and effectiveness. In other cases a close tie to the government and its official party also seems to have been favourable to the peasant cause at certain stages of organizational development, as in Mexico during the Cardenas regime. As the organization became increasingly consolidated, however, this tie facilitated a deterioration of its militancy and effectiveness. This happened when the political party in control came increasingly under the influence of groups that did not place a high priority on the peasants' interests. While the influence of leftist political groups in most cases strengthened peasant organizations, in other cases the strong counter-forces provoked by such radical political groups led to the destruction of potentially powerful movements. This happened in India and, finally, in Indonesia. In some cases, such as in Japan, India and the Philippines, ideological division within the party supporting the movement weakened its effectiveness.

The financing of organizations can also be problematic. In some cases the membership fees play a minor role, but some strong, cohesive groups managed their own affairs without outside support. Some did this through the management of various types of cooperative enterprises, with profits used wholly or partly for the union. Most organizations received financial support from political parties, urban unions or federations with which the peasants' organization was directly or indirectly affiliated. These sources included the Ministry of Labour or other government agencies, international organizations, foundations or NGOs. Top leaders in permanent service to certain organizations were sometimes paid by outside supporters. This situation all too often implied that the paying institution had a great deal of control over the organization, leading to goals that did not necessarily coincide with those of the peasant membership. In some cases, competition between financing agencies and other interests trying to gain control over peasant organizations led to organizational rivalry and to the buying-off of leaders between organizations.

IMPLEMENTATION OF LAND REFORM

As noted above, it was not infrequent for rather specific, initially modest demands related to tenancy improvement or higher wages – once they had successfully brought the peasants of a certain area together – to be gradually transformed into demands for a drastic change of the social order at the local, regional or even national level, with stress on land distribution. Most of the cases studied suggest that the demands related to specific grievances launched most regional or even nationwide movements, such as the Zapata rebellion, the Japanese movement, the Huk movement in the Philippines, the BTI in Indonesia, and the Bolivian and Cuban peasant federations.

In most cases land redistribution was the most strongly desired objective. This was especially so in areas where large *latifundios* or plantations had recently been established or extended to land that belonged to local or indigenous peasants. The more recent the despoliations and usurpations, the more strongly injustice was felt. And when tension was high, small acts of provocation by the landless could bring the whole issue of 'recovery' of formerly lost lands into the foreground in a dramatic way.

Some form of direct action from the peasants often served to make clear to the authorities, as well as to other vested interests and land-holding groups, that peasant demands were serious. As was shown by the MST in Brazil and the *Aksi Sefihak* in Indonesia, the occupation or invasion of lands considered to be expropriable were the most effective direct actions, and the most frequently practised. However, this happened frequently, threatening social and political stability, and occasionally at the cost of many lives, particularly on the side of the peasants.

When land reform was effectively being implemented, the role of peasant organizations took various forms. According to the law in Mexico, Bolivia, Japan and Taiwan, community-level peasants' unions or commissions had to present a petition for land. A minimum number of members was generally required, and a representative or executive committee with which the land reform agency could deal had to be elected. After land was distributed, this committee (or a newly elected one with a different structure) generally played an important role in the management of the land received by the members of a community, either individually or jointly.

An important function of these peasants' unions or commissions after land distribution was to fill the vacuum created by the disappearance of the large landowner as the central figure in or behind local power structures. Specifically, the leader of the local peasants' organization took over part of the former landowner's functions. And because the leader was (generally) democratically elected, he depended on the membership for his support. Thus a democratization of the local government was often a result of agrarian reform. This was obviously the case in Mexico, Japan, Bolivia and Cuba. There is considerable evidence that where the struggle for agrarian reform encountered many obstacles, peasants' organizations achieved greater cohesiveness and strength. This proved to be an important asset in overcoming the subsequent difficulties related to improving the agricultural productivity of the newly obtained lands.

There are many indications that where a peasants' organization played a role in the distribution of land (and the preceding struggle), post-reform measures and programmes – such as the formation of a cooperative or a credit society, or a community development initiative – could be carried out much more easily. Where local leaders had considerable experience in dealing with official agencies and harnessing support from the peasantry, post-reform initiatives tended to be more successful. This was particularly obvious in China after 1949, and to some extent in Bolivia and Mexico, and was also the case in Japan where the peasanty gained considerable political clout at local and national levels.

When a peasants' organization (such as in China, Japan, Mexico and Bolivia) was tied to the political party running the government (and its land distribution programme), the land distribution also functioned as a kind of proselytizer for the party. As peasants were generally obliged to be members of a union or committee affiliated with the predominant peasants' federation, this could lead to political control over the peasantry. It some-times happened that the newly elected leaders abused their power in ways reminiscent of the former *hacendado*. More recently, especially in Mexico, the *caciquismo* has taken on considerable proportions, sometimes to such a degree that peasants saw little difference between the pre- and post-reform situations. Such acute frustrations may lead to new radical move-ments, as occurred in the case of the Zapatistas in Chiapas.

An intangible but very important effect of militant peasants' organiza-tions that have achieved reforms or other benefits was the respect that the organized peasants gained from their opponents, as well as from other peasants. This psychological factor has received far less attention than it deserves. The enthusiasm and directed will to change which are part of this phenomenon are human resources that can make a valuable contribution to development efforts when they are channelled toward constructive goals. The development fever that seems to have existed in Morelos when Zapata ruled that state at the height of peasant pressure indicated such important, untapped human resources. Also, in the first stages of the post-revolutionary land reform process in China, Japan and Cuba, peasants made considerable development advances. Extreme confidence in such militancy in China, however, led to such disastrous policies as the Great Leap Forward and the Cultural Revolution.

CONCLUSIONS

The Russian, Chinese, Indonesian, Bolivian and Cuban movements demonstrate how peasants' movements can become radicalized. The peas-ants reacted to elite expansion or resistance by becoming a class-conscious, revolutionary force at the national level. This occurred not because the peasantry was, by nature, revolutionary, but despite its pru-dent, traditional and evolutionary approach. Movements in these countries had considerable success because they were not violent explosions of peasants' discontent, repressed as quickly as they came up. With few excep-tions, they all began with a careful grassroots organization that took up the most strongly felt grievances of the peasants – the 'counterpoints' within the dominant traditional system – and slowly built strength around those grievances. Only by proceeding carefully, and remaining well within the rules of the game, were the first steps taken toward creating representative interest groups against the heavy weight of traditional patronage and eco-nomic and political repression. And only after the rural elite reacted to minor peasants' demands and organizational success in ways clearly against the prevailing laws (often including violence), did the peasants' organizations become more radical. It is quite probable that at any stage during the process of radicalization and the escalation of demands, peas-ants' organizations would have accepted a compromise if the rural elite had been willing to give them a fair chance. Elites generally did not do this. Elite intransigence, more than anything else, was the reason that peasants' organizations finally took a revolutionary stand, demanding the radical overthrow of the system as a whole, and acting accordingly. It is surprising that in view of so much historical evidence, elites have followed the same fatal course to the present day. Is this because they form part of, and are supported by, the trend of globalization of the capitalist economy?

There is a growing awareness and some mobilization around this dilemma. In this connection, it is remarkable that some of the current, strongly agitating peasant movements, such as the Zapatistas, the Philippine KMP and the Brazilian MST, came together in a joint effort with other farmers', indigenous peoples' and women's organizations and NGOs in the First Conference of the Peoples' Global Action against 'Free' Trade and the World Trade Organization (Geneva, 23–25 February 1998). This indicates a social mobilization for 'globalization from below', in reaction to imposed 'globalization from above'.

CHAPTER EIGHT

The Role of Peasants' Organizations in Managing Agrarian Conflict

Jose Noel D. Olano

INTRODUCTION: AGRARIAN CONFLICT AND AGRARIAN REFORM

Agrarian reform provides the overall framework and context for the discussion on management of agrarian conflict by grassroots organizations. The argument is that agrarian conflict, whether it be between peasant and landlord, peasant and government, or peasant and fellow peasant, is influenced by the agricultural tenurial situation of society. The land tenure situation influences the nature, intensity and extent of the conflict, and how it is resolved or unresolved.

This chapter is based on the case of the Philippines, where the state has played a major role in the implementation of an agrarian reform programme. This social justice measure enshrined in the Constitution has been enacted into law by Congress. An executive branch of government, the Department of Agrarian Reform (DAR), has been implementing it for more than 10 years.

The relationship between agrarian reform and agrarian conflict is such that even the Republic Act 6657, otherwise known as the Philippine Comprehensive Agrarian Reform Programme, defines agrarian conflict or dispute as:

> *Any controversy relating to tenurial arrangements, whether leasehold, tenancy, stewardship or otherwise, over lands devoted to agriculture, including disputes concerning farm-workers' associations or representation of persons in negotiating, fixing, maintaining, changing or seeking to arrange terms or conditions of such tenurial arrangements.*

It includes any controversy relating to compensation of lands acquired under this Act and other terms and conditions of transfer of ownership from landowners to farm-workers, tenants and other agrarian reform beneficiaries, whether the disputants stand in the proximate relation of farm operator and beneficiary, landowner and tenant, or lessor and lessee (DAR, 1992, p.5).

> *Agrarian conflict stems from change: a change from one tenurial status to another, or a change in possession and ownership of land. The majority of conflicts between*

and among peasants revolve around the issue of land. Some conflicts arise from issues such as credit uptake or irrigation rights, yet these issues still fall within the overall purview of agrarian reform.

The law mentioned above provides a definition of agrarian reform. It is defined as the redistribution of lands, regardless of crops or fruits produced, to farmers and regular farm workers who are landless, irrespective of tenurial arrangement, to include the totality of factors and support services designed to lift the economic status of the beneficiaries, and all other arrangements alternative to the physical redistribution of lands such as production or profit sharing, labour administration, and the distribution of shares of stock, which will allow beneficiaries to receive a just share of the fruits of the lands they work.

Hayami et al. (1990) further distinguish between the terms 'land reform' and 'agrarian reform'. Land reform refers specifically to government policies that intend to redistribute the whole or a part of the bundle of property rights on land, while agrarian reform refers more broadly to the reform of agrarian institutions, including credit and marketing institutions, and to the redistribution of land property rights.

Agrarian conflict cannot be examined in isolation, and must be viewed within the context of agrarian reform. History has shown that peasant uprisings in different parts of the world have emanated from conflict between powerful landowners and transnational corporations and landless farm workers and tenants. Agrarian unrest has stemmed from the clamour for change by the peasants against a government that more often than not tries to maintain the status quo.

The first part of this chapter provides information on the agrarian reform situation in the Philippines. Past and prevailing laws and programmes are also examined. The role of peasants' or grassroots organizations in agrarian reform is discussed briefly, followed by an extensive discussion on agrarian conflict and how the peasants manage conflict using both legal and extralegal channels. There is a wide array of peasants' initiatives and experiences in the Philippines from which case studies can be derived. The case studies in this chapter were chosen because of the author's familiarity with and personal involvement in the cases.

This chapter highlights the Philippine experience in implementing agrarian reform and the experience of Filipino peasants and peasants' organizations in managing agrarian conflict. The experience will show that implementing agrarian reform is a very difficult task, especially in a democratic setting. Even with the presence of a comprehensive agrarian reform law being implemented by a government bureaucracy, agrarian reform remains a gigantic and overwhelming task unless efforts are made to make peasants' organizations major stakeholders of the programme. They must be at the forefront of the programme, providing proper guidance and direction. This chapter will also show that the same principle holds true for conflict management. Peasants' organizations are much more effective in addressing individual or group conflicts than farmers left on their own.

THE STATE OF AGRARIAN REFORM IN THE PHILIPPINES

The present state of land distribution

According to a report by the World Bank (1996), two-thirds of the poor are engaged in the agriculture, fishery and forestry sectors. In the agricultural sector, farm sizes and cultivable land per agricultural worker have fallen in recent decades, even with additional land brought under cultivation through deforestation. And in 1988, 86 per cent of all landowners owned farms of 7 ha or less, accounting for 23 per cent of agricultural land, while fewer than 2 per cent of landowners had farms exceeding 24 ha but controlled 36 per cent of all farm land.

The Philippines has a total land area of around 30 million ha. Of this, approximately 11 million ha are cultivated land. Around 11 million Filipinos (or 43 per cent of the labour force) depend on agriculture for their employment. The agriculture labour force – the farmers, tenants and farm workers who constitute the majority of the poor in the Philippines – are the target beneficiaries of the Comprehensive Agrarian Reform Programme (CARP).

It is difficult to determine the exact number of farmers or farm households standing to benefit from CARP. The DAR's figures on farmer beneficiaries pertain to those to whom land titles have been awarded. The same difficulty is true of land records. The Land Registration Authority does not have a master list of agricultural land titles that are subject to agrarian reform. In 1988 DAR undertook a *Listasaka* or voluntary land registration process nationwide. Unfortunately, the exercise failed to come up with the data needed to determine the exact scope of CARP. Why would landowners go forward to register their lands when they knew the government intended to expropriate them? Thus in 1992, on the assumption of the Ramos Government, DAR undertook a CARP Scope Validation which involved securing, validating and computerizing land records at the village, municipal and provincial levels. These data were then organized, for management purposes, to determine the actual land acquisition and distribution status per area. Table 8.1 shows the national land acquisition and distribution status as of February 1998.

The land categories in Table 8.1 follow the categories and phasing prescribed by law. Phase one includes tenanted rice and corn lands, idle and abandoned lands, private lands voluntarily offered by owners, lands foreclosed by government financial institutions, and lands owned by government, to be distributed within a four-year period beginning 1988. Phase two includes all alienable and disposable public agricultural lands and pri-

Table 8.1   Land acquisition and distribution status as at February 1998

Land category	Scope (ha)	Accomplishment (ha)	Balance (ha)
Tenanted rice and corn lands	575 011	515 813	59 198
Private agricultural land over 50 ha	721 466	317 203	404 263
Private agricultural land 24–50 ha	253 266	68 527	184 739
Private agricultural land 5–24 ha	750 760	333 044	417 716
Private agricultural land less than 5 ha	47 539	37 408	10 131
Government-owned lands	871 045	793 326	77 719
Landed estates and settlement	718 535	689 252	29 283
Grand total	3 937 622	2 754 573	1 183 049

Source: DAR, 1998.

vate agricultural lands in excess of 50 ha, to be completed also within a four-year period. Phase three covers all private agricultural lands, commencing with large landholdings and proceeding to medium and small landholdings under the following schedule: (a) landholdings above 24 ha up to 50 ha, to begin in 1992 and to be completed in 1995; (b) landholdings from the retention limit up to 24 ha, to begin in 1994 and to be completed in 1998.

The figures in Table 8.1 provide some information on the status of agrarian reform implementation. Based on a total scope of close to four million ha, the government has been able to accomplish 70 per cent of its target. The remaining 30 per cent (about 1.1 million ha) remain to be distributed. This balance, however, is composed mainly of private agricultural land. Private lands over 50 ha comprise 34 per cent of the balance and, combined with private lands between 24 and 50 ha, constitute 50 per cent of the balance. This fact is significant because the heart of agrarian reform is the distribution of private agricultural lands; it is in these types of lands where farmers experience extreme poverty and oppression. Even the government has admitted that the remaining private lands, especially the large sugar haciendas, have offered stiff landlord resistance and opposition. Thus agrarian conflicts between landlords and peasants in these areas are expected to be numerous and intense.

Agrarian reform from past to present

History will show that attempts to implement agrarian reform in the past have been feeble and token. Policies and programmes were implemented by various administrations to quell peasant unrest. More significantly, there was no attempt to encourage peasant participation in the implementation of agrarian reform. Table 8.2 provides a summary of these policies and programmes, which produced insignificant results and little impact. A 1985 Ministry of Agrarian Reform report showed that in a 42–year period

Table 8.2   Summary of agrarian reform policies and programmes

Year	Administration	Policy/programme	Main features
1933	Governor General Theodore Roosevelt	Rice Share Tenancy Act (Public Act 4054)	50–50 sharing of crop; interest rate ceiling of 10% per crop; safeguard against arbitrary dismissal
1933		Creation of National Land Settlement Administration (NLSA)	Tasked with resettlement projects
1935–41	President Manuel Quezon	Anti-usury law/tenancy relations regulation/landed estates/free patents	Negotiated purchase of large land holdings for resale to tenants
1950	President Elpidio Quirino	Establishment of Land Settlement and Development Corporation (LASEDECO)	land to Huk rebels at resettlement sites
1954	President Ramon Magsaysay	Agricultural Tenancy Act (RA 1199) Land Reform Act (RA 1400)	Enforce fair tenancy practices Expropriate and redistribute large estates
1963	President Diosdado Macapagal	Agricultural Land Reform Code	Establish owner cultivatorship and economic family size farm; creation of Agriculture Credit Administration and Agricultural Productivity Commission
1971–72	President Ferdinand Marcos	Code of Agrarian Reform (RA 6389)	Declared Philippines as land reform area; automatic conversion of tenancy to leasehold; establishment of Department of Agrarian Reform (DAR)
		Presidential Decree (PD 27)	Entire country as land reform area Distribution of tenanted rice and corn lands

only 99 000 ha of land were covered and given to some 52 000 beneficiaries. The failure may be attributed to several factors.

A major factor is the lack of political will on the part of the government to implement a genuine and comprehensive agrarian reform. The land reform programmes were not meant to radically alter the prevailing oppressive and unjust agricultural structure. Rather, they were used as quick-fix solutions to political problems, such as neutralizing agrarian unrest sporadically occurring in Luzon, or as a means to economically disempower political rivals, as in the case of President Marcos.

Past programmes have also been limited in terms of coverage of agricultural land types, in particular to tenanted rice and corn lands. The programmes focused on tenancy regulation and resettlement. Some owners of vast rice and corn lands changed the crops planted in their farms in order to evade the programme. The limitation has also excluded the large tracts of coconut lands and sugar haciendas where most of the poorest farm workers can be found.

The policies are riddled with loopholes or provisions which make implementation difficult and disadvantageous to the poorer farmers. For example, the Rice Share Tenancy Act could take effect only in provinces where municipal councils petitioned the Governor-General for its implementation. These municipal councils, however, were very much influenced, if not controlled by landlords. The Land Reform Act of Magsaysay allowed the Land Tenure Administration to expropriate large estates, but only those petitioned by tenants. However, tenants were so indebted to their landlords and had become so dependent on them for almost all their needs that no one dared make a petition.

The agencies created to carry out the programmes were generally inefficient and lacked adequate funding. Magsaysay's Land Tenure Administration was able to expropriate only less than 20 000 ha after six years, and the National Land Settlement Administrations accomplished only 6000 ha during the Commonwealth period.

Basic features of the Comprehensive Agrarian Reform Programme

On 10 June 1988, President Corazon Aquino signed into law Republic Act (RA) 6657, otherwise known as the CARP. There were diverse reactions to Republic Act 6657. Positions among peasants' groups ranged from outright and total rejection to uncompromising acceptance of the law. It is clear, however, that CARP was an improvement over previous laws for the following reasons, amongst others.

- Coverage and schedule of implementation – CARP covers all public and private agricultural lands, regardless of tenurial arrangement and commodity produced. The distribution of these lands shall be implemented and completed within 10 years from effectivity of the law.

■ Retention and distribution limits – retention by the landowner shall not exceed 5 ha and 3 ha to each qualified child of the landowner. Qualified farmer beneficiaries, on the other hand, may own not more than 3 ha of land.

■ Qualified beneficiaries – lands shall be distributed to landless residents of the same village or municipality subject to the following priority: (a) agricultural lessees and share tenants; (b) regular farm workers; (c) seasonal farm workers; (d) other farm workers; (e) actual tillers or occupants of public lands; (f) collective or cooperatives of beneficiaries; (g) others directly working on the land.

■ Determination of just compensation to the landowner – factors considered are: the cost of acquisition of the land, current value of like properties, its nature, actual use and income, the sworn valuation by the owner, the tax declarations, and the assessment made by government assessors. The Land Bank of the Philippines (LBP) shall compensate the landowner in cash and in bonds.

■ Payment by beneficiaries – lands awarded shall be paid for by the beneficiaries to the LBP in 30 annual amortizations at 6 per cent interest per annum. Payments for the first three to five years may be reduced and should not exceed 5 per cent of the value of the annual gross production.

■ Support services to the beneficiaries – farmer beneficiaries shall be provided with the following support services: (a) land surveys and titling; (b) liberalized terms on credit facilities and production loans; (c) extension services by way of planting, cropping, production and post-harvest technology transfer, as well as marketing and management assistance and support to cooperatives and farmers' organizations; (d) infrastructure, such as access trails, mini-dams, public utilities, marketing and storage facilities; and (e) research, production and use of organic fertilizers and other local substances necessary in farming and cultivation.

Problems in implementation

CARP experienced rough sailing in its first few years of implementation. In 1992, midway through the programme, only 20 per cent of lands had been distributed. More alarming was the fact that large tracts of private land had not gone through the first step of land acquisition. Furthermore, a substantial portion of the Agrarian Reform Fund had already been used within the first six years.

Certain significant events and incidents in the political arena transpired between 1986 and 1992 which affected programme implementation. One major factor was the frequent changes in Department Secretaries. In a period of five years (1988–92) the DAR went through five changes in leadership. Such changes in a bureaucracy are devastating: the organization is rendered useless and unstable. There is no continuity of programmes, policies and personnel assignments, thus making everyone in the organization nervous and insecure.

A second political factor was the exemption of Hacienda Luisita, a large landholding owned by the family of President Aquino. The owners colluded with government officials to exempt the property from agrarian reform. President Aquino had earlier announced that agrarian reform was going to be the centerpiece programme of her government. The exemption of their land, however, elicited strong reactions from the peasant groups.

Many believe that the 1986 revolution by the Epiphanio de los Santos Avenue (EDSA) which ousted the dictator, President Marcos, and installed President Aquino, ushered in opportunities to implement radical social reforms. Having popular backing, the revolutionary government of President Aquino provided opportunities for executive issuances and decisive action on such an important issue as land reform. However, the elite that had remained at the helm of government conspired and prevented this from happening. Worse, the exemption became a symbol of the government's lack of political will to implement genuine agrarian reform. This also emboldened landowners to defy agrarian reform following the example set by the highest official of the land.

A third political factor is the strong resistance from the landlords. The landlords wield political and economic power and have used this to obstruct and hinder the implementation of land reform in their own lands. Some examples of the abuse of power by landlords are cited below. In 1993, a provincial agrarian reform officer of DAR in the province of Davao Oriental was shot and killed in front of his own house. The execution was ordered by a landowner from Davao province. In the northern Cebu province landlords put up barbed wire and 'No Trespassing' signs on their properties after the Municipal Agrarian Reform Officer (MARO) sent them Notices of Acquisition. In the case of a MARO in Cadiz City in Negros Occidental, six lawyers of a landowner descended upon her when a Notice of Coverage was sent to the landowner. In Batangas province, the Operation Sugarlands being conducted by the Field Operations Group of DAR to expedite the distribution of sugarlands was stopped after Congress passed a resolution opposing the conduct of such an operation. In Ormoc city in Leyte, the local DAR had to open its office until midnight to allow farmers to come out under the cover of darkness to enlist themselves as agrarian reform beneficiaries.

Policies emanating from government have also affected the programme. Pro-farmer policy pronouncements from top government officials were made, but the translation of these pronouncements into executive and administrative orders, issuances and ordinances have caused conflict and confusion.

For instance, while RA 6657 is certainly better than previous laws, it has its share of provisions that are questionable and disadvantageous to farmers. Most notable are the provisions on exemptions and exclusions, and the stock distribution option. Section 10 of RA 6657 enumerates the types of lands that qualify for exemption. This provision has been the subject of legal tussles between and among government departments and agencies. Examples include the conflict between DAR and the Department of Education and Culture over coverage of excess school and university lands that have agricultural workers; and the conflict between DAR and the Department of Environment and Natural Resources over lands proclaimed as forest or mining reserves or lands which have Timber Lease Agreements or Pasture Lease Agreements but are actually being cultivated and farmed by settlers and other occupants.

As mentioned above, the stock distribution option has allowed estates such as Hacienda Luisita to evade actual distribution, as the law states that 'corporations or associations which voluntarily divest a proportion of their capital stock, equity or participation in favor of their workers or other qualified beneficiaries under this section shall be deemed to have complied with the provisions of this Act'.

In October 1997 farmers from Sumilao, Bukidnon went on a hunger strike to protest the conversion from agricultural to industrial land which had already been awarded to them by DAR. This incident is discussed further in the Case Study section of this chapter; it is cited here to exemplify the conflict within government itself in the interpretation of policy. In this case DAR maintains its position based on a certain set of administrative orders and guidelines enacted by the Office of the President on the conversion of agricultural land. The other side, local government and the Office of the President through the Executive Secretary, maintain their position based on the power of local government to reclassify agricultural land into other uses. Further aggravating the situation is the issuance of the Department of Justice Opinion No. 44, which states that lands reclassified into industrial and commercial uses by local government before 1988 are exempted from CARP. This opinion has led to the unabated and extensive conversion of prime agricultural lands in the countryside.

Finally, there are operations-related factors or problems related to the actual conduct of land reform from the time the land is expropriated to the moment it is awarded to the farmer. The experience in implementing CARP shows that the nuts and bolts, the minute details of operationalizing the programme, are important factors to be considered.

A major bottleneck is the complex land acquisition and distribution process. The steps and procedures from the moment a landholding is identified under CARP to the actual distribution of the title to the farmer is a drawn-out and complicated process. This is partly due to the fact that agrarian reform in the Philippines is being implemented in a democratic setting whereby the so-called 'due process' must be given to the landowners. The other major reason is the involvement in the process of numerous agencies belonging to different departments within government. Although

DAR is the lead agency it has to coordinate with the following agencies: the Land Registration Authority under the Department of Justice for securing and cancelling old titles, transferring them in the name of the Republic of the Philippines, and registering new titles in the name of the farmer beneficiaries; the Land Management Service of the Department of Environment and Natural Resources for the validation of land classification and approval of survey plans; the Geodetic Engineers' Association of the Philippines for the conduct of perimeter and subdivision surveys; and the Land Bank of the Philippines for the valuation and payment of the property. While these agencies are being supported financially by the Agrarian Reform Fund in the execution of the tasks assigned to them, the fact that they are not under the administrative control of one Department Secretary or Undersecretary produces administrative nightmares, especially as the whole effort is national in character. A slight backlog in one agency can affect the whole process. Papers and folders tend to go back and forth between agencies varying in their institutional capacity, which in turn determines the speed (or lack of speed) of the land acquisition process.

Technical difficulties also plagued the programme. 'The polygon will not close' is an expression, even if inherently contradictory, often heard among DAR technicians and surveyors when asked about the backlogs in the completion of surveys. When these occur the technicians are forced to undertake further technical research on the subject of landholding. The system for filing and storing land records in the local Register of Deeds is also far from ideal (the system is often the butt of jokes among DAR field people who describe the filing system as 'biblical', i.e. 'search and thou shalt find').

Completing agrarian reform

Despite the setbacks and obstacles encountered, agrarian reform still remains a development imperative that must be completed. A most recent development is the signing by President Ramos of an amendment to RA 6657, which extends the implementation of the Comprehensive Agrarian Reform Programme for another 10 years with an additional allocation of 50 billion pesos. The state must therefore seize this opportunity to acquire and distribute the remaining private agricultural lands, especially the sugar haciendas and the commercial farms. Then government must focus its attention on the farmers who, in the past 10 years of CARP implementation, have been given land. An evaluation must be made of the adequacy of support services given to these farmers. Government must ensure productivity of the distributed lands by providing the necessary technical support such as agricultural extension, credit, marketing, irrigation and other infrastructure facilities.

In the end, however, agrarian reform must make a difference in the life of the farmer. It must be a programme that provides tangible benefits and improves quality of life. And because the farmer is the prime beneficiary of this programme, he/she must be able to identify with the programme, participate meaningfully in its implementation, and finally assume ownership over his/her development process. This process can be facilitated by the active involvement of farmers in their own organizations. Then, and only then, can agrarian reform be a truly sustainable and empowering process.

ROLE OF PEASANT ORGANIZATIONS IN AGRARIAN REFORM

The previous section has shown the importance of the state in the implementation of an agrarian reform programme. The state is a necessary part of the equation. Yet another important part of the equation which may spell the success or failure of an agrarian reform programme are the peasants' organizations.

In 1979 the World Conference on Agrarian Reform and Rural Development (WCARRD) came out with a recommendation to promote people's organizations, including rural workers' associations and cooperatives, to strengthen the participation of the rural poor in decision-making, implementation and evaluation of agrarian reform and rural development programmes. The purpose of such organizations is to provide a continuing mechanism for the pursuit of the interests of its members as collectively perceived by them.

The role of peasants' organizations, the nature of their struggle for agrarian reform, and the degree and quality of their participation in agrarian reform depend on the objective conditions prevailing in society at a given time. Where the state is closely aligned with the landowning class, the struggle by the grassroots organizations may be more radical and revolutionary. Where a government is strong in implementing social reforms, the peasants' organizations may be more open to participating actively in implementing the programme. The following section looks at the history of peasant unrest in the Philippines, and how the forms of struggle and participation have evolved over the years.

Philippine peasant unrest and struggle

Rather than provide a chronological narration of events in the history of agrarian unrest in the Philippines, this section provides some interesting features characterizing peasant unrest and struggle.

Peasants' uprisings have been associated with movements for liberation. The uprisings during the Spanish era (1565–1896) were related to the growing dissent against Spanish authorities and the moves towards freedom and democracy. Victor Karunan (1984) lists some of the revolts, which include the Dagohoy and Tamblot rebellions in Bohol during the period 1744–1829; the Banco rebellion in Limasawa; and the Sumoroy rebellion in Samar (1649–50). These revolts were easily crushed by the superiority of Spanish arms. While Karunan attributes the revolts as uprisings against land grabbing, increase in land rent, and exploitation by friars and the *principalía*, these revolts cannot be dissociated from the growing anti-colonialist sentiment building up over the years due to various forms of oppression by the Spanish colonizers, eventually leading to the Philippine revolution of 1896–98.

The same can be said for the resistance movements during the American and Japanese occupations. Karunan again provides some historical data. In 1904 Macario Sacay led a Tagalog resistance composed of forces from the provinces of Rizal, Cavite, Laguna, and Batangas to fight American forces. In 1942, when the Japanese army occupied the Philippines, an underground resistance movement named Hukbalahap (Hubko ng Bayan Laban sa Hapon – The People's Army Against the Japanese) was formed and engaged in a guerrilla war with the Japanese.

The peasant uprisings in the Philippines had religious undertones. Sturtevant (1976) provides a detailed narration and analysis of some of the popular uprisings in the Philippines during the period, and describes a very revealing feature of these peasant uprisings:

> . . . *Few if any movements between 1840 and 1930 were organized around purely economic symbols. Few if any, furthermore, made the redistribution of land a basic objective. If a connecting link or common theme existed in the outbreaks, it was a religious or supernatural element (Sturtevant, 1976, p.17).*

It is interesting to note that the church played a major role in peasant organization, especially during the Martial Law years of President Marcos. Basic Christian Communities were organized in parishes throughout the country. This effort was complemented by community organizing work done by development NGOs. The church, including its leaders, became critics of government repression.

Perhaps more than the religious undertones, the fate of peasants' uprisings and movements was heavily influenced by their leaders, such as Luis Taruc and Jeremias Montemayor, who were at the head of strong peasants' organizations. Taruc was the leader of the Huks which, after leading a peasant-based rebellion during the Japanese war, shifted to fighting for land reform after the war. Montemayor was head of the Federation of Free Farmers (FFF), which became one of the strongest advocates for land reform during the regime of President Ferdinand Marcos. Both the Huks and the FFF presented a strong peasant lobby to the government's agrarian reform policies. When President Marcos declared martial law in 1972, the democratic space contracted and it became more difficult to lobby for reforms without being branded a communist. Peasant federations such as the FFF were eventually co-opted by the government, especially after the latter embarked on rural development programmes, such as the green revolution and *samahang nayons* (rural cooperatives).

Peasants' organizations have remained divided and fragmented. There is only one point in the history of the peasants' movement when different peasants' organizations of varying ideological persuasions united and formed a common front to pursue policy advocacy with the government. This occurred in 1986 after the EDSA revolution which ousted President Marcos, at a time when President Corazon Aquino had both legislative and executive powers. Twelve federations, claiming a total membership of 1.5 million farmers, united and formed the Congress for a People's Agrarian Reform (CPAR). CPAR's advocacy heightened during the period when President Aquino came out with Presidential Proclamations on Agrarian Reform, and when Congress deliberated and passed the Comprehensive Agrarian Reform Law. This unity, however, was short-lived. Members of CPAR agreed to disband in 1993 after organizational, personal and ideological differences became insurmountable.

In the beginning it was easy for the 12 federations to come together under the banner of CPAR because there was a basis for unity. The common agenda was to pressurize the government for a policy and programme on land reform. When the government promulgated CARP, the member federations of CPAR took different positions, some largely influenced by the political ideologies they belonged to. Some groups held the position that, although CARP was imperfect and had loopholes, it was certainly more progressive than other laws and it contained 'windows of opportunity' for peasant participation. The communist-backed groups, on the other hand, completely rejected CARP and called for more radical peasant initiatives such as land occupations. Furthermore, when the government started supporting and even financing some members of CPAR, the basis for unity withered and disappeared.

Continuing role of peasants' organizations

Although there is division and diversity among peasants' organizations in the Philippines today, the sector as a whole has developed and adapted itself to the prevailing socio-political and economic situation. Peasants' organizations and their leaders have matured, as evidenced by the respect shown to each other despite differing positions taken on agrarian issues or in relations with the government.

The lines are still very much drawn. The communist-backed peasant groups still reject CARP, and have condemned the government's agrarian and agricultural policies. Other peasants' groups have maintained critical, selective and principled partnerships with government. They have chosen to sit in government bodies or on committees where their agenda can be advanced. They have participated in programmes where maximum benefits for their members can be secured. In the process of working with the government, these groups have also been able to translate on-the-ground experiences into concrete policy proposals.

An ongoing phenomenon in the rural areas is the 'mushrooming' of rural organizations of farmers, farm workers, tribal communities, women, co-operatives, livelihood associations and multisectoral groups. Many of these organizations are not affiliated to any national federation, yet they have engaged government in their localities and have been effective in doing so. While the massive increase in government, foreign and NGO programmes over the past few years has contributed to this phenomenon, the main factor has been a growing consciousness among the rural poor that organizing themselves to meaningfully participate in their own development is their right and obligation under a democracy.

AGRARIAN CONFLICT

Before Spanish colonization, Philippine society was governed by a local chieftain (*Datu*) who rendered judgement in disputes among his people. His word was final and executory. Such was the manner in which the people managed their conflicts.

Present-day Philippine rural society is very different. Conflicts, especially those related to land, abound between and among rural folk. Whereas before the word of the *Datu* was law of the land, now numerous laws enacted over the past 100 years serve to guide those who render judgement. Whereas the *Datu* was closely involved with the people he ruled, the current judicial system is complicated, inaccessible and alien to the rural people.

Agrarian conflict has been defined in RA 6677 as any controversy relating to tenurial arrangements. In the rural villages, controversies include conflicts arising from subleasing arrangements, that is, a farmer leasing land from another farmer who possesses an ongoing lease from the original owner; land boundary disputes, especially in the absence of defined boundaries between home lots; subdivision of land inheritance; illegal trespassing; and illegal squatting by landless people in large properties of landowners.

There are agrarian conflicts that occur during the conduct of the land transfer process. These controversies include conflicts arising from delineation of lands covered by land reform and those retained by the landowner; identification of farmer-beneficiaries, especially in cases where a landowner or a corporation has a preference for former tenants, employees or workers; and conflicts among farmer-beneficiaries over choice of the most productive lands awarded to them.

There are channels, mechanisms and processes open to peasants in the settlement of disputes. There are both formal and informal structures and processes. The former consists of the regular courts, judicial processes and quasi-judicial structures and processes prescribed and afforded by law; the latter consists of peasants' organizations, indigenous structures, and extralegal means and activities employed by the peasants to settle disputes or secure favourable decisions and victories in their agrarian struggle. This section takes a cursory look at these two channels, and their inherent strengths and weaknesses.

Peasants and the judicial system

Two major mechanisms are worth examining. The first is the regular judicial process using the regular courts, but emphasis will be placed on the *Katarungang Pambarangay* (*barangay* or village court). The second is the system established by RA 6657 which includes two basic and important mechanisms: the Barangay Agrarian Reform Council (BARC) and the Department of Agrarian Reform Adjudication Board (DARAB).

Katarungang Pambarangay *(village justice)*

Farmers dread the idea of going to court, which involves setting aside time normally used for productive activities on the farm, and spending what little money they have for transportation fares to attend never-ending hearings. The proceedings in court and even the consultations with lawyers are equally horrifying experiences.

Michael Fremerey expounds on the alienation of villagers from the formal justice system:

> *Whereas the villager is fully aware of those customary rules which accompany him throughout his lifetime, and defines by commonly accepted norms and sanctions his role within a confined community, he hardly conceives the standards which are set for his rights and duties by modern law. The 'remoteness' of modern law is symbolized by the physical absence of legal institutions in the village . . . Adding to this is the demoralizing experience that, whenever contact with the legal system is established, the villager mostly appears to be on the losing side (Fremerey, 1990, p.33).*

It was in response to this situation that, in 1978, the Philippine government enacted a law to 'delegalize' the justice system. Presidential Decree No. 1508, Establishing a System of Amicably Settling Disputes at the Barangay Level, was signed into law by President Ferdinand E. Marcos on 11 June 1978. The primary objectives of the *Katarungang Pambarangay* Law are: to promote the speedy administration of justice; to perpetuate the time-honoured tradition of settling disputes amicably for the maintenance of peace and harmony; to implement the constitutional mandate to preserve and develop Filipino culture; and to relieve the courts of docket congestion and thereby enhance the quality of justice dispensed by them.

This decree established in each *barangay* a body known as *Lupon Tagapayapa*, composed of the *barangay* captain (village chief) as chairman and not less than 10 nor more than 20 members who are appointed by the *barangay* captain and constituted as a group every two years. A conciliation panel is constituted for each dispute brought before the *Lupon*. This panel is called the *Pangkat ng Tagapagkasundo*, consisting of three members who are chosen by agreement of parties to the dispute from the list of *Lupon* members. The *Lupon* members in the *Pangkat* mediate and conciliate disputes at the village level, with the basic principle being to resolve the conflict at the lower level before it is elevated to the next level. In the light of this, the *Lupon* has authority to settle all disputes except for those involving government bodies, public officials, as well as cases where there is no private offended party, or where other municipalities or residents of other *barangays* are involved.

The Barangay Agrarian Reform Council (BARC) and the Department of Agrarian Reform Adjudication Board (DARAB)

The BARC is composed of representative(s) of farmer and farm-worker beneficiaries and non-beneficiaries; agricultural cooperatives and other farmer organizations; the Barangay Council; non-governmental organization (NGOs); landowners; and officials from the Department of Agriculture (DA), Department of Environment and Natural Resources (DENR), DAR officials assigned to the area; and the Land Bank of the Philippines.

With regard to conflict mediation, BARC has three main roles which involve giving support to the implementation of the agrarian reform programme; mediating, conciliating and arbitrating conflicts and issues brought to it for resolution; and acting as a conflict-mediator in agrarian disputes over tenurial and financial arrangements. Further to these tasks, BARC helps identify qualified beneficiaries and landowners within the *barangay*, facilitates their demands to obtain credit from lending institutions, as well as coordinating the delivery of support services to them. It also assists DAR by evaluating the accuracy of the initial parcellary mapping of the concerned village, and its value, as well as by preparing periodic reports on how the implementation of CARP is progressing in a certain area.

BARC is also required to mediate, conciliate and settle agrarian disputes lodged before it within 30 days from recognition of the case. If no settlement is arrived at after the prescribed period, the BARC shall issue a certification of proceedings and furnish copies to the concerned parties.

The next recourse for peasants, agrarian reform beneficiaries or affected landowners, after the BARC, is the Department of Agrarian Reform Adjudication Board (DARAB). Similar to the process employed by the *Katarungang Pambarangay* in the elevation of cases to the higher courts, the DAR will not recognize any agrarian dispute or controversy unless a certification is presented from the BARC that the dispute has been submitted to it for mediation and conciliation without any success of settlement.

Thus a distinctive feature of RA 6657 is the assignment of quasi-judicial powers to the DAR through the creation of the DARAB, which has parallel structures at the provincial level (the judge of which is called a Provincial Adjudicator or PARAD), the regional level (judge is called a Regional Adjudicator or RARAD), and the central level. Section 50 of RA 6657 vests upon DAR the jurisdiction to determine and adjudicate agrarian reform matters. The law even goes further, saying that the DAR shall have exclusive original jurisdiction over all matters involving the implementation of agrarian reform.

Performance of the formal structures

To what extent have these formal legal structures benefited the peasants, or how far have they been used by peasants to settle agrarian disputes?

A report by the Ministry of Local Government on the performance of the *Katarungang Pambarangay* for the period 1979–83 states that 179 398 disputes were brought to the *Lupons* for action (Sosmena, 1985). Eighty-seven per cent (156 527) of the total number of cases were amicably settled at the *barangay* level, while 13 704 disputes were forwarded to the courts. Accordingly, these settlements have resulted in the decongestion of cases in courts, which is one of the objectives of the law, and have also contributed to government savings.

Unfortunately, the report does not provide a breakdown of the types of disputes settled by the *Lupons*. Such information would have revealed the magnitude of agrarian disputes *vis-à-vis* the non-agrarian disputes brought before the *Lupons*. Jopillo (1989), in a study on dispute settlement in two *barangays* in Bago City, province of Negros Occidental, provides interesting information on the types of cases brought before the *Lupons* in the two *barangays*. In a six-year period the study recorded 170 cases filed in Barangay Napoles and 72 cases filed in Barangay Lag-asan. The cases were classified into two categories, namely criminal and civil, and each category was further broken down into specific types of cases. Jopillo also devotes a whole chapter to the disputes involving public policy, defined in her paper as 'a guiding rule or course adopted and pursued by actors in dealing with a problem or matter of public concern'. Table 8.3 shows the breakdown of disputes per *barangay*.

An official document issued in April 1983 expanded the scope of the *Katarungang Pambarangay* programme to include complaints or petitions involving disputes. Jopillo attributes the number of disputes to the agricultural nature of the *barangays* studied. She further states that there were more agrarian disputes in Barangay Napoles and none in Barangay Lag-asan because there were more residents in Napoles who were either sugar-farm workers or beneficiaries of agrarian reform, in particular the Operation Land Transfer programme (PD 27). The disputes involved sub-leasing arrangements among farmers and some land boundary and land inheritance disputes. According to the study, some of the disputes were amicably settled by the *barangay* captain, while the unresolved disputes were passed on to the local DAR office.

Table 8.3   Number and kinds of disputes regarding public policy brought to the *Lupon* in two *barangays* from the period 1983–88

Cases	Barangay Napoles	Barangay Lag-asan
Ejection	3	11
Demand for payment of debt	18	7
Breach of contract	1	2
Demand for specific performance	8	1
Boundary disputes	2	2
Agrarian disputes	15	0
Total	47	23

Source: Jopillo, 1989.

Other than the number of BARCs already organized, DAR does not have any evaluation report on the functional effectiveness of the BARC. Some DAR field technicians, however, say that the BARCs were helpful only in so far as farmer beneficiary identification was concerned.

In relation to the DARAB, the DAR (1996) report states that from the start of CARP up to 1996, regular and land valuation cases adjudicated have reached 71 551, 86 per cent of all cases filed during the period. In addition the report provides some figures on their 1996 accomplishment, reproduced in Table 8.4. There is no accompanying explanation on the distinction between the types of cases found in this Table. Although everything is found under the section 'Delivery of Agrarian Justice', an ordinary person will not be able to distinguish between what is judicial, what is DARAB, and what is agrarian law implementation. Furthermore, while DAR claims to have overshot its targets in terms of cases, it is not clear how targets were set and established in the first place. Also, when is a particular case considered resolved? The report fails to provide a clear picture on how the DARAB as a mechanism for administering agrarian justice is responding to the plight of the peasants.

Table 8.4   Delivery of agrarian justice: resolution by type of case (January to November 1996)

Type of case	Cases resolved	Target
Judicial	895	3094
DARAB	21 458	14 240
Agrarian law implementation	8319	8000
Total	30 672	25 334

Source: DAR (1996).

Peasants and the extralegal struggle

There is a tradition of activism among peasants' organizations in the Philippines. Farmers have marched in the streets, barricaded government agencies, organized protest rallies, boycotted products, occupied lands, and staged hunger strikes. As discussed above, peasants' organizations fall under the informal mechanism category for agrarian conflict resolution. The tactics they employ, which deviate from legal norms but are not illegal, may be called the extralegal struggle. The case studies in the next section showcase two peasants' organizations and their strategies, tactics and activities in addressing conflict situations.

CASE STUDIES

Case 1 – role of the Katipunan ng Samahang Magsasaka (KASAMA) in resolving conflicts related to tenancy in the sugarlands of Batangas

This case study demonstrates how a grassroots organization manages conflicts between its farmer members and landowners, and between farmer subtenants and tenants, as a result of a shift from share tenancy to leasehold.

Background of the organization

Katipunan ng Samahang Magsasaka (KASAMA) is a permanent, democratic and independent union organized and managed by peasants to protect and promote their rights and interests; to develop their working conditions in their place of work; and to uplift their standard of living in society through organized action. Membership consists of small owner–cultivators, tenants and subtenants, leaseholders, and landless rural workers.

KASAMA envisions a society of justice, freedom and democracy where people own or control the primary means of production to be able to provide for their basic needs, and have enough power to participate at all levels of decision-making in society towards development for their common good. Its mission is to form a broad and strong peasants' federation in the Southern Tagalog region that will advocate and implement a genuine agrarian reform and rural development programme, in order to be able to respond to their present and historical problems of poverty and injustice so that they can fully participate in the act and process of social transformation.

The ultimate goal of KASAMA is the rationalization of agrarian relations in the area through the implementation of genuine agrarian reform, that is, land to the tiller. A step towards this goal is the conversion of share tenancy system to leasehold and the reduction of land rental. They believe that such goals can be achieved only through broadening and strengthening the federation by organizing and training its members and leaders.

The activities of KASAMA include organizing and maintaining local chapters; providing legal assistance in agrarian disputes and court cases, and representing peasants in collective negotiations; conducting education and training programmes for members and leaders; establishing linkages with other private or government agencies and organizations; fund raising; mobilizing at local, provincial and national levels towards the attainment of KASAMA's goals and objectives, especially those that would secure pro-peasant laws; managing and supervising income-generating projects for the benefit of members; and the formation of a province-wide cooperative.

Today KASAMA is a peasant federation with over 2500 household members located in 146 village chapters in eight municipalities of Western Batangas.

Socio-economic profile of KASAMA members

A KASAMA member is generally a male sugarcane farmer with an average age of 50 years. The majority have either finished or started elementary school education. In terms of tenurial status, 45.5 per cent are leaseholders, 44.2 per cent are tenants, and 5.7 per cent are holders of the Certificate of Land Ownership Award (CLOA).

Farming is the main source of income, and is usually augmented by income from off-farm activities. The primary crop produced is sugarcane, followed by rice. The average area of land tilled is between 1.6 and 2.5 ha. Average income received annually is about 25 000 pesos (Php25 000, equivalent to US$675).

Managing conflict through legal assistance

In a survey conducted by KASAMA among its members, the legal assistance programme rated highest among all the services provided by the organization. Satisfaction was high because it dealt directly with the member's tenurial situation.

The predominant agrarian situation in Batangas is tenancy in sugar farms. KASAMA's legal programme is aimed at transforming the share tenant into leaseholder and eventually into small owner–cultivator. In the process of working towards this transformation, KASAMA has to assist in settling the dispute at two levels: first between tenant and landlord, and second between tenant and subtenant.

In a share tenancy relationship, the practice is for a tenant to share expenses and produce with his landlord on a 50–50 basis. More often than not actual sharing amounts to 70–30 in favour of the landlord. Share tenants have little or no control over the management of the farm. The type of crop to be planted is determined by the landlord, who also handles milling of sugar. Therefore the tenant often has no control, and no information on the milling and selling transactions, especially with regard to the price at which the sugar was sold. It is also common for a tenant to be heavily indebted to the landlord because the latter lends money for production expenses that including land preparation, seeding, weeding, fertilizers, fertilizer application, trucking and hauling.

The shift from share tenancy to leasehold immediately produces an average 50 per cent increase in the income of the farmer per hectare. In leasehold a tenant pays a fixed rate of 25 per cent of net income to the landlord. The tenant also enjoys more control over management of the farm, especially the type of crops planted.

KASAMA's Legal Assistance Programme reports that for the period 1990–92 the programme facilitated the filing of 134 petitions with the DARAB. Some 437 petitions were involved with 120 landowners in 735 ha, and have so far resulted in three cases involving five leasehold petitioners settled amicably; four cases involving 87 petitioners resolved with petitioners becoming CLOA holders; 58 cases with decision to mill sugarcane in the names of petitioner and landowner with proceeds divided on a 75–25 sharing in favour of the farmers; and 12 members awarded Emancipation Patents under the Operation Land Transfer Programme.

Figures taken from the 1995 KASAMA plan also indicate the performance of the Legal Assistance Programme. For instance, of the targeted 30 leasehold cases to be submitted to DARAB for decision, 38 cases were actually submitted; and of the targeted submission of leasehold pleadings to the DARAB for 70 petitioners, 132 new pleadings were actually submitted. The report, however, does not indicate how yearly targets were set.

How satisfied are the farmer-members with KASAMA's Legal Assistance Programme? Is the programme assisting them in settling agrarian disputes? Data from KASAMA's Impact Evaluation Report provide some relevant information. While the report does not provide clear distinctions on the difference among the types of legal assistance provided and the reasons for the respective percentages per assistance, it can be deduced that the high uptake by members of the fixed rental assistance is due to KASAMA's strategy of transforming share tenants to leaseholders as a transition before becoming owner–cultivators.

Several observations can be drawn from Table 8.5. One interesting factor is the way the reasons have been constructed and worded. Availability of assistance, membership and KASAMA's understanding are not mutually exclusive factors. In other words, a member can take up KASAMA's services for all the reasons cited, and a farmer has no compelling reason of the three. Uptake due to membership is also difficult to understand: is this reason cited to infer the advantages of being a member as compared to not being a member?

Interpreting the data, however, shows that availability of assistance is a key factor in making farmers go to KASAMA for legal assistance. This means that such services are not readily available elsewhere, especially

Table 8.5   Reasons for approaching KASAMA for legal assistance

Reason	Number of respondents	Percentage
Availability of assistance	184	72.7
Due to membership	57	22.5
KASAMA understands	12	4.8
Total	253	100.0

from government, the formal justice system, or the private sector. It would have been helpful to find out if farmers also went to KASAMA because its legal services are inexpensive. Private lawyers and law firms might be as readily accessible as KASAMA were it not for the expensive rates they charge. The term 'KASAMA understands' also connotes the perception among farmers that their own organization is sympathetic to their cause and is therefore friendlier to them. Perhaps this is indicative of how alien the formal courts, including the *Katarungang Pambarangay*, have become to them.

Case 2 – MAPALAD farmers

This case study demonstrates how a peasants' organization can employ both legal and extralegal means to settle a dispute with the landlord and with the government. The issue is primarily concerned with conflict in land use, that is, whether prime agricultural land is to be awarded to farmers under agrarian reform, or whether the land can be converted to industrial and commercial purposes. There are several levels of conflict: between a peasants' organization and the landlord; between the peasants' organization and a branch of government; between the landlord and a branch of government; and between one branch of government and another.

Background

The MAPALAD farmers are beneficiaries of the CARP over a 144 ha parcel of agricultural land in Barangay San Vicente, Sumilao, Bukidnon. They were issued a CLOA on 25 September 1995 by the DAR.

The land formerly belonged to Norberto Quisumbing Sr Management and Development Corporation (NQSRMDC), and was covered by Compulsory Acquisition issued by the DAR as early as 3 January 1990 and a Notice of Acquisition issued on 25 October 1991.

On 11 December 1993, Mr Gaudencio Beduya, for the Bukidnon Agro-industrial Development Association (BAIDA), filed an application before the office of the DAR for conversion of holding from agricultural to agro-industrial.

On 20 October 1994, in a letter addressed to Mr Gaudencio Beduya, DAR Undersecretary Jose C. Medina, Jr, Chairman of the Presidential Agrarian

Reform Council Land Use Technical Committee, informed Mr Beduya that the application for conversion could not be given due course, stating that:

> It was deemed that since the area is found to be agriculturally productive and irrigated, it actually falls within the non-negotiability provision on conversion, as provided under AO No. 20, Series of 1992, hence, conversion should not be given due course.

On 14 November, DAR Secretary Ernesto D. Garilao issued an Order denying the application for conversion of the subject property from agricultural to industrial on the grounds that: (a) the area is considered as a prime agricultural land with irrigation facility, (b) the subject landholding has long been covered by a Notice of Compulsory Acquisition (NCA) and the existing policy on withdrawal or lifting on areas covered by NCA is not applicable under the given circumstances, and (c) there was no clear and tangible compensation package or arrangements for the beneficiaries whichever group they might be, primarily due to the pending case of the DARAB.

In the same order Secretary Garilao stated that:

> Accordingly without delay, the subject property shall be placed under CARP compulsory coverage in accordance with the schedule of implementation prescribed in Section 7 of RA 6657, and distribute the same to all qualified beneficiaries.

A Motion for Reconsideration denying the application for conversion was filed by the former landowner on 9 January 1995, but this motion was denied on 7 June 1995. Subsequently, a CLOA was generated and issued in the name of the MAPALAD farmers. Thereafter, Norberto Quisumbing filed an Appeal on the Order of Secretary Garilao before the Office of the President.

On 29 March, Executive Secretary Ruben D. Torres, 'by authority of the President', rendered a decision which set aside the appealed order of Secretary Garilao and approved the application for conversion of NQSR-MDC/BAIDA. On 24 May 1996 DAR moved for a reconsideration of the Decision of the Office of the President.

On 10 April 1997, pending resolution of the Motion for Reconsideration filed by DAR, NQSRMDC/BAIDA filed before the Regional Trial Court of Malaybalay, Bukidnon, a complaint for cancellation and annulment of title, damages and injunction, naming the MAPALAD farmers as private defendants.

Despite a Motion to Dismiss based on lack of jurisdiction filed by the MAPALAD farmers, an order was issued on 27 June 1997 enjoining the farmers from entering and occupying the disputed property. Thereafter, the MAPALAD farmers filed a petition for Certiorari and Prohibition requesting the issuance of a temporary restraining order and writ of preliminary injunction before the Court of Appeals.

Meanwhile, on 23 June 1997, more than one year after DAR filed its

Motion for Reconsideration, Executive Secretary Ruben Torres issued an Order dismissing the Motion for Reconsideration filed by DAR on 24 May 1996, on the grounds that the said Motion was filed beyond the 15 days prescribed period by law and declaring that the Decision dated 29 March 1996 had become final and executory.

On 14 July 1997 the DAR filed a second Motion for Reconsideration on the Order of Executive Secretary Ruben Torres.

Managing conflict through legal and extralegal means

It was clear from the start that the MAPALAD farmers used the existing legal system to attain their objectives. They participated in the land acquisition and distribution process established by the DAR. When the landlord used the legal procedures in DAR, the Office of the President, and the regular courts to question and overturn the orders given, the MAPALAD farmers put their faith in the same system. However, when the same legal system started contradicting itself, the farmers had to resort to extralegal means of struggle.

The legal battle   The legal processes of the case are aptly described in the previous section. The MAPALAD farmers would have had a difficult time were it not for the legal assistance provided by various support groups. The legal assistance provided by the NGOs was crucial to the legal and extralegal struggle. Lawyers from development NGOs such as Balay Mindanaw Foundation (BMFI), and legal NGOs such as Sentro para sa Alternatibong Lingap Panlegal and KAISAHAN (a local term meaning unity), provided the much-needed legal tactics, strategies and representations in hearings and meetings.

In presenting their side to the public and to the government bodies including the courts, the MAPALAD farmers argued as follows.

■ The law on the side of the farmers is clear by virtue of the land being irrigated with an irrigation canal which passes through the centre of the land. It is not a mere right of way. It has numerous outlet canals to irrigate the land. It is in fact part of the 600 hectare irrigation project of the National Irrigation Administration for the province of Bukidnon.

■ Conversion of these irrigated lands seriously endangers the capability of the country to answer its own food needs. Administrative Order No. 20, series of 1992, issued by President Ramos, says that irrigated lands where water is available to support rice and other crops are non-negotiable for conversion.

■ The farmers were issued a CLOA through the proper process. A Notice of Coverage was issued by the DAR on 3 January 1990. A Notice of Acquisition was issued on 25 October 1991. They were selected to be the rightful beneficiaries since they were farm workers of the same land. Mr Quisumbing has never attempted to deny this. Once a title has been issued this should be respected until cancelled by the courts. There has been no cancellation order, and yet the landowner claims ownership to the land and has prevented the farmers from entering the land.

■ It is claimed that the decision of Executive Secretary Ruben Torres allowing the conversion of the land is final and executory and must be respected. However, there is a pending Motion for Reconsideration filed by the DAR which awaits Mr Torres' ruling. Secondly, the farmers were never made a party when NQSRMDC–BAIDA first appealed the DAR's decision to the Office of the President. How can a decision be rendered which may deprive the farmers of the land when they were not even given a chance to answer the appeal? This is against their constitutional right to due process. There is therefore no 'Presidential Mandate' in favour of the conversion. In fact, any Presidential Mandate will be found in the issuances of President Ramos to preserve prime agricultural land.

■ The power of local government units to reclassify prime agricultural lands at any cost must not be allowed. When this is exercised, national needs, such as balanced and sustainable development, must be borne in mind.

■ It is also claimed that the power of local government to reclassify lands must be upheld against the power of the DAR. But this should not be regarded as a conflict between the power of local government and the DAR.

■ The farmers are not against development. In fact, they support any programme that is people-led, sustainable and environmentally sound. The NQSRMDC–BAIDA project, which was endorsed by Governor Carlos Fortich of Bukidnon, cannot be called people-led as this was made without proper consultations with those who will be affected, including the farmer beneficiaries of CARP.

■ The farmers have long dreamed of improving their income and generating jobs from agriculture. From increased productivity derived from the land, new industries will rise. Agro-processing plants will convert raw materials into finished products. Schools and universities will be filled with happy, well fed and empowered students who are proud of their farmer parents who struggled to have secure tenure over the land. These dreams were made possible when the land was declared as an agrarian reform community in 1994.

The extralegal battle   Based on the events that transpired, the MAPALAD farmers employed two major and crucial extralegal activities. The first was the attempted land occupation that happened on 15 July 1997. The second was the month-long hunger strike in October 1997 which caught the attention of the whole nation.

On 14 July 1997, after the expiration of the Temporary Restraining Order and with no injunction served on them, 78 MAPALAD farmers entered the property and started tilling the land. They did so on the strength of the CLOA which had already been awarded to them. Security guards were taken by surprise and, although shots were fired into the air, the farmers remained in the property.

The next day the guards of NQSRMDC harassed the farmers. The guards burned the farmers' huts and streamers, destroyed the farm plot fences, confiscated farm implements, and let loose some 60 carabaos to attack the farmers and trample on their farms. At the same time, additional guards with powerful guns arrived to augment the security force. On the third day of the land occupation, Norberto Quisumbing Jr, accompanied by an ex-Colonel and commander of the security force, drove the farmers away from the land.

The violence and force used by the landowner during the land occupation had a traumatic effect on the farmers. Ruling out the use of counter-violence against the landowner, the farmers decided to follow their tribal custom of *lugol* or fasting. The farmers belonged to an indigenous group called *Higaonons* and, as part of their custom, they would fast, sometimes to the point of death, as a form of protest against any member of the community or household. It was their belief that fasting or hunger strike was the highest form of protest they could make in response to the violence used against them by the landowner and in response to the deadlock reached by instrumentalities of government on their case.

The farmers, together with NGO workers involved in the campaign, organized the hunger strike in two areas. One group composed of 11 hunger strikers camped out in front of the DAR in Manila, while the second group of seven hunger strikers staged their strike in the town plaza of Cagayan de Oro City. The hunger strike officially started on 9 October 1997. The hunger strikers had a clear demand: Reverse the Order of the Office of the President (signed by Executive Secretary Torres) and give back the land to them. The target of the protest was President Ramos. In effect, the message of the demand was for the President to change his previous order approving conversion of the land, honour the titles already given to the farmers by the DAR, and ensure their installation on the land.

Various preparations were made before the hunger strike. Three NGOs led the support group in Cagayan de Oro: BMFI, Kaanib Foundation, and the Philippine Partnership for the Development of Human Resources in Rural Areas (PhilDHRRA). The support group in Manila was led by a group of NGOs and a peasant federation called ARNow! (People's Campaign for Agrarian Reform Network). A command structure which coordinated, planned tactics and made decisions was established between the Manila and Cagayan de Oro support groups. In ARNow!, groups were established to undertake specific functions, including the Media Group which handled all media-related matters; the Camp Management Group which handled day-to-day activities and concerns in the strike area; the Legal Group which handled the preparation of legal documents and argumentations; the Finance Group which handled fund-raising activities; and the Education and External Relations Group which handled the mobilization of other sectors, such as the church, students, workers, the urban poor, women, professionals and others. A negotiation panel was also formed to spearhead any talks with the government.

The most important preparation, however, was the spiritual preparation made by the farmers to ready themselves for the hunger strike. They knew that they were going to go through a very difficult physical, mental and emotional ordeal. But they were willing to sacrifice even their own lives so that justice would be given to them, their families and the other farmer beneficiaries of MAPALAD.

The campaign and the hunger strike lasted for 27 days. On 5 November President Ramos reversed his previous order and awarded 100 ha out of the contested 144 ha to the MAPALAD farmers. The remaining 44 ha were given to the landowner for development into an agro-industrial area. The 100–44 formula was recommended by the inter-agency task force organized by order of the President. This task force, which was headed by Secretary Salvador Escudero of the Department of Agriculture, conducted hearings and negotiated with the landowner and the farmers.

The campaign, described by one national newspaper as 'the most successful mass campaign during the administration of President Ramos', was effective because of several factors. First and foremost was the sincerity and bravery of the MAPALAD farmers. No one doubted their seriousness in seeing the hunger strike to its very end, to the point of death, unless their case was resolved. Pictures of their emaciated faces and worn-out figures occupied almost all the major newspapers during the campaign. Their plight, and the whole issue of agrarian reform and land conversion, became hot topics on the radio and television and in the newspapers. The campaign gained strength when Cardinal Sin, the highest official of the church in the land, made a pastoral visit to the farmers. Members of different religious congregations followed suit and even joined the strikers in the camp. Masses were held nightly in a makeshift tent beside the tent of the hunger strikers. Soon various politicians and personalities started showing up in the strike area. Members of Congress and the Senate also started calling for hearings and inquiries on the case.

Public opinion was swayed in favour of the farmers, and the government had no option but to listen to their demands. Thus on 21 October the President met with the farmers in Malacanang Palace. When the President gave his assurance that he would decide on their case within 10 days, the farmers agreed to eat crackers and soup with the President. The farmers also agreed to bring down the level of the protest to fasting. During the hunger strike they took nothing but water. During the 10–day fast they took biscuits and soup in the evenings. On 30 October, when no decision had come from the President, the farmers resumed their hunger strike. This decision was reached by the farmers despite assurances from government envoys that the President would be making a decision within a few days.

The first days of November were tense. By this time the health of the farmers had deteriorated to dangerous levels. Some members of the support group assigned to the camp even asked the command structure to be relieved of their duties in the camp because they could no longer bear seeing the suffering of the hunger strikers. The situation reached a point where one of the hunger strikers, Linda Ligmon, out of despair and frustration, announced that she would also stop taking water. Then, on 5 November, the President announced his decision in favour of the farmers. After celebrating their initial triumph by breaking their hunger strike and taking a bowl of soup, the farmers went back to their homes expecting that the DAR would process their titles and install them on their farms based on President Ramos' order. The Quisumbings, however, lost no time in filing a case in the Supreme Court contesting the Order of the President.

From November 1997 to April 1998 nothing happened. Although the DAR continued to generate the new titles, these were not given to the farmers because of the pending case in the Supreme Court. Then in April the Second Division of the Supreme Court came out with a controversial decision that affirmed the previous order of Executive Secretary Torres approving the conversion on the grounds of technicality. This decision in effect set aside the order of President Ramos.

The farmers have resumed their legal and extralegal battle. They have filed, through their counsel, a Motion for Reconsideration asking the Supreme Court to sit *en banc* and decide on the case based on its merits and not on merely technical issues, as the issue at hand is one of substantive justice. On the extralegal front they have set up camps in front of DAR and the Supreme Court, and have called their protest an 'anger strike'. A big event that caught national and international media attention was the visit of incoming Philippine President Joseph Estrada to their camp. On 8 June, President Estrada had lunch with the farmers and announced his support to their cause. Furthermore, he made an announcement that his administration would put priority on food security and would go slow on land conversions.

At the time of writing, the Supreme Court has passed a resolution asking the Quisumbings to respond to the Motion for Reconsideration filed by the farmers and the Office of the President. In the meantime the farmers are still camped outside the Supreme Court.

CONCLUSIONS

Agrarian reform is a contentious programme which creates conflict and division between and within classes. Agrarian disputes necessarily arise, and are often related to tenancy relations and claims to ownership of the land. When these conditions prevail in a rural setting, what mechanisms may be used to settle and manage these conflicts? The chapter has shown two major categories: the formal and the informal mechanisms. The formal mechanism consists of the regular courts and the judicial and quasi-judicial processes prescribed and afforded by law. More specifically these pertain to the *Katarungang Pambarangay*, the BARC and the DARAB. The informal mechanism, on the other hand, consists of peasants' organizations, indigenous structures, and extralegal means and activities employed by peasants to settle disputes or secure favourable decisions and victories in their agrarian struggle. The case studies discussed above fall under the informal mechanism. The matrix below aims to aid analysis of the effectiveness of these mechanisms.

	Formal mechanism	Informal mechanism
Individual farmer	Quadrant 1	Quadrant 2
Peasants' organization	Quadrant 3	Quadrant 4

Quadrant 1 (individual farmer–formal mechanism)

Jopillo (1989) gives an indication of how many individual farmers utilize the village justice system or *Katarungang Pambarangay*. In her study of one *barangay* which had an agrarian reform character, 15 agrarian disputes were submitted to the *Lupon* for resolution. It is hard, however, to conclude that this is characteristic of the agrarian villages in the Philippines. It would also be useful to know how many agrarian disputes were not brought before the *Lupons*.

The assessment by the DAR that the BARCs function more as mechanisms to assist in beneficiary identification, rather than in dispute resolution, eliminates the BARC as a formal mechanism that will be used by an individual farmer. In this case farmers go direct to the DAR municipal and provincial offices to seek help in resolving the conflict. This probably explains why there are numerous cases docketed in the DARAB. Consequently, DARAB's solution to the problem is curative rather than preventive. Instead of strengthening the capacity of BARCs to settle local disputes, DARAB's proposal is to strengthen its own structure and system by adding more lawyers and increasing their salaries.

Regardless of whether an individual farmer will utilize the *Lupon* and regular courts or the BARC and the DARAB, another major problem is the question of jurisdiction in agrarian reform implementation. Cana (1993) states this as 'a problem because the apparent ambiguity in our laws with respect to jurisdiction results in multiplicity of suits or litigations which could otherwise be heard in one forum . . . This jurisdiction problem seems to spring from the legal question: is it possible to segregate or differentiate the purely civil aspects of a case from the strictly agrarian?'

Thus in the formal mechanism it is possible that a municipal trial court's decision on an agrarian case is in conflict with the decision of the DARAB. Contending parties, such as landlord and tenant, can wage legal battles in more than one court. This creates confusion and becomes disadvantageous to farmers, who have very limited resources.

Quadrant 2 (individual farmer–informal mechanism)

Individual farmers have a better chance of using or accessing the informal mechanisms if they are members of a peasant organization. The case study on KASAMA showed that the organization's services and resources were geared primarily to their members. Legal assistance was provided to tenants and subtenants who were members of their local chapters.

Individual farmers who are not organization members can, however, benefit from the extralegal action of peasants' organizations. In the case study on MAPALAD, while only 18 farmers engaged in a hunger strike, the decision to award 100 ha of land would benefit even those farmers who are not members of MAPALAD, as long as they qualify as beneficiaries. In the long run, however, these non-members will be assimilated by MAPALAD.

Quadrant 3 (peasants' organization–formal structure)

The performance records of the *Katarungang Pambarangay* or the DARAB do not segregate individual from organizational cases. More research is needed in this area. It is important to find out if DARAB prioritizes cases filed by peasant organizations over cases filed by individual farmers. There is a weakness in the performance evaluation system of DARAB adjudicators which encourages prioritization of individual cases rather than organizational cases. The number of cases he/she decides on measures the performance of an adjudicator. The more cases resolved, the higher the evaluation rating. There is no distinction, however, on the nature of cases. A case involving one farmer is equal to a case involving 100 farmers. Ten individual cases therefore are better than one case involving hundreds of farmers. By resolving the former an adjudicator gains a score of ten, while resolving the latter only gives a score of one. This system fails to consider the gravity a case may have and the potential impact of its resolution.

The MAPALAD farmers made full use of the formal mechanism. The support provided by the legal NGOs was crucial to the effectiveness of their engagement in the formal arena.

Quadrant 4 (peasants' organization–informal structure)

The legal assistance provided by KASAMA is an example of how a peasant organization can set up its own mechanism to settle disputes. When

KASAMA helps a member to become a leaseholder, it has to first settle several relationships. If the leasehold applicant is a tenant, KASAMA makes sure that the subtenant is not in a disadvantageous position after conversion to leasehold. Arrangements acceptable to all parties are worked out. The same holds true if the applicant is a subtenant. Some farmer-leaders were trained by KASAMA to handle conflict resolution and provide legal assistance. These types of training and development required financial resources. In 1997, 80 per cent of KASAMA's expenses of 1.5 million pesos went to support farmer paralegals and paralegal training. This is an area not commonly funded by international donor agencies. More financial support should go to these kinds of programmes.

The MAPALAD case is an example of how effective a peasants' organization can be in using extralegal means to mobilize wide public support for its cause, and in ensuring that agrarian legislation delivers what it is legally supposed to.

Final note

The formal mechanisms provided by the state, especially in a democracy, will always be present. The state, because of changes in governments, will initiate changes that would either strengthen or weaken the formal mechanism. Peasants' organizations must always advocate improvement of the formal mechanisms to make them more responsive to the needs of peasants.

Peasants' organizations must take care of their own. They must be well equipped to operate within the arena of the formal mechanisms (that is, in Quadrant 3). In this respect, NGOs and legal aid groups have a lot of work to do. However, when everything else fails a Quadrant 4 situation must be a ready option. Peasants' organizations must be able to muster their internal strengths and creativity and believe in their own capability to solve their problems.

Notes

CHAPTER 1

1. With research input from Uzma Hashmi, United Nations Research Institute for Social Development.
2. This work is formally animated by the Popular Coalition to Eradicate Hunger and Poverty in Rome (an IFAD-led consortium of bilateral/multilateral agencies and NGOs working in the area of rural poverty alleviation and agricultural reforms).
3. Many of these aspects were brought up and heatedly discussed between representatives of grassroots organizations participating in IFAD's network and concerned IFAD staff at an open meeting marking the formal launch of the network in Rome in February 1998. The author also participated in this meeting.
4. The Vatican itself has recently called for an improved and just land redistribution (Vatican, 1997).
5. Land restitution has at times also meant giving back the land to the previous landlords or landowning classes, as is currently the case in several of the Eastern European countries. To a limited extent, this seems to be happening in Nicaragua, Mozambique and Ethiopia as well.
6. At present there is little open international debate on the flexible use of available arable and other land areas for food production and livelihood sustenance. International concern regarding global warming and biodiversity protection is frequently contradictory to local priorities for resource use (Ghimire, 1997; Ghimire and Pimbert, 1997). The possible environmental impacts of land extension, reclamation and extensive sustainable use of various types of local natural resources should be considered from the initial planning phase, together with the development of appropriate mechanisms to limit the negative ones. However, to completely overlook the prospects for food production and other livelihood activities because of the perceived fear of environmental degradation is historically unrealistic, and also shows a lack of imagination and social empathy on the part of environmental planners and activists.
7. The GTZ, in a study of land tenure, notes that nearly 1000 people have been killed in Brazil over the past decade due to land conflicts, with most being indigenous peoples; in northern Ghana more than 2000 people died in 1994 alone for the above reason with 25 000 others having to flee the country; in Malaysia and Indonesia the contradictions between indigenous and state laws regarding land are also causing severe rural unrest, as is the case in most of sub-Saharan Africa (GTZ, 1998, pp.21–22).

CHAPTER 3

1. Translated from Spanish to English by Mariana Mozdzer.
2. Phase I originated in Decrees 153 and 154 of March 1980. This phase was characterized by the formation of large cooperatives operating in the form of collective land tenure and production, and which were created after the expropriation of estates of over 350 ha. In April 1980, Decree 207 (also called Phase III) was passed. (Phase II was designed but never implemented.) In Phase III small leaseholders became landowners. In 1992, as a result of the Peace agreements between the Frente Farabundo Martí de Liberación Nacional and the government, the Programme of Land Transfers was initiated in order to benefit the demobilized armed forces on both sides of the conflict.
3. According to the 1993 Agricultural Census, 44 per cent of real estates were declared as totally owned by the producer (Salgado, 1996, p.96).
4. In the case of Nicaragua agrarian reform could re-emerge, considering the existence of new armed groups working in rural areas who claim that the government did not fulfil its pledge to redistribute land to ex-combatants.
5. This happened in Honduras, although with a different intensity, during military rule in the 1970s; in El Salvador during the civil–military governments (1979–83); and in Nicaragua during the Sandinista period.
6. Even in those cases where the production units were legally cooperatives in which the members contracted debts with the state for the transferred property, 'the high degree of state control made these cooperatives look like estates run by the state' (Pelupessy, 1998, p.145).
7. Phase III benefited some 38 000 producers. However, Prosterman, who inspired the law for Phase III (29 April 1980), expected to reach between 137 000 and 183 000 families (Prosterman, 1985, p.99).
8. Prosterman is the author of works such as *Land Reform and Democratic Development*, Johns Hopkins University Press, Baltimore, 1987. His pro-agrarian reform approach relied on the belief that providing small individual plots would be the best antidote against the advance of communism. He followed the ideas of Ladejinsky (1977), an anti-Communist Russian immigrant to the USA and adviser to the government on how to stop the advance of the Red Army led by Mao Ze Dong in China. He also advised on the preparation of a law on agrarian reform in Japan as well as several other Asian countries.
9. This is more evident in Nicaragua, where the first law on land reform was practically ready to be executed soon after the first political advent of the Sandinistas, but for political reasons it was postponed until July 1981.
10. The supporters of this new technological approach believe that it has more chance of implementation on medium-scale peasant holdings: those who have very little land need extra work outside their plot to increase their income; and alternative technologies are inconvenient for the better-off sectors employing contractual workers as they are more intensive. In Nicaragua, the average plot of land ranges from 10 to 15 ha. Considering the extensive character of Nicaraguan agriculture, peasants would be in the medium size category and, in consequence, be potentially interested in new technologies.
11. ECODEPA was created by UNAG with the support of the Swedish Centre for Cooperation in the mid-1980s. During the Sandinista revolution it concentrated on emergency activities and the provisioning of rural areas. In the 1990s it became involved in coffee exports and the import of inputs and

machinery. It was badly in debt with different banks and stopped operating in 1996. SOCRA in El Salvador was a CONFRAS project supported by international cooperation. In the early 1990s it built a modern coffee plantation and started exporting coffee purchased from CONFRAS cooperatives. In 1998 its financial situation was very precarious due to increasing multiple debts.
12. The theory behind this alternative was conceived in the Programa de Formacion y Seguridad Alimenticia which contributed to the creation of the Asociación Centroamericana de Organizaciones Campesinas para la Cooperación y el Desarrollo.

CHAPTER 4

1. I wish to acknowledge with deep gratitude the help provided by several colleagues at the Land Tenure Center, University of Wisconsin–Madison: William Thiesenhusen, Don Kanel and Herman Felstehausen. They provided suggestions for references to be consulted and made many helpful comments on earlier drafts.

CHAPTER 5

1. This contractual obligation, in effect, means that the World Bank and the IMF have become key policy-makers in these adjusting countries, contradicting the aims of their establishment at Bretton Woods in 1944. The programmes of economic liberalization and policy reform contain both short-term 'stabilization' or the reform of fiscal and monetary policies, involving cuts in government spending, devaluation and interest rate liberalization, and long-term structural adjustment programmes designed to improve resource-use efficiency, including privatization of the public sector and promotion of the production and export of tradable goods. The short-term measures are the responsibility of the IMF; long-term programmes fall in the domain of the World Bank. The two are connected with each other: indebted countries' acceptance of IMF terms is a precondition for the World Bank's financial support and for the rich donor countries' provision of new loans.
2. In modern times the view of a large section of Muslim society of Western-style interest-bearing credit as a form of usury has been gradually replaced with a partnership between the lending institution and the borrower. The bank charges administrative fees for transactions, and both parties share in the profit and loss of the credit-financed activity (*musharakah*). For an understanding of the practical aspects of Islam-based credit transactions in the land market, see a careful study of the situation in Sudan by Abdalla (1993).
3. The Gini index, or coefficient, is a statistical summary of the degree of inequality. It ranges from a minimum of zero (absolute equality) to a maximum of one (absolute inequality), i.e., the larger the index, the greater the inequality or degree of concentration. The South Korean Gini index is taken from El-Ghonemy (1990a, Table 6.4).
4. Under the heading 'Great proprietors are seldom great improvers' Adam Smith explains how the British absentee landlords neglected the improvement of production, compared to small proprietors (*The Wealth of Nations*, Book III, Chapter II, especially p.364).
5. These estimates are only an indication of the probable order of magnitude to reduce rural poverty by half. See the results of my estimate of poverty in Egypt

(El-Ghonemy, 1990a, p.247) and for 1965 by Adams (1985). These relationships are presented for 20 countries in El-Ghonemy (1990a, Figure 5.3 and 1993b, pp.11–13) and for 21 countries in El Ghonemy et al. (1993, pp.359–364). Poverty estimates were based on head-count ratio of total rural population. Size distribution of land relates to holdings/ownership per household. For agricultural growth, two measurements were used in two separate analyses: agricultural GDP per head of agricultural population using the official exchange rate, and agricultural GDP per head using purchasing power parity exchange rates, i.e., expressed in constant international comparable purchasing power dollars. In the regression analysis, poverty is the dependent variable and both agricultural growth per head and the Gini index of inequality in land distribution are the independent variables. The estimates of proportionate changes in the text are based on an elasticity (the slope of the curve) of poverty level with respect to the Gini index for the concentration of land of (positive) 1.65, which is substantial.

6. The short-term exceptions were Bolivia, China, Cuba, Iraq, Nicaragua and Tunisia, which experienced falls in production during their early years of land reform implementation. In Bolivia the reason was the hasty implementation of the programme without providing the beneficiaries with credit and marketing services. In China, it was the disagreement among the leaders within the Communist Party with regard to the institutional organization of agricultural production, including the mobilization of rural labour. Unfavourable weather and mismanagement of state farms were behind the fall in sugar production in Cuba (1959–65). In Nicaragua, social unrest, civil war and US trade sanctions following the 1979 Sandinista revolution contributed to falling food production in 1980–89. A combination of institutional organizational uncertainty and unfavourable weather resulted in a production decline in Tunisia: the droughts of 1961–62 and 1967, and the government experimentation with collective cooperatives which was resisted by farmers. In Iraq, it was soil salination in the south and political instability manifested in three coups d'état in the 1960s (El-Ghonemy, 1990a, pp.211–215).

7. Kenya did not participate in the 1990 World Census of Agriculture. The latest published data, from 1981, show that land concentration increased between 1971 and 1981. Of the total number of 2 112 000 holdings in the small-farm sector, 83 per cent are less than 2 ha. At the other extreme, the large farm sector comprises 2192 farms (landholdings) with a total area of 2.6 million ha; 81 per cent of the farms are over 200 ha, 930 of which are each 500 ha and over.

8. I am grateful to Professor Alex Duncan of Oxford Policy Management for providing useful information on current land policy in South Africa.

9. Other foreign professionals, however, do not share this view. Robert Chambers has remarked: 'One first step is for outside professionals, the bearers of modern scientific knowledge, to step down off their pedestals, and sit down, listen and learn' (Chambers, 1985, p.101). For a comprehensive discussion of the theoretical and empirical justification of indigenous customary tenure, see Bromley (1989); Platteau (1995).

10. Estimates of the costs of new irrigation schemes per hectare at 1985 prices show that the average capital cost was US$4196 in North Africa and the Middle East, compared to US$2366 in South Asia and the Far East, and US$2420 in Latin America. On scarcity of water in the Middle East and the projected rates in 2025, see El-Ghonemy (1998, p.55).

11. These adjusting countries are Algeria, Egypt, Jordan, Mauritania, Morocco, the Sudan, Tunisia and Turkey. See El-Ghonemy (1998, Appendix Tables 10.10, 10.11 and 10.12). See also a recent study on Latin America edited by Berry (1998).

12. These data were first collected in 1950 for my PhD thesis (El-Ghonemy, 1953), then extended to 1986 and analysed in El-Ghonemy (1992, 1993a, ch. 6).

13. 'Minute' refers to landholdings of less than 1 ha. The results of the world agricultural censuses of 1970, 1980 and 1990 show an increase in these holdings in developing countries. The increase is faster in those holdings below 0.5 ha, accounting for an average of nearly 30–45 per cent of the total number. Many of these very small holdings are fragmented into four to nine plots, constraining production and incomes in this peasant sector. It is in the interest of the large-farm sector to keep the peasant sector as a reservoir of cheap labour.

CHAPTER 6

1. I am grateful to Uzma Hashmi for her assistance with literature analyses and her valuable comments.
2. In 1997, the UN Economic and Social Council (ECOSOC) Commission on Human Rights convened a Sub-Commission on the Prevention of Discrimination and Protection of Minorities. An Expert Seminar held in Geneva in June 1997 discussed forced evictions and emphasized the obligation of the state to provide security of tenure, as well as protection, in cases of unjust forced eviction, with 'special consideration given to the rights of indigenous peoples, children and women and other vulnerable groups' (E/CN.4/Sub.2/1997/7). The landless, tenants and agricultural labourers were not mentioned. Gross violations of peasants' human rights (death, imprisonment, police and landowner harassment, unfair labour conditions, etc.) tend to go unnoticed by many human rights advocacy groups. Amnesty International, for example, advocates human rights protection but rarely, if ever, mentions violations of the land rights of the rural poor in developing countries and the food and livelihood insecurity that may result.
3. The above examples are based on responses to a questionnaire on land reform conducted in 1997 by the United Nations Research Institute for Social Development and the Popular Coalition to Eradicate Hunger and Poverty.
4. On 24 April 1998, in an unexpected move, the Supreme Court declared the presidential decision null and void and the future of MAPALAD peasants has again been thrown into confusion. This shows the complexity of land reform process in the Philippines, as well as the peasants' need for continued legal and extra-legal support from NGOs, farmers associations and other progressive actors.

CHAPTER 7

1. The present report is based mainly on field research and advisory work for the International Labour Organization during the 1960s and early 1970s, particularly the data on Mexico, Bolivia, Brazil, Japan, Taiwan, Indonesia and the Philippines. Other material has been derived from literature or field visits in relation with academic research or NGO activities, particularly the data on Russia, China, India, Cuba and Zimbabwe. More extensive collections of most of those data plus sources and bibliographies are presented in Huizer, 1967, 1972, 1980, 1991.

References

Abate, A. and F. Kiros (1983) 'Agrarian reform, structural changes and rural development in Ethiopia', in *Agrarian Reform in Contemporary Developing Countries*, A.K. Ghose (ed.), Croom Helm, London.

Abdalla, A. (1993) *Formal and Informal Organization of Agricultural Land Markets in the Sudan*, FAO, Rome.

Adams, M. (1997) *The Importance of Land Tenure to Poverty Eradication and Sustainable Development in Africa*, Oxford Management Policy, Oxford (mimeo).

Adams, R. Jr, (1985) 'Development and structural change in rural Egypt, 1952–1982', *World Development*, Vol.13, pp.705–723.

Affonso, A., S. Gómez, E. Klein and P. Ramírez (1970) *Movimiento Campesino Chileno*, Chilean Agrarian Reform Research and Training Institute (ICIRA), Santiago.

Agarwal, B. (1994) *A Field of One's Own: Gender and Land Rights in South Asia*, Cambridge University Press, Cambridge.

Alamgir, M. and P. Arora (1991) *Providing Food Security for All*, IFAD Studies in Rural Poverty No. 1, International Fund for Agricultural Development (IFAD), New York University Press, New York.

Alcántara Ferrer, S. (1997) 'Cardenismo y cultura campesina: el caso de la Comarca Lagunera', in *México en Movimiento: Concierto Mexicano 1910–1940. Repercusión e Interpretaciones, Actas del tercer Encuentro de Mexicanistas en Holanda organizado en Groninga, el 7 de noviembre de 1996*, H. Hermans, R. Papousek and C. Raffi-Béroud (eds), Centro de Estudios Mexicanos, Groningen.

ALRD (1993) *Voice of the Landless*, Association for Land Reform and Development (Bangladesh), Shamsul Huda, Dhaka.

ANGOC (1997) *Country Overview: The Philippines*, paper prepared for Knowledge Networks on Grassroots Initiatives on Land and Tenurial Reforms, South-East Asia Regional Planning Meeting, Quezon City, 25–26 November, Asian NGO Coalition for Agrarian Reform and Rural Development.

ANGOC (1998) *How Much Land Does a Peasant Need? A Regional Report and Overview on Agrarian Reform in South-East Asia*, Asian NGO Coalition for Agrarian Reform and Rural Development/IFAD/UNRISD, Geneva (mimeo).

Anon. (1988) *HUNGRY for What is Right*, No. 12, FoodFirst Information and Action Network (FIAN), Heidelberg.

Anon. (1996a) 'Clouds of plenty, clouds of doubt', *Financial Times*, 22 October.

Anon. (1996b) 'Fastlease: fast tracking a long delayed right: cases and experiences in PO implementation of leasehold', *Peasant Initiatives*, No.4, March, NGO PAKISAMA.

Anon. (1996c) *Financial Times*, 23 September.

Anon. (1997a) *Manila Times*, 18 April; 23 April; 7 November; 8 November.

Anon. (1997b) 'Farmers to face Noble's guards', *Sun Star*, Cagayan de Oro, The Philippines, 22 April.

Anon. (1997c) Farm News & Views, *Journal of the Philippine Peasant Institute,* Quezon City, Manila, Vol.10, May–June.
Anon. (1997d) Farm News & Views, *Journal of the Philippine Peasant Institute,* Quezon City, Manila, Vol.10, September–December.
Anon. (1997e) *FIAN Magazine,* FoodFirst Information and Action Network, May.
Anon. (1998a) 'Noticias sobre FEMUPROCAN (Federación de Mujeres Productoras del Campo de Nicaragua)', *Boletina,* Vol.35, pp.68–69.
Anon. (1998b) 'COPALMA hacia la Excelencia', *Reconversión en Marcha,* Vol.1(2), April–June, Managua.
Anon. (1998c) AR Now, *Mapalad Agrarian Reform Monitor,* Quezon City, January.
Anon. (1998d) *The Economist,* 9 June.
Anon. (undated) *Land Conversion Case: Sumilao, Bukidnon,* publisher not given.
Barraclough, S. (1973) *Agrarian Structure in Latin America: A Résumé of the CIDA Land Tenure Studies,* Lexington Books, Lexington.
Barraclough, S.L. (1991) *An End to Hunger? The Social Origins of Food Strategies,* Zed Books, London.
Barraclough, S. (1992) *The Struggle for Land in the Social Dynamics of Deforestation,* paper prepared for the Fundacão Memorial da America Latina Conference (São Paulo, 25–27 March 1992), UMA Estratégia Latino-Americano para a Amazõnia, UNRISD, Geneva.
Barraclough, S.L. and A. Affonso (1972) *Critical Appraisal of the Chilean Reform,* (transl. from Spanish), Universidad Catolica de Chile, Santiago (mimeo).
Barraclough, S. and M.F. Scott (1987) *The Rich Have Already Eaten: Roots of Catastrophe in Central America,* Transnational Issues No. 3, Transnational Institute, Amsterdam.
Barraclough, S., A. van Buren, A. Gariazzo, A. Sundaram and P. Utting (1988) *Aid That Counts: The Western Contribution to Development and Survival in Nicaragua,* Transnational Institute/Coordinadora Regional de Investigaciones Económicas y Sociales, Amsterdam.
Barraclough, S.L. and K.B. Ghimire (1995) *Forests and Livelihoods: The Social Dynamics of Deforestation in Developing Countries,* Macmillan, London.
Barraclough, S.L, K.B. Ghimire and H. Meliczek (1997) *Rural Development and the Environment,* UN Research Institute for Social Development (UNRISD), Geneva.
Barry, T. (1995) *Zapata's Revenge,* South End Press, Boston.
Baumeister, E. (1994) *La Reforma Agraria en Nicaragua (1979–1989),* Katholieke Universiteit, Nijmegen.
Baumeister, E. (1996) *Evaluación del Programa Campesino a Campesino de Nicaragua,* Oxfam, Managua.
Baumeister, E. (1998) *Estructura y Reforma Agraria en Nicaragua (1979–1989),* Ediciones CDR-ULA, Managua and San José.
Berry, A. (ed.) (1998) *Poverty, Economic Reform and Income Distribution in Latin America,* Lynne Rienner, London.
Berry, A. and R. Cline (1979) *Agrarian Structure and Productivity in Developing Countries,* Johns Hopkins University Press, Baltimore.
BLAST (1996) *Annual Report 1995,* Dhaka.
BLAST (1997) *Annual Report 1996,* Dhaka.
Bowles, C. (1954) *Ambassador's Report,* Harper & Brothers, New York.
Brockett, C. (1990) *Land, Power, and Poverty. Agrarian Transformation and Political Conflict in Central America,* Unwin Hyman, Boston.
Bromley, D. (1989) 'Property relations and economic development: the other land reform', *World Development,* Vol.17, pp.867–877.
Bruce, J.W. and S.E. Migot-Adhola (eds) (1994) *Searching for Land Tenure Security in Africa,* Kendhall/Hunt Publishing Co., Dubuque.

Cana, L.P. (1993) 'Legal and judicial impediments to agrarian reform implementation in Negros Occidental', *Agrarian Reform Implementation in Negros Occidental: Innovations, Lessons, and Experiences*, Jaime V Ongpin Institute of Business and Government Institute for Social Research and Development (ISRAD), University of St La Salle, Bacolod City.

Carruthers, I. and C. Clark (1981) *The Economics of Irrigation*, University Press, Liverpool.

Carter, M.R. and B.L. Barham (1996) 'Level playing fields and *laissez faire*: postliberal development strategy in inegalitarian agrarian economies', *World Development*, Vol.24(7), July.

Carter, M.R. and D. Kanel (1985) *Collective Rice Production in Finca Bermudez: Institutional Performance and Evolution in the Dominican Agrarian Reform Sector*, LTC Research Paper No. 83, Land Tenure Center, University of Wisconsin, Madison.

Carter, M.R., B.L. Barham and D. Mesbah (1995) 'Agricultural export booms and the rural poor in Chile, Guatemala and Paraguay', *Latin American Research Review*, Vol.31(1).

Castillo, L. and D. Lehman (1983) 'Agrarian reform and structural change in Chile', in *Agrarian Reform in Contemporary Developing Countries*, A.K. Ghose (ed.), Croom Helm, London.

Chambers, R. (1985) *Rural Development: Putting the Last First*, Longman, London.

Chambers, R. (1991) 'The state and rural development: ideologies and an agenda for the 1990s', in *States or Markets: Neo-liberalism and the Development Policy Debate*, C. Colclough and J. Manor (eds), Clarendon Press, Oxford.

Chavez, H. and M. Childress (1994) *Informe sobre el Sondeo en el Sector Reformado*, Proyecto para el Desarrollo de Politicos Agricolas de Honduras, Tegucigalpa.

Childress, M. (1997) *Experiencias con los Mercados de Tierras de Honduras y El Salvador*, Land Tenure Center, Madison.

Chiriboga, M., A. Faune, F. Campillo and R. Grispan (1995) *La Política del Sector Agropecuario y la Mujer Productora de Alimentos en Centroamérica*, Inter-American Institute for Agricultural Co-operation/Banco Interamericano de Desarrollo, San José, Costa Rica.

Chonchol, J. (1989) 'El desarrollo y la reforma agraria en America Latina', *Boletin de Estudios Latinoamericanos y del Caribe*, No. 46, June.

Cleveland, H. (1985) 'The passing of remoteness', *Hubert H. Humphry Institute Newsletter*, University of Minnesota, Vol.8(1), May.

Collier, G.A, with E.L. Quaratiello (1994) *BASTA! Land and the Zapatista Rebellion in Chiapas, A Food First Book*, Institute for Food and Development Policy, Oakland, CA.

Collier, P. and D. Lal (1986) *Labour and Poverty in Kenya, 1900–1980*, Clarendon Press, Oxford.

Coltart, D. (1993) 'The Legal Resources Foundation, Zimbabwe', in *Empowering People: Building Community, Civil Associations, and Legality in Africa*, R. Sandbrook and M. Halfani (eds), Centre for Urban and Community Studies, University of Toronto.

Commons, J.R. (1957) *Legal Foundations of Capitalism*, University of Wisconsin Press, Madison (originally published in 1924 by Macmillan).

CONFRAS (1997) *Problemas y Proyecciones*, Confederación de Federaciones de la Reforma Agraria de El Salvador, Equipo Técnico, Documento para Discusión, San Salvador (mimeo).

Conrad, A.H. and J.R. Meyer (1964) *The Economics of Slavery*, Aldine, Chicago.

Cornelius, W. (1992) 'The politics and economics of reforming the ejido sector in Mexico: an overview and research agenda', *LASA Forum*, Vol.23(3).

Cornia, G.A. (1985) 'Farm size and yields and agricultural production: an analysis for fifteen developing countries', *World Development*, Vol.13, pp.513–534.

Cruz, R. and M. Muñoz (1997) *Situación Actual de la Conversión y el Arrendamiento de Tierras en Grupos del Sector Reformado de Cuatro Regiones de Honduras*, PRODEPAH, Tegucigalpa.

DAR (1990) *Agrarian Reform Programme: Salient Features and Progress Made*, Report of an International Colloquium, Department of Agrarian Reform, Government of the Philippines, Quezon City.

DAR (1992) *Comprehensive Agrarian Reform Programme Handbook*, Department of Agrarian Reform, Region 4, Government of the Philippines, Manila.

DAR (1996) *State of Agrarian Reform, 1996*, Department of Agrarian Reform, Government of the Philippines, Office of the Secretary, Quezon City.

DAR (1997a) *Medium-term Development Plan (1999–2004) for the Comprehensive Agrarian Reform Program*, Department of Agrarian Reform, Government of the Philippines, Diliman, Quezon City.

DAR (1997b) *1997 Accomplishment Report*, Department of Agrarian Reform, Government of the Philippines, Planning Service, Policy and Planning Office, Diliman, Quezon City.

DAR (1998) *Land Acquisition and Distribution Status as of February 28, 1998*, Department of Agrarian Reform, Government of the Philippines, Quezon City.

DAR (undated) *Comprehensive Agrarian Reform Program (CARP), RA No. 6657, Presidential Issuances*, Department of Agrarian Reform, Government of the Philippines, Diliman, Quezon City.

DARAB (1997) *Complaint (Carruf Agricultural Corporation)*, Department of Agrarian Reform Adjudication Board, Government of the Philippines, Malaybalay, Bukidnon (mimeo).

Deere, C.D. (1985) 'La reforma agraria como revolución y contrarrevolución: Nicaragua y El Salvador', *Polémica*, No.7–8, pp.61–76.

Dias, C.J. (1987) 'Obstacles to using law as a resource for the poor: the recapturing of law by the poor', in *Report of the Seminars on Legal Services for the Rural Poor and Other Disadvantaged Groups, South-East Asia and South Asia*, International Commission of Jurists, Geneva.

Dong Wan and Yang Boo (1984) *Alleviation of Rural Poverty in the Republic of Korea*, Poverty Studies Series No.12, FAO, Rome.

Dorner, P. (1986) 'Technology, institutions, global economy and world peace', *Transactions Wisconsin Academy of Sciences, Arts and Letters*, Vol.74.

Dorner, P. (1992) *Latin American Land Reforms in Theory and Practice: A Retrospective Analysis*, University of Wisconsin Press, Madison.

Dorner, P. (1997) 'Food, population, energy and the environment in the global economy of the twenty-first century', *Journal for the Study of Peace and Conflict*, 1997–1998 Annual Edition, The Wisconsin Institute.

Dorner, P. and D. Kanel (1971) 'The economic case for land reform', in *Land Reform in Latin America: Issues and Cases*, P. Dorner (ed.), Land Economics Monograph Series No. 3, Land Tenure Center, University of Wisconsin, Madison.

Dorner, P. and W.C. Thiesenhusen (1990) 'Selected land reforms in East and South-east Asia: their origins and impacts', *Asian Pacific Economic Literature*, Vol.4(1), March.

Edwards, E.E. (1940) 'The first three hundred years', in *Farmers in a Changing World: The Yearbook of Agriculture, 1940*, Government Printing Office, Washington, DC.

El-Ghonemy, M.R. (1953) *Resource Use and Income in Egyptian Agriculture Before and After Land Reform*, PhD thesis, North Carolina State University, Raleigh.

El-Ghonemy, M.R. (1984) *Development Strategies for the Rural Poor*, Economic and Social Development Paper No.44, FAO, Rome.

El-Ghonemy, M.R. (1990a) *The Political Economy of Rural Poverty: The Case for Land Reform*, Routledge, London.

El-Ghonemy, M.R. (1990b) 'Egyptian land reform and its relevance to the Philippines' in *International Issues in Agrarian Reform: Past Experience and Future Prospects*, Government of the Philippines, Institute of Agrarian Studies, University of Los Baños, Laguna/FAO, Rome.

El-Ghonemy, M.R. (1992) 'The Egyptian state and agricultural land market, 1810–1986', *Journal of Agricultural Economics*, Vol.43, pp.175–190.

El-Ghonemy, M.R. (1993a) *Land, Food and Rural Development in North Africa*, Westview Press, Boulder/IT Publications, London.

El-Ghonemy, M.R. (1993b) *Land Reform and Rural Development in North Africa*, Working Paper No.6, International Development Centre, University of Oxford, Oxford.

El-Ghonemy, M.R. (1998) *Affluence and Poverty in the Middle East*, Routledge, London.

El-Ghonemy, M.R., G. Tyler and K. Azam (1986) *Yemen Arab Republic: Rural Development Strategy and Implementation – An Assessment*, UN Economic and Social Commission for Western Asia, Beirut.

El-Ghonemy, M.R., G. Tyler and Y. Couvreur (1993) 'Alleviating rural poverty through agricultural growth', *Journal of Development Studies*, Vol.29, pp.358–363.

ESCWA/FAO (1986) *Landlessness: Dynamics, Problems and Policies*, report of Economic and Social Commission for Western Asia Expert Consultation, FAO, Rome.

Facultad Latinamericana de Ciencias Sociales (FLACSO) (1995) *Centroamérica en Cifras 1980–1992*, San José.

FAO (1984) *Poverty Alleviation in People's Democratic Republic of Yemen*, Poverty Study No.9, FAO, Rome.

FAO (1985) *Production Yearbook*, Vol.39, FAO, Rome.

FAO (1986a) *Production Yearbook*, Vol.40, FAO, Rome.

FAO (1986b) *FAO Investment Centre Study*, FAO, Rome.

FAO (1987) *Second Progress Report on WCARRD Programme of Action, Including the Role of Women in Rural Development*, 24th Session of FAO Conference, Paper C87/19, FAO, Rome.

FAO (1988) *Impact of Development Strategies on the Rural Poor*, FAO, Rome.

FAO (1991) *Country Tables: Basic Data on the Agricultural Sector*, FAO, Rome.

FAO (1993a) *Rural Poverty Alleviation*, FAO Economic and Social Development Paper 113, FAO, Rome.

FAO (1993b) *Country Tables: Basic Data on the Agricultural Sector*, FAO, Rome.

FAO (1993c) *Agriculture: Towards 2010*, conference publication, FAO, Rome.

FAO (1995) *Fourth Progress Report on WCARRD Programme of Action*, conference publication, FAO, Rome.

FAO (1996a) *FAO Fact Sheets*, World Food Summit, FAO, Rome.

FAO (1996b) *Production Yearbook*, Vol.50, FAO, Rome.

FAO (1997) *Report of the 1990 World Census of Agriculture: International Comparison and Primary Results by Country, 1986–1995*, FAO, Rome.

FAO/WHO (1992) *Nutrition and the Global Challenge*, Publication of the International Conference on Nutrition, December 1991, FAO, Rome.

Faruquee, R. and K. Carey (1997) *Research on Land Markets in South Asia: What Have We Learned?*, Policy Research Working Paper 1754, World Bank, Washington, DC.

Fatheuer, T. (1997) 'Die Wiederkehr des Verdrängten – Agrarreform uns soziale Bewegungen in Brasilien', in *Lateinamerika: Land und Freiheit. Analysen und Berichten 21*, Horleman, Bad Honnef, pp.66–80.

Fedder, G. and R. Noronha (1987) 'Land rights systems and agricultural development in sub-Saharan Africa', *World Bank Research Observer*, Vol.2, pp.143–169.

Feder, E. (1971) *The Rape of the Peasantry. Latin America's Landholding System*, Double Day/Anchor Books, New York.

Fernández Q. (1997) *Reforma Agraria y Reversión de las Grandes Extensión Ganaderas de Zonas Bajas: Referencia sobre las Condiciones de Evolución y Limitantes de los Sistemas de Producción Campesinos*, Proyecto Proderbo, Unión Europea y Gobierno de Nicaragua, Rio Blanco.

Fremerey, M. (1990) 'Legal education in rural development: notes from an "outsider"', in *Law As Weapon: Alternative Approaches to Distributive Justice*, Jose Ventura Aspiras (ed.), Participatory Research, Organization of Communities, and Education towards Struggle for Self-Reliance, Inc. (PROCESS), Makati City, The Philippines.

Funez, F. and R. Ruben (1993) *La Compra-Venta de Tierras de la Reforma Agraria*, Editorial Guaymuras, Tegucigalpa.

Ganz, E. (1996) 'Indigenous peoples and land tenure: an issue of human rights and environmental protection', *Georgetown International Environmental Law Review*, Vol.19(1), Fall.

García-Sayan, D. (ed.) (1987) *Derecho Humanos y Servicios Legales en el Campo*, Comision Andina de Juristas y Comision Internacional de Juristas, Lima.

Geisler, C.C. and F.J. Popper (eds) (1984) *Land Reform American Style*, Rowman & Allanhold, Totowa, NJ.

Ghai, D. and C. Hewitt de Alcántara (1994) *Globalization and Social Integration: Patterns and Processes*, UN Research Institute for Social Development (UNRISD), Geneva.

Ghai, D. and S. Radwan (1983) *Agrarian Policies and Rural Poverty in Africa*, International Labour Organization, Geneva.

Ghimire, K.B. (1997) 'Land use options for rural development', *Development in Practice*, Vol.7(4), November.

Ghimire, K.B. and M.P. Pimbert (eds) (1997) *Social Change and Conservation: Environmental Politics and Impacts of National Parks and Protected Areas*, Earthscan, London.

Ghose, A.K. (1983) *Agrarian Reform in Contemporary Developing Countries*, Croom Helm, London.

Gordillo de Anda, G. (1990) 'Modernizacion del campo y apertura', *Expansion*, Diciembre.

Gordillo de Anda, G. (1997) *The State and the Market: The Missing Link*, presented at the International Seminar on Agricultural and Sustainable Development in the Mediterranean (Montpellier, France, 10–12 March 1997), FAO, Rome.

Gore, C. (1994) *Social Exclusion and Africa South of the Sahara: A Review of the Literature*, International Institute for Labour Studies, Geneva.

Government of South Africa (1995) *The Composition and Persistence of Poverty in Rural South Africa: An Entitlement Approach to Poverty*, Policy Paper No.15, Land and Agriculture Policy Centre, Pretoria.

Griffin, K. (1996) *Studies in Globalization and Economic Transitions*, Macmillan, London.

Griffin, K. and A. Rahman Khan (1992) *Globalization and the Developing World*, UN Research Institute for Social Development (UNRISD), Geneva.

Grzybowski, C. (1994) 'Movimentos populares rurais no Brasil : desafios e perspectivas', in *A Questiâo agrária hoje*, Joâo Pedro Stédile, Editora da Universidade/UFRGS, Porto Alegre, pp.285–297.

GTZ (1998) *Land Tenure in Development Cooperation: Guiding Principles*, Deutsche Gesellschaft für Technische Zusammenarbeit, Eschborn.

Hansen, R.D. (1971) *La Política del Desarrollo Mexicano*, Siglo Veintiuno Editores, SA, Mexico, DF.

Hayami, Y. and V. Ruttan (1971) *Agricultural Development: An International Perspective*, Johns Hopkins University Press, Baltimore.

Hayami, Y., M.A. Quisumbing and L. Adriano (1990) *Toward an Alternative Land Reform Paradigm: A Philippine Perspective*, Ateneo de Manila University Press, Quezon City.

Herzog, J.S. (1960) *Breve Historia de la Revolución Mexicana: Los Antecedentes y la Etapa Maderista*, Fondo de Cultura Económica, Mexico, DF.

Hewitt de Alcántara, C. (ed) (1994) *Economic Restructuring and Rural Subsistence in Mexico: Corn and the Crisis of the 1980s*, UNRISD/Center for US–Mexican Studies, University of California at San Diego, La Jolla, Calif.

Hindley, D. (1964) *The Communist Party of Indonesia, 1951–1963*, University of California Press, Berkeley/Los Angeles.

Huda, S. (ed.) (1993) *Voice of the Landless*, Association for Land Reform and Development (ALRD), Dhaka.

Huizer, G. (1967) *On Peasant Unrest in Latin America*, ILO–Comite Interamericano de Desarrollo Agricola, Washington, DC.

Huizer, G. (1972) *The Revolutionary Potential of Peasants in Latin America*, Heath–Lexington Books, Lexington, Massachussetts. (Spanish edition: *El Potencial Revolucionario del Campesino en America Latina*, Siglo XXI, Mexico, 1973).

Huizer, G. (1980) *Peasant Movements and their Counter-forces in South-East Asia*, Marwah Publications, New Delhi.

Huizer, G. (1991) *Folk Spirituality and Liberation in Southern Africa*, Centre d'Etude d'Afrique Noire, Bordeaux.

ICJ (1997) *Legal Services in Rural Areas in Africa*, International Commission of Jurists, Geneva.

IFAD (1992) *The State of World Rural Poverty*, International Fund for Agricultural Development, Rome.

IFAD (1993) *The State of World Rural Poverty: A Profile of Latin America and the Caribbean*, International Fund for Agricultural Development, Rome.

IFAD/World Bank/FAO (1997) *Network Proposal on Negotiated Land Reform*, International Fund for Agricultural Development, Rome (mimeo).

IFPRI (1995) *A 2020 Vision for Food, Agriculture and the Environment*, International Food Policy Research Institute, Washington, DC.

INA (1994) *Información Básica de los Grupos Campesinos*, documento de trabajo, Instituto Nacional Agrario (Honduras), Tegucigalpa.

ISTA (1997) *Cooperativas del Sector Reformado con Trámites de Areas en Venta*, documento de trabajo interno, Instituto Salvadoreño de Transformación Agraria, El Salvador.

IUF (1998) *Report on the IUF Land and Freedom Project Planning Workshop* (Bangalore, India, 24–26 July 1998), International Union of Food, Agricultural, Hotel, Restaurant, Catering, Tobacco and Allied Workers' Associations, Geneva.

Jacoby, E. (1961) *Agrarian Unrest in South-East Asia*, Asia Publishing House, Bombay.

Jannuzi, F.T. (1994) *India's Persistent Dilemma. The Political Economy of Agrarian Reform*, Westview Press, Boulder/San Francisco/Oxford.

Jannuzi, F.T. and J.T. Peach (1994) 'Bangladesh: A Strategy for Agrarian Reform', *Land*, Vol.1(1), February.

Jansen, E.G. (1990) *Rural Bangladesh: Competition for Scarce Resources*, University Press, Dhaka.

Janvry, A. de (1981) 'The role of land reform in economic development: policies and politics', *American Journal of Agricultural Economics*, Vol.63(2), May.

Janvry, A. de (1997) 'Land reform revisited', *WIDER Angle*, No.1, World Institute for Development Economics Research.

Janvry, A. de and E. Sadoulet (1989) 'Investment strategies to combat rural poverty: a proposal for Latin America', *World Development*, Vol.17(8), August.

Jazairy, I., M. Alamgir and T. Panuccio (1992) *The State of World Rural Poverty: An Inquiry into its Causes and Consequences*, published for the International Fund for Agricultural Development by New York University Press, New York.

Jopillo, M.S.G. (1989) *Third-Party Mediation: Application in Public Policy Disputes*, Institute of Philippine Culture, Ateneo de Manila University, Quezon City.

Kabir, K. (1994) 'Question of land reforms and role of NGOs in Bangladesh', *Land*, Vol.1(1), February.

Kanel, D. (1974) 'Property and economic power as issues in institutional economics', *Journal of Economic Issues*, Vol.VIII(4), December.

Kanel, D. (1985) 'Institutional economics: perspectives on economy and society', *Journal of Economic Issues*, Vol.XIX(3), September.

Kanel, D. (1988) 'The human predicament: society, institutions and individuals', *Journal of Economic Issues*, 22(2), June, pp.427–434.

Karunan, V.P. (1984) *If The Land Could Speak, It Would Speak for Us, Volume 1: A History of Peasant Movements in Thailand and the Philippines*, Plough Publications, Hong Kong.

Karunan, V.P. (1992) *Peasant Protest and Rural Elite Strategies in Asia: Case Studies of India, the Philippines, and Sri Lanka*, PhD dissertation, Katholieke Universiteit Nijmegen, Nijmegen.

Kay, C. (1983) 'The agrarian reform in Peru: an assessment' in *Agrarian Reform in Contemporary Developing Countries*, A.K. Ghose (ed.), Croom Helm, London.

Keidel, A. (1981) *Korean Farm Production and Income, 1910–1975*, Korea Development Institute, Seoul.

Khan, S.A. (1989) *The State and Village Society: The Political Economy of Agricultural Development in Bangladesh*, University Press Limited, Dhaka.

Kikuchi, M. and Y. Hayami (1978) 'Agricultural growth against a land resource constraint: a comparative history of Japan, Taiwan, Korea and the Philippines', *Journal of Economic History*, Vol.38, December.

Korten, D.C. (1995) *When Corporations Rule the World*, Earthscan Publications, London/Kumarian Press, Hartford/Berrett-Koehler, San Francisco.

Künnemann, R. (1997) 'Agrarian reform: a fulfilment-bound states' obligation', *HUNGRY for What is Right*, No.10, FoodFirst Information and Action Network (FIAN), Heidelberg.

Künnemann, R. (1998) 'Agrarian reform: a fulfilment-bound states' obligation', *HUNGRY for What is Right*, No.12, FoodFirst Information and Action Network (FIAN), Heidelberg.

Ladejinsky, W. (1977) 'Too late to save Asia' in *The Selected Papers of Wolf Ladejinsky: Agrarian Reform as Unfinished Business*, L.J. Walinsky (ed.), Oxford University Press, New York/World Bank, Washington, DC.

Lan, D. (1983) *Making History. Spirit Mediums and the Guerrilla War in the Dande Area of Zimbabwe*, PhD thesis, London School of Economics, London.

Land Tenure Center (1989) *Viabilidad de las Cooperativas del Sector Reformado del Norte de Honduras*, documento de trabajo borrador, Land Tenure Center, Madison.

Landsberger, H.A. (1969) *Latin American Peasant Movements*, Cornell University Press, Ithaca/London.

Lewis, A. (1963) *The Theory of Economic Growth*, Allen and Unwin, London.

Lipton, M. (1985) Land Assets and Rural Poverty. World Bank Staff Working Paper No. 744, World Bank, Washington, DC.

Livingstone, I. (1986) *Rural Development, Employment and Incomes in Kenya*, Gower, Aldershot.

Loveman, B. (1976) *Struggle in the Countryside: Politics and Rural Labor in Chile, 1919–1973*, Indiana University Press, Bloomington and London.

LRC (1995) *Annual Report*, Legal Resources Centre, Johannesburg.

Luu, N.N. (1982) 'Agrarian revolution in North Vietnam' in *Rural Poverty and Agrarian Reform*, S. Jones, P.C. Joshi and M. Murmis (eds), R.N. Sachdev at Allied Publishers Private Ltd, New Delhi.

Mafeje, A.B.M. (1993) 'Where the theory doesn't fit', *Ceres*, January/February.

Mançano, H.B. (1996) *MST, Movimiento dos Trabalhadores Rurais Sem Terra. Formaçâo e Territorializaçâo em Sâo Paulo*, Editora Hucitec, Sâo Paulo.

Mannan, M. (1990) 'The state and the formation of a dependent bourgeoisie in Bangladesh', *South Asia Journal*, Vol.3(4), pp.391–410.

Mao Ze Dong (1971) 'Report on an investigation of the peasant movements in Hunan', in *Selected Readings from the Works of Mao Ze Dong*, Foreign Language Press, Peking.

Martin, D. and P. Johnson (1981) *The Struggle for Zimbabwe: The Chimurenga War*, Zimbabwe Publishing House, Harare.

Matus, J., M.L. Padilla and F. Diaz (1993) *Diagnóstico de Campo. Identificación de un proyecto de Apoyo a la Problemática de la Propiedad en Nicaragua*, Comisión de las Comunidades Europeas, Managua.

Melmed-Sanjak, J.S. and M. Carter (1991) 'The economic viability and stability of 'capitalized family farming': an analysis of agricultural decollectivization in Peru', *Journal of Development Studies*, Vol.27(2), January.

Ministry of Home Affairs (1969) *The Causes and Nature of Current Agrarian Unrest*, Ministry of Home Affairs, Research and Policy Division, New Dehli (mimeo).

Montgomery, J.D. (1984) 'Land reform as an international issue', in *International Dimensions of Land Reform*, J.D. Montgomery (ed.), Westview Press, Boulder/London.

Municipality of Valencia (1997) *1996 Socio-Economic Profile*, Valencia.

Nichols, W.H. (1964) 'The place of agriculture in development', in *Agriculture in Economic Development*, C. Eicher and L. Witt (eds), McGraw-Hill, New York.

Nijera Kori (1996) *Profit by Destruction*, report on a workshop on Ecology, Politics and Violence of Shrimp Cultivation, Nijera Kori, Dhaka.

Nijera Kori (1997a) *Activity Report Nijera Kori*, Nijera Kori, Dhaka (mimeo).

Nijera Kori (1997b) *Annual Report 1996–97*, Nijera Kori, Dhaka.

Nitaplan (1995) *Informe Ejecutivo para el Proyecto de Tecnología Agraria y Ordenemiento de la Propiedad Agraria*, Equipo de Investigación Sectorial Rural, Managua.

Nsabagasani, X. (1997) *Land Privatization, Security of Tenure and Agricultural Production: The Ugandan Experience*, Institute of Social Studies, The Hague.

Nye, J.S., P.D. Zelikow and D.C. King (eds) (1997) *Why People Don't Trust Government*, Harvard University Press, Cambridge.

Otero, G. (1989) 'Agrarian reform in Mexico: Capitalism and the state' in *Searching for Agrarian Reform in Latin America*, W.C. Thiesenhusen (ed.), Unwin Hyman, Boston.

Owen, L.A. (1937) *The Russian Peasant Movement 1906–1917*, King & Son, London.

Owen, W.F. (1966) 'The double development squeeze on agriculture', *American Economic Review*, Vol.56, March.

Parsons, K.H. (1984) 'The place of agrarian reform in rural development policies' in *Studies on Agrarian Reform and Rural Poverty*, M. Riad El-Ghonemy (ed.), FAO, Rome.

Pearse, A. (1980) *Seeds of Plenty, Seeds of Want: Social and Economic Implications of the Green Revolution*, United Nations Research Institute for Social Development (UNRISD), Geneva.

Pelupessy, W. (1998) *Políticas Agrarias en El Salvador (1960–1990)*, EDUCA, San José.

PERA (1991) *X Evaluación de la Reforma Agraria en El Salvador*, Proyecto Planificación y Evaluación de la Reforma Agraria (PERA), Oficina Sectorial de Planificación Agropecuaria, Ministerio de Agricultura y Ganadería, San Salvador.

PhilDHRRA (1997) *TriPARRD Series No. 1: Making Agrarian Reform Work: Securing the Gains of Land Tenure Improvement; TriPARRD Series No. 2: Making Agrarian Reform Work: Animating Peasant Organizations*, Philippine Partnership for the Development of Human Resources in Rural Areas.

Piña, C. (1998) *Globalization and the Agrarian Reform/Land Tenure Crisis*, United Nations Research Institute for Social Development (UNRISD), Geneva (mimeo).

Plant, R. (1993) 'Land rights in human rights and development: introducing a new ICJ initiative', *International Commission of Jurists, The Review*, Vol.51, December.

Platteau, J.P. (1995) *Reforming Land Rights in Sub-Saharan Africa*, Discussion Paper No. 60, United Nations Research Institute for Social Development (UNRISD), Geneva.

Posas, M. (1981) *El Movimiento Campesino Hondureño. Una perspectiva general*, Colección Cuadernos número 2, Editorial Guaymuras.

Posas, M. (1996) 'El sector reformado y la política agraria del estado', in *El Agro Hondureño y su Futuro*, Baumeister, E., C. Wattel, L. Clerx, M. Posas, R. Salgado and D. Kaimowitz (eds), Editorial Guaymuras, Tegucigalpa.

Prosterman, R. (1985) 'Reforma agraria en El Salvador', *Polémica*, No.7–8, San José, Costa Rica.

Radwan, S. (1977) *Agrarian Reform and Rural Poverty in Egypt, 1952–75*, International Labour Organization, Geneva.

Radwan, S. and E. Lee (1986) *Agrarian Change in Egypt: An Anatomy of Rural Poverty*, Croom Helm, London.

Rahman, H.Z. (1995) 'Land Reform Agenda 1990s', *Land*, Vol.2(2), December.

Ranger, T.O. (1967) *Revolt in Southern Rhodesia 1896–7: A Study in African Resistance*, Heinemann, London.

Ravindran, D.J. (ed.) (1988) *A Handbook on Training Paralegals: Report of a Seminar on Training of Paralegals*, International Commission of Jurists, Geneva.

Reed, J. (1977) *Ten Days That Shook the World*, Penguin, London.

Reijntjes, C., B. Haverkort and A. Waters-Bayer (1996) *Farming for the Future: An Introduction to Low-External-Input and Sustainable Agriculture*, Information Centre for Low-External-Input and Sustainable Agriculture, Leusden, The Netherlands/Macmillan, London (first published 1992).

Restrepo, I. and S. Eckstein (1975) *La Agricultura Colectiva en México*, Siglo Veintiuno Editores SA, Mexico, DF.

Riedinger, J. (1990) 'Philippine land reform in the 1980s', in *Agrarian Reform and Grassroots Development: Ten Case Studies*, R.L. Prosterman, M.N. Temple and T.M. Hanstad (eds), Lynne Rienner Publishers, Boulder.

Ruben, R. (1997) *Making Cooperatives Work. Contract Choice and Resource Management within Land Reform Cooperatives in Honduras*, PhD thesis, Universidad Libre de Amsterdam.

Saha, B.K. (1997) *Agrarian Structure and Productivity in Bangladesh and West Bengal*, University Press Ltd, Dhaka.

Salgado, R. (ed.) (1994) *El Mercado de Tierras en Honduras*, Centro de Documentación de Honduras, POSCAE–Wisconsin, Tegucigalpa.

Salgado, R. (1996) 'La tenencia de la tierra en Honduras' in *El Agro Hondureño y su Futuro*, Baumeister, E., C. Wattel, L. Clerx, M. Posas, R. Salgado and D. Kaimowitz (eds), Editorial Guaymuras, Tegucigalpa.

Salmon, J.D. (1968) 'The Huk rebellion', *Solidarity*, Vol.III(12).

Sanchez Hernandez, M. (1987) *Local Organization in Rural Development Programs: The Case of The Puebla Project*, PhD dissertation, Development Studies, University of Wisconsin–Madison.

Schönleitner, G. (1997) *Discussing Brazil's Agrarian Question: Land Reform is Dead, Long Live Family Farming*, MSc dissertation, London School of Economics, London.

Schuh, G.E. (1985) *The International Capital Market as a Source of Instability in*

International Commodity Markets, paper presented at the XIX International Conference of Agricultural Economists (Malaga, Spain, August–September).

Schultz, T.W. (1964) *Transforming Traditional Agriculture*, Yale University Press, New Haven.

Scott, J.C. (1985) *Weapons of the Weak: Everyday Forms of Resistance*, Yale University Press, New Haven.

Seigel, M. (1997) *Structures in the International Economy That Promote the Concentration of Land Ownership*, Service of Documentation and Study (SEDOS), Rome.

Sen, S. (1982) *Peasant Movements in India*, Bagchi & Co, Calcutta.

SENTRA (Sentro Para Sa Tunay na Repormang Agraryo) (1997) 'Market-oriented CARP in the Philippines: a recipe for failure', *Agrarian Trends*, special issue, September.

Shaw, C. (1997) 'Rural land markets', *El Salvador: Rural Development Study*, Vol.II, World Bank, Washington, DC.

Shillinglaw, G. (1974) 'Land reform and peasant mobilization in Southern China, 1947–1950' in *Peasants, Landlords and Governments: Agrarian Reform in the Third World*, D. Lehmann (ed.), Holmes & Meier, New York.

Smith, A. (1977) *The Wealth of Nations*, Dent, London.

Sobhan, R. (1993) *Agrarian Reform and Social Transformation*, Zed Books, London.

Soliman, H.D. (1987) 'A critical analysis of legal services for the rural poor and other disadvantaged groups', *Report of the Seminars on Legal Services for the Rural Poor and Other Disadvantaged Groups, South-east Asia and South Asia*, International Commission of Jurists, Geneva.

Sosmena, G.C. (1985) 'Barangay justice: delegalization mechanism', in *Dispute Processing in the Philippines*, R. Mojares (ed.), Bureau of Local Government Supervision, Metro Manila.

Stacey, J. (1979) 'When patriachy kowtows: the significance of the Chinese family revolution for feminist theory', in *Capitalist Patriarchy and the Case for Socialist Feminism*, Z.R. Eisenstein (ed.), MR Press, New York/London.

Stewart, F. (1995) *Adjustment and Poverty: Options and Choices*, Routledge, London.

Stiefel, M. and M. Wolfe (1994) *A Voice for the Excluded. Popular Participation in Development: Utopia or Necessity?*, UNRISD/Zed Books, Geneva/London.

Strasma, J. (1985) *Employment, Crop Mix, and Membership Capacity in Agrarian Reform Cooperatives: El Salvador*, University of Wisconsin–Madison, Madison.

Sturtevant, D.R. (1976) *Popular Uprisings in the Philippines 1840–1940*, Cornell University Press, Ithaca.

Sundarayya, P. (1979) 'The communist movement in Andhra: terror regime 1948–51', in *Peasant Struggles in India*, A.R. Desai (ed.), Oxford University Press, Bombay.

Tantawy, M. (1992) *al-Halal wal-Haram fi Mu'amalat al-Bunouk* (Permitted and Prohibited Banking Transactions), al-Ahram al-Iqtissadi, Cairo.

Tawney, R.H. (1932) *Land and Labour in China*, Allan and Unwin, London.

Thiesenhusen, W.C. (ed.) (1989) *Searching for Agrarian Reform in Latin America*, Unwin Hyman, Boston.

Thiesenhusen, W. (1993) 'New players, new rules', *Ceres*, January/February.

Thiesenhusen, W.C. (1995) *Broken Promises: Agrarian Reform and the Latin American Campesino*, Westview Press, Boulder.

Uddin, G.S. and S. Akhter (1997) 'Landless labourers in Bangladesh: a sociological analysis', *Land*, Vol.3(3), December.

UNAG (1997) *1992–1997: Informe Evaluativo al III Congreso* (first draft), Unión Nacional de Agricultores y Ganaderos, Managua.

UNAG/FENACOOP (1989) *Autodiagnóstico Cooperativo and Dirección General de Reforma Agraria*, Unión Nacional de Agricultores y Ganaderos–Federación Nacional de Cooperativas Agropecuarias y Agroindustriales, Managua.

UNESCCHR (1997) *The Realization of Economic, Social and Cultural Rights: Expert Seminar on the Practice of Forced Eviction*, UN Economic and Social Council Commission on Human Rights, Sub-Commission on Prevention of Discrimination and Protection of Minorities, Geneva, 11–13 June, 1997, Report of the Secretary General, E/CN.4/Sub.2/1997/7.

UNRISD (1995) *States of Disarray: The Social Effects of Globalization*, United Nations Research Institute for Social Development, Geneva.

Vaessen, J. (1997) 'The transformation of cooperative organisation in Nicaragua', *Contract Choice, Pathways of Change and Agricultural Perfomance among Agricultural Production Cooperatives*, NIRP, Managua.

Valera, A.S., R.P. Ledesma and J.R. Plantilla (1987) 'An integrated approach in providing legal services to the rural poor and other disadvantaged groups: SALAG (Structural Alternative Legal Assistance for Grassroots)', *Report of the Seminars on Legal Services for the Rural Poor and Other Disadvantaged Groups, South-East Asia and South Asia*, International Commission of Jurists, Geneva.

Van der Haar, G. and A. Zoomers (1998) *Land in Latin America: New Context, New Claims and New Concepts*, Wageningen/Amsterdam (mimeo).

Vatican (1997) *Towards a Better Distribution of Land: The Challenge of Agrarian Reform*, Pontiful Council for Justice and Peace, Libreria Editrice Vaticana, Vatican City.

Via Campesina (1998) *A Three-Year Plan: Strengthening the Via Campesina 1999–2001*, Tegucigalpa, MDC, Honduras.

Vogelgesang, F. (1996) 'Property rights and the rural land market in Latin America', *CEPAL Review*, Vol.58, April.

Von Blanckenburg, P. (1994) 'Land reform in Southern Africa: the case of Zimbabwe', *Land Reform, Land Settlement and Cooperatives*, FAO, Rome.

Walinsky L.J. (ed.) (1977) *The Selected Papers of Wolf Ladejinsky: Agrarian Reform as Unfinished Business*, Oxford University Press, New York/World Bank, Washington, DC.

Walt, B.R. de and M.W. Rees, with A.D. Murphy (1994) 'The end of agrarian reform in Mexico: past lessons, future prospects', in *Transformation of Rural Mexico*, No.3, Ejido Reform Research Project, Center for US–Mexican Studies, University of California at San Diego, La Jolla, CA.

Warman, A. (1976) *Y Venimos a Contradecir: Los Campesinos de Morelos y el Estado Nacional*, Ediciones de la Casa Chata, Mexico, DF.

WCARRD (1979) *Programme of Action of the World Conference on Agrarian Reform and Rural Development*, FAO, Rome.

Westergaard, K. (1994) *People's Empowerment in Bangladesh: NGO Strategies*, CDR Working Paper 94.10, Centre for Development Research, Copenhagen.

Wolf, E. (1969) *Peasant Wars of the Twentieth Century*, Harper and Row, New York.

Womack Jr, J. (1969) *Zapata y la Revolución Mexicana*, Siglo Veintiuno Editores, SA, Mexico, DF.

World Bank (1983) *China. Socialist Economic Development*, World Bank, Washington, DC.

World Bank (1990) *World Development Report 1990*, World Bank, Washington, DC.

World Bank (1992) *World Development Report*, Oxford University Press, Oxford.

World Bank (1996) *A Strategy to Fight Poverty: Philippines*, The World Bank Country Operations Division, Country Department I, East Asia and the Pacific Region, East Asia Pacific External Affairs, World Bank, Washington, DC.

World Bank (1997a) *World Development Report*, Oxford University Press, Oxford.

World Bank (1997b) *El Salvador: Rural Development Study*, Technical Annexes, Vol.II, World Bank, Washington, DC.

Zeeuw, H. de, E. Baumeister, E. Kolmans and M. Rens (1997) *Promover la Agricultura Sostenible en América Central*, ICCO–Pan para el Mundo, Managua.

Index